Percy Alport Molteno

A Federal South Africa, a comparison of the critical period of American history with the present position of the colonies and states of South Africa, and a consideration of the advantages of a Federal Union

Percy Alport Molteno

A Federal South Africa, a comparison of the critical period of American history with the present position of the colonies and states of South Africa, and a consideration of the advantages of a Federal Union

ISBN/EAN: 9783337114893

Printed in Europe, USA, Canada, Australia, Japan

Cover: Foto ©Suzi / pixelio.de

More available books at **www.hansebooks.com**

A

FEDERAL SOUTH AFRICA

A COMPARISON OF THE CRITICAL PERIOD OF AMERICAN
HISTORY WITH THE PRESENT POSITION OF THE
COLONIES AND STATES OF SOUTH AFRICA, AND
A CONSIDERATION OF THE ADVANTAGES
OF A FEDERAL UNION

BY

PERCY ALPORT MOLTENO, LL.B.
OF THE INNER TEMPLE, BARRISTER-AT-LAW,
AND ADVOCATE OF THE SUPREME COURT OF THE CAPE OF GOOD HOPE

WITH MAPS

LONDON
SAMPSON LOW, MARSTON & COMPANY
Limited
St. Dunstan's House
FETTER LANE, FLEET STREET, E.C.
1896

Dedication.

TO THAT NOBLE ENGLISHMAN,

SIR GEORGE GREY,

WHO FIRST ENDEAVOURED TO COMBINE THE SCATTERED
EUROPEAN POPULATIONS OF SOUTH AFRICA,
AND WHO, IN A SUPREME DEGREE,
HAS SHOWN HIS APPRECIATION OF, AND HIS SYMPATHY WITH,
ALL THAT IS BEST, ALL THAT IS MOST NOBLE,
ALL THAT IS MOST TRUE,
AMONG WHATEVER PEOPLE AND IN WHATEVER PORTION OF
THE WORLD HIS LOT HAS BEEN CAST,
DURING A LONG AND SPLENDID CAREER,
THIS LITTLE WORK IS BY PERMISSION DEDICATED.

PREFACE.

THE following pages embody an attempt to give definition to the vague ideas of union which are in the air in South Africa. There is a strong feeling that union is necessary, but the motives of this feeling are not clearly grasped or understood, while the conception of the manner in which it may be brought about is still more vague. The summary of the events which led America to deal with the problem will help us to appreciate the dangers of disunion, and the wonderful success of the machinery devised in 1787 for avoiding the inevitable results of a wantof a central controlling authority, will give us confidence to proceed to a similar remedy for the growing dangers of disunion in South Africa.

We have heard constantly of racial difficulties in South Africa. The difficulties are not racial so much as political. In America the homogeneous populations were becoming hostile to each other owing to being grouped in states with divergent interests; it is the same in South Africa—coterminous states and no central authority to bind them together. As a proof that the difficulty is not racial, we may refer to the fact that the two Dutch Republics have never succeeded in uniting together.

The most powerful factor which makes for disunion at present is the interference of the British Government in the internal affairs of South Africa. This interference naturally has a bias in favour of the two colonies as against the states. The result is that, while human nature remains what it is, the Republics will inevitably desire to have a champion to set against England, the champion of the colonies. Germany has taken advantage of this feeling for her own purposes. It is most important that English statesmen should realize this fact, and should refrain from interference in the internal concerns of South Africa. If they will rely more fully upon the great principles of local self-government and freedom, which have been England's own strength, and which have, when applied to the self-governing colonies, given such excellent results, and will permit to South Africa, as a whole, the same freedom to manage its own internal affairs, they will be rewarded by seeing the various difficult problems solve themselves gradually and naturally in accord with local circumstances. England's periods of active interference in South Africa have always been disastrous to herself and to South Africa—indeed the present troubles may all be traced directly to Lord Carnarvon's attempt to force his policy on South Africa. Let English statesmen remember that, as Sir John Seeley points out, there was no such thing as a Crown colony, in which Englishmen are governed administratively without representative assemblies, in the old colonial system which preceded the revolt of the American colonies ("Expansion of England," p. 67); much more, then, is it fatal to-day to attempt to treat South Africa, regarded as a whole, as if it were a Crown colony governed through the machinery of an Imperial Secretary and a High Commissioner. I may adduce the high authority of Mr. Porter against the separation of the function of High Commissioner from that of Governor of the Cape Colony.

Mr. Porter had been Her Majesty's Attorney-General of the Cape of Good Hope for twenty-six years, from 1839 to 1865, thus holding this office long before the name High Commissioner had ever been used in connection with South Africa. During the course of a debate in the Cape Parliament, of which he had then become a member, Mr. Porter, in the year 1873, pointed out that the High Commissioner and Governor are really one, that the name had first arisen when Sir Henry Pottinger was Governor in 1847, and had been introduced then only to give a friend of the Governor's a high sounding title of Secretary to the High Commissioner—there was no distinction of duties or function, and no salary. "I do not know," said Mr. Porter, "that there is any political necessity for the office of High Commissioner, I could see it abolished to-morrow without the slightest possible regret. . . . I do not think that the High Commissioner, who is also Governor, ought to do anything for which his responsible advisers are not responsible. I apprehend this to be a constitutional principle. . . . I think whether you retain the name, or whether you discard the name, his responsible advisers should be responsible for his proceedings."

To those who think the High Commissioner necessary for guarding Native interests, I would commend a consideration of the fact, that the ablest, the most consistent, the wisest, and the most effective guardian that the Natives of South Africa have ever had, Mr. Saul Solomon, joined in Mr. Porter's protest against the danger of creating the function of the High Commissioner; and that he had in an earlier Parliament moved and carried a resolution abolishing the salary of the High Commissioner, which had been first drawn when the Governor of the Cape became Governor of British Kaffraria. Had this wise policy been adopted, the history of South Africa would have been entirely different. The purposes of English statesmen would have been modified by the ripe experience of colonial statesmen, who were also Englishmen; there would have been no forcible annexation of the Transvaal—for the late Sir John Molteno, the then Premier of the Cape, was utterly and entirely opposed to it—and none of that ill-feeling in South Africa which is directly traceable to that monstrous and iniquitous act.

Let Englishmen remember that English hearts beat high and truly even where English judgment has been informed by African experience, and I would commend to them and to all men, whether in England or South Africa, the noble words of Saul Solomon, who, in protesting against the Act annexing British Kaffraria, which had been passed by the English Parliament at the instance of the autocratic

Sir Philip Woodehouse, and which was being held *in terrorem* over the Cape Legislature, said, "I admit the change is necessary, but, I say, let it be submitted to us like men. I am sure the colony is proud to be connected with Great Britain;—(cheers)—to live under the flag of England, which speaks of material wealth and commercial enterprise, and a power of arms which have been the admiration of the world. But it speaks also of better and higher things. It speaks of a system of laws and principles which have been the growth of ages, and which are the glory of England's people. These laws and principles we ought not to surrender if we possess the power of defending them. These laws and principles are the heritage of England's children and her children's children. Such constitutional resistance as we are now offering will not be looked upon by the people or the Parliament of England as a proof of disloyalty, but as a proof of our loyalty, and that we will not allow their rights to be invaded in our persons, nor their principles to be trampled upon in the colony of the Cape of Good Hope."

If a Federal union be formed of all the colonies and states, England can then step aside and allow this Federation to manage all its internal affairs. Until this union is formed it is not easy for England to withdraw, as it is desirable that it should do in its own interest, and in the interest of the peaceful and united development of South Africa.

This little work was about to go to press when the terrible news of recent events at the Cape came to hand. It will be for the reader to judge how far the dangers which I have there foreshadowed have in some instances been brought into active operation, and he will gain a keener appreciation of the arguments in the text for the necessity of union.

I have made more than the usual drafts upon the actual text of the writers upon whose assistance I have so greatly relied, particularly in describing the machinery of the American Constitution, and I must at once acknowledge my extreme indebtedness to the American author, Professor Fiske, whose valuable works have given us such a clear insight into the critical periods of American history; and I am equally indebted to Mr. Bryce, whose monumental work on the American Constitution has done more than any other to arouse an interest in, and afford a source of knowledge to the student of American history and institutions. The *Federalist* has always been at hand, and I have taken the liberty of drawing largely on that splendid collection of arguments on Federal government; while Freeman's " Federal Government," unfortunately never completed, has given me useful aid.

I have to thank Sir George Grey for valuable help and encouragement, and Mr. W. F. Sheppard for his careful criticisms made while the work was passing through the press.

P. A. MOLTENO.

Jan., 1896.

CONTENTS.

CHAPTER I.

INTRODUCTORY.

Statement of problem—Successful solution of similar problem in America—Value of these results for South Africa—Origin of separate states in South Africa—Unwise policy of British Government—Re-union never lost sight of—Unfavourable influence of Sir Philip Woodehouse's action—Favourable influence of grant of Responsible Government to Cape Colony—Fatal effects of Lord Carnarvon's policy—Present position of colonies and states—Practically autonomous—Dangers of this condition—Similar condition of American colonies after independence won and before union formed—Value of American precedent for South Africa   1

CHAPTER II.

THE CRITICAL PERIODS OF AMERICAN AND SOUTH AFRICAN HISTORY.

Condition of American colonies when war broke out—Similar condition of South African colonies and states—Forms of government—Congress sole bond after war—Weakness of Congress—Fate predicted for colonies in Europe—Patriotism of leading statesmen—No central authority—Colonies retain power of taxation

—Failure to pay interest on public debts—Army unruly—Commercial war between colonies—Selfish policy of New York—Isolated policy of Transvaal—Quarrel between New York and Connecticut over duties—Similar tariff war between Cape and Transvaal—Closing of drifts—Feeling of Uitlander population—Dangers of this—Necessity for peaceful fusion of races—Fine qualities of Boers—English and Dutch traits complementary—Both necessary for development of South Africa 9

CHAPTER III.

THE CRITICAL PERIODS—*Continued.*

Territorial troubles in America—Quarrel between Connecticut and Pennsylvania over Wyoming—Between New York and New Hampshire over Green Mountains—Territorial troubles in South Africa—Washington's remedy—Financial distress after war—Legislative attempts to remedy—Serious troubles in Rhode Island and Massachusetts—Armed risings—Attack on Federal arsenal—Army of 4000 men called out—Congress unable to restore order—Currency legislation at Cape—Trouble due to want of central power—Dangers of similar position in South Africa—America applied remedy—Will South African statesmen apply similar remedy—Danger of enmities if delayed—Common commercial interests brought states together in America—Similar operations of commercial interests in South Africa 27

CHAPTER IV.

CONDITIONS WHICH FAVOUR UNION IN SOUTH AFRICA.

One continuous territory—No great natural barriers—Healthy climate—Boundaries of South Africa defined—Republics populated from Cape Colony—European population uniformly dispersed—Assimilating power of Africander population — Similar distribution of English and Dutch languages throughout South Africa—Similar institutions—Same common law—Racial distinctions quickly disappear—Local patriotism supplants national antipathies—Distance from Europe favours freedom from European complications—Monroe Doctrine for South Africa . . . 38

CHAPTER V.

ADVANTAGES CONFERRED BY UNION.

Preservation from evils of dissension — Arguments of *Federalist* applicable—Dangers from hostile duties and commercial rivalry—Territorial disputes—Loss of northern territories to South African system—Union would provide remedy—Northern territories compared with western territory of America—Surrender of claims of individual states to union—Precedent for South Africa—Necessity of dealing with the question —Success of American plan—Chartered Company's rule only temporary—Union would remove danger of hostile commercial action—Jealousies of South African states—Cost of collection of customs reduced by union—Abolition of internal customs' boundaries—Stimulus to commerce by internal free trade—Free interchange of products—Prosperity of each adds to prosperity of all—South Africa would present to world united front in matters of commerce . . . 42

CHAPTER VI.

ADVANTAGES CONFERRED BY UNION—*Continued.*

Native question—Importance of combined action—Saving effected by one common administration instead of several—Form of government guaranteed to each colony and state — Law and order guaranteed—Security against native risings—Uitlander population in Transvaal—New population of Rhodesia—Importance of dealing with these questions in early stage—Objection that freedom of states would be destroyed met by *Federalist* 61

CHAPTER VII.

THE EXCLUSION OF FOREIGN INTERFERENCE.

Danger of foreign interference—Arguments of *Federalist* — Interference of Germany — Deliberate plan — German annexations—Danger of adding interference of another power in South Africa—Estrangement of Transvaal—Territory necessary for South African system — Similar question in America in 1787 — Successful solution in America—Loss of valuable territories owing to supineness of British Government —Walwich Bay—Delagoa Bay—Union necessary to enforce claims—Failure of English statesmen to understand South Africa—Mr. Gladstone's opinion—Complication of many factors—Difficulty of discovering true South African opinion—A neglected warning—Sir Owen Lanyon's military rule—Disastrous results—The late Sir John Molteno's views on exclusion of foreign interference 72

CHAPTER VIII.

THE FORM OF FEDERAL UNION.

Maintenance of present governments—Attachment to governments—Feeling at Cape—Feeling in America —How far present governments must part with rights —Two forms of Federation—Essentials of Federation —Independence in matters of local concern—Dependence in matters of common concern—Examples from history—Relation of states to Federal government — One class of Federation represents only several members of Union—Viciousness of this form—Example of America before present union formed—Evil results—Analysis of causes of weakness—These of universal operation—Other class of Federation operates on governments and on citizens as well—Latter good form of Federation—America since union formed on this principle has prospered—Importance of subject—Argument of *Federalist*—If operation of central government be on separate states, only force can compel obedience to Federal mandate—Evils of resort to force—Remedy, operation of central government on individuals—If opposition to central government offending party must take aggressive action—Impossibility of providing for every contingency — Application of *Federalist* argument to Africa 93

CHAPTER IX.

FEDERAL OBJECTS AND FEDERAL MACHINERY.

Objects described as Federal by United States Constitution—By Constitution of Dominion of Canada—Constitution written—Not subject to legislature—Supreme over all authorities—Contrast to flexible constitution of England—Historical origin of American Constitution—Similar written and supreme constitution for South African Federation—Idea familiar owing to existence of constitution ordinances in colonies and grondwets in republics—Provision in constitution for discharge of duties by Federal government—President—Mode of election and powers — Administration by Cabinet preferable—Principles of Cabinet government—Senate—Powers and functions—Has succeeded—Desirable in South Africa—House of Representatives—Powers and duties—Desirable in South African Federation . 117

CHAPTER X.

THE FEDERAL COURTS.

PAGE

Necessity for federal courts—Established by constitution —Jurisdiction of courts—Courts have worked well— Provide means of operation of federal government on individuals—Civil process for securing authority of state against infringement—Success of these provisions—Further function of federal courts—Maintain the supremacy of the constitution—Give effect to relative validity of federal constitution, of federal statutes, of state constitutions and state statutes—Court acts as international arbiter between states—Has preserved peace among states—Unanimous verdict in favour of success of courts—Valuable precedent for South African Federation 138

CHAPTER XI.

GENERAL PROVISIONS OF THE AMERICAN CONSTITUTION.

Preface—No export taxes—No preferential commercial regulations—No titles of nobility—Importance of excluding titles from South Africa—No state shall make law impairing the obligation of contract—Importance of this provision—No state can impose duties on exports or imports—Value of this article for securing internal free trade—No state may make war or make engagements with foreign powers—Recognition of judicial records of courts throughout Union— Citizens of each state entitled to all privileges of citizens in any other state—Mutual extradition—Congress to have power to legislate for common territory— Guarantee of form of government and internal order in each state—Mode of amending constitutions—No religious tests—Freedom of speech, of press, of assembly and petition—Security from unlawful arrest or search—Adoption of these principles in Federal Constitution for South Africa 150

CHAPTER XII.

THE PROVED ADVANTAGES OF FEDERAL GOVERNMENT.

Arguments for federation used in case of America—Provides union for national purposes—Separate state government for state purposes—Federalism best means for developing new countries—Sir John Seeley's opinion—Self-government stimulates political life—Secures good administration of local affairs—Diminishes difficulty of governing great areas—Relieves central legislature of much work better dealt with by local legislation—All above advantages hold good for South Africa—Sir George Grey's opinion—Only road to safety and success in South Africa—Bryce's opinion on success of federalism in America—Fiske's opinion—Freeman's eulogy—Federal success in case of Switzerland—Value of Swiss precedent for South Africa—Sir Henry Maine's tribute to success—Lesson plain to South Africa—Rapid movement of questions in South Africa—Direction of development towards powerful union—Importance of seizing right moment—Value of federation to enable South Africa to occupy proper position in regard to Europe—To realize its legitimate aspirations 159

CHAPTER XIII.

OUR CONNECTION WITH EUROPE.

Must be connected with some European power—Which power—Spanish, French, and English systems tried in America—England's colonies self-governing—French and Spanish despotically ruled—Victory of English system—Collapse of French Canada when attacked by English colonies—Despotic rule—Cause of collapse—Same despotic rule in Portuguese and German colonies in South Africa—Consequent stagnation—English colonies in America resist England when she coerces—America after independence adopts English system—Special mechanism by which England has avoided despotism—Develops principle of representation and local self-government—Origin of principle—Territorial as opposed to Græco-Roman city system—Failure of Græco-Roman system—Goths introduce free institutions to Europe—Loss of this freedom on Continent, save in Holland and Switzerland—Cause of loss—Necessity for military organization—Insular position of England—Permits development of freedom—Contact with sea increases tendency to freedom—Importance of principle of self-government—Attempt by Sir Philip Woodehouse to destroy at Cape—Instances of safety of England due to insular position—Expansion of English institutions in America—Revolt against arbitrary rule in America—Similar revolt at Cape—Anti-convict agitation—Constitutional struggle—Sir Bartle Frere—Despotism—War of Independence—Dangers of interference in internal affairs of South Africa—Importance of using great principles of self-government and Federation at Cape—For above reasons connection must be with England 174

CHAPTER XIV.

CONNECTION OF SOUTH AFRICAN WITH UNIVERSAL HISTORY.

Gradual consolidation leads to widening peace area—War at first favours internal peace—Pax Romana—Civiliz-

CONTENTS. xxi

PAGE

ing result of Roman peace—Gradual removal of
barbaric frontier from Europe—Similar work in Africa
—Barbarism rolled back from Cape Peninsula—
Country won for civilization and peace—Emigrant
farmers put an end to murderous rule of Dingaan and
Moselikatse—Terrible effects of Chaka's operations—
800,000 natives destroyed—Boer settles between
hostile clans—Saves remnant of mountain tribes—
Boer colonization—Admirable system—Boer views
of natives—No intermixture—Importance of this—
Dutch and English native policy compared—Dr.
Wallace's views—Boer taken his full share in costly
work of civilization—As Rome moved frontier of
barbarism eastward, so South African colonies and
states are moving it northwards 200

CHAPTER XV.

A NOBLE IDEAL.

Society at first militant type—*Contract* or industrial type
replaces *Status* or military type—State now exists for
members, not members for state—Coercion decreases
and representation arises—Society no longer compelled to be self-contained—International commerce
arises—Divisions between nations disappear—Consolidation now takes place by Federation—Advance
in civilization dependent on cessation of war—
Peaceful Federation is only further Consolidation—
Cessation of war unwelcome to most—Action of High
Commissioner—Character of rank and file—Hope of
few—Historical development of peaceful Federation
—Results achieved by United States—War of
Secession—Fought to secure principle of decisions
between states by judicial process, no longer by war
—American system given peace to a vast area—
Africa's ideal similar to give peace to area south of

CONTENTS.

	PAGE
Zambesi and Cunene—Area as great as Europe omitting Russia—South Africa thus fitted to take its place among great federated groups of the world—Christian principles and ethical theory unite to confirm ideal—Words of Washington in conclusion .	. 210

APPENDICES.

I.—AREA OF UNITED STATES AND OF SOUTH AFRICA   223

II.—DR. A. R. WALLACE'S COMPARISON OF ENGLISH AND DUTCH METHODS OF NATIVE TREATMENT   225

III.—THE TEXT OF THE CONSTITUTION OF THE UNITED STATES OF AMERICA 230

INDEX   251

MAPS.

POLITICAL MAP OF SOUTH AFRICA .   .   *to face page*   1

MAP OF AMERICA SHOWING ACQUISITIONS OF TERRITORY BY ORIGINAL THIRTEEN STATES   81

MAP OF SOUTH AFRICAN SYSTEM   .   .   ,,   81

A FEDERAL SOUTH AFRICA.

CHAPTER I.

INTRODUCTORY.

Statement of problem—Successful solution of similar problem in America—Value of these results for South Africa—Origin of separate states in South Africa—Unwise policy of British Government—Re-union never lost sight of—Unfavourable influence of Sir Philip Woodehouse's action—Favourable influence of grant of Responsible Government to Cape Colony—Fatal effects of Lord Carnarvon's policy—Present position of colonies and states—Practically autonomous—Dangers of this condition—Similar condition of American colonies after independence won and before union formed—Value of American precedent for South Africa.

THE thoughtful student of South African events must have been struck by the fact that the time is rapidly approaching when the people of this southern extremity of the continent will be called upon to decide whether their political development is to be in the direction of a number of separate states or confederacies, or of a strong and powerful union.

We may put the question in the identical words used by Jay in the second number of the famous *Federalist*: " It is well worthy of consideration, therefore, whether it would conduce more to the interest of the people of America [South Africa] that they should to all general purposes, be one nation, under one federal government, or that they should divide themselves into separate confederacies, and give to the head of each the same limit of power which they are advised to place in one national government."

It will be the object of this series of papers to discuss this momentous question.

We must then inquire why the solution of this problem is becoming urgent, what are likely to be the advantages and what the disadvantages of a closer union, what are the conditions which favour such a union, and, further, in what form this union may be effected?

We are not called upon to face for the first time the great problem "whether societies of men are really capable or not of establishing good government from reflection and choice, or whether they are for ever destined to depend for their political constitution on accident and force." This has been solved by the history and practice of the United States of America for more than one hundred years. These results have recently been made available by means of several learned and interesting works. South Africa is therefore in the fortunate position of having a precedent to follow and an easy means of access to all the information necessary to completely analyze and comprehend the manner in which these results have been attained. The difficulties with which the authors of this great American confederation had to contend were by no means light, indeed at one time the closer union appeared all but hopeless. The results, however, of disunion and the dangers into which the states were rapidly led, were such that the patriotic and far-seeing men in all the states realized that the time had come when smaller differences and ambitions must be sunk in face of the necessity of securing the whole country against the manifold dangers with which it was threatened by disunion.

So well known is the extent, power, wealth, influence and progress of the United States of America that I need not dwell upon it here. It is a magnificent example to South Africa, and well worthy of her careful and anxious consideration in contemplating her own future.

It is only in comparatively recent years that any question of union of colonies and states could arise in South Africa, as there was only one state—the "Old Colony" or Cape Colony. The policy of the English Government, which at first forbad the settlers to follow out the necessary and inevitable movement towards expansion, led to the seizure of Natal, and the subsequent abandonment of these settlers gave rise to the Free State and the Transvaal.

In 1845 Natal was erected into a separate government under a lieutenant governor. In 1852 the independence of the South African Republic was recognized by Great Britain, and in 1854 the Orange Free State was formed upon the abandonment of the Orange River sovereignty by Great Britain.

Thus in the same year in which representative institutions were granted to the Cape, there were in existence several colonies and states. The question of their reunion to the old colony was never lost sight of by the leading men of the Cape Parliament. Indeed Mr. Solomon discussed it in his first election address in 1854. In 1858 the Orange Free State Volksraad had passed a resolution in favour of annexation to the Cape, but Sir E. Bulwer Lytton informed Sir G. Grey[1] "that her Majesty's Government were not prepared to depart from the settled policy of their predecessors by advising the resumption of British sovereignty in any shape over the Free State."[2] Between 1860 and 1865 the question of the voluntary reannexation of the Free State and Transvaal was again freely mooted in those states, but the arbitrary and high-handed proceedings of her Majesty's High Commissioner, Sir Philip Woodehouse, both in regard to the interference in the Basuto War in favour of the Basutos— an act the far-reaching consequences of which have not yet been fully developed—and in regard to the domestic affairs of the Cape Colony, nipped this feeling in the bud.

When, however, the question of Responsible Government was being brought to an issue in the Cape Parliament in 1871, the Free State openly said that it was prepared to join the Cape if responsible government were accepted, but not otherwise, and the congratulations of the Presidents of the Free State and the Transvaal to the first Premier of the Cape, the late Sir John Molteno, on his accession to office were warm and significantly worded. The President of the South

---

[1] See note at end of chapter.
[2] Parliamentary Papers, C. 508, pp. 12, 14.

African Republic wrote after conveying his congratulations, " I feel assured that the change brought about in this respect (responsible government) by the united actions of her Majesty's representative and the representatives of the people of the Cape Colony will tend to the good of South Africa at large as well as the Cape Colony in particular; while at the same time I am confident it will direct the spirit of the nation in that proper channel which will ultimately lead to a closer union between the different colonies and states of South Africa."

Federation was looked upon as the certain result of the grant of Responsible Government to the Cape, and Lord Kimberley gave Sir Henry Barkly authority to summon a meeting of all the colonies and states to consider the "conditions of union."[1] The rapprochement, however, was soon clouded over by the action of the High Commissioner in the case of the Diamond Fields annexation, which was not approved by Cape statesmen, indeed was opposed by them as far as was possible; and finally the whole matter was shipwrecked by Lord Carnarvon's ill-conceived and ill-advised attempt at a forcible confederation. On this we cannot dwell; no darker period ever passed over South Africa. Force and fraud were rampant, peoples were deprived of their constitutional rights—their chosen form of government, and the country deluged in blood. In the words of the divine poet: " non ragioniam di lor ma guarda è passa." It was an attempt to force a plant in place of allowing it to grow. The hurricane is over, its effects are still with

[1] Parliamentary Papers, C. 508, p. 14.

us; but a wiser policy and the lapse of time are healing the wounds, and the plant of natural growth, which was so ruthlessly torn up between 1875 and 1881, is now quietly rooting once more under the favouring sunshine of prosperity and peace.

Thus the question of union has ever been before the people of South Africa as a natural desire springing out of their common feeling for unity. Had the working of responsible government, which was being watched with anxious interest by the other states, been allowed to proceed untrammelled in the Cape, it would have been a solution of all South African troubles, and the states, seeing the freedom of management of all local affairs enjoyed by the Cape, would have been long since ready to come in under the same system.

The problem now is a very different one, and at the same time a more urgent one. History is being made rapidly in South Africa, almost too rapidly for those on the spot, accustomed to the slower development which was the normal course of affairs before the discovery of the Diamond Fields in 1870, to follow up and keep pace with.

A great change has come over the affairs of South Africa since 1872, when the Cape first entered upon responsible government. The colonies and states of South Africa are to-day in large measure independent powers, sovereign in their own territories and in their relation with each other. The Cape with its responsible government has full control of its internal affairs and its commerce, while it practically controls its relations with the neighbouring colonies and states. The Transvaal has, by recourse to arms, convinced England of her desire for independence and freedom from foreign control, while the immense wealth pouring into her coffers has given her the means and dignity which at some period of her history she stood much in need of. The Free State was abandoned by England against the wishes of her inhabitants, but having prospered and developed under her independent government, she also is free from foreign interference. Within the last year or two Natal has entered upon responsible government, and has already given ample evidence of her fitness to shape her own course. Thus the control of all the states in their internal affairs as well as their external and internal fiscal relations has been entrusted to those who are responsible to local public opinion for their acts, and, so far as these questions are concerned, they are practically free to control their own destiny.

A strong local attachment to their several governments has grown up in each colony and state, just as was the case with the people of the various states of America. While this factor has its advantages it has also its evils to be guarded against, and with a view to bringing out the dangers which now threaten these colonies and states, owing to their acquisition of practical autonomy, we will point out the very close analogy which exists between their condition and that of the American colonies immediately after their independence had been acknowledged by Great Britain. Similar conditions give rise to similar results; the newly-won freedom has in each case given rise to the pursuit by the various states of a separate and frequently hostile policy in regard to their neighbours. The comparison will serve to bring out in concrete form and with admirable clearness and force the dangers of the position, and will also point to the remedy which, if applied in good time, will doubtless have the like effective and glorious result of founding the basis of a great and united South African Federation.

NOTE.—When Sir George Grey brought the resolution of the Orange Free State in favour of union before the Cape Parliament in his opening speech in 1859, he suggested a federation of the colonies and states. For this action he was reprimanded and summarily recalled by Sir E. Bulwer Lytton and Lord Carnarvon, the latter being Under Secretary for the Colonies, and largely entrusted with the conduct of the department owing to Lytton's bad health.

CHAPTER II.

THE CRITICAL PERIODS OF AMERICAN AND SOUTH AFRICAN HISTORY.

Condition of American colonies when war broke out—similar condition of South African colonies and states—Forms of government—Congress sole bond after war—Weakness of Congress—Fate predicted for colonies in Europe—Patriotism of leading statesmen—No central authority—Colonies retain power of taxation—Failure to pay interest on public debts—Army unruly—Commercial war between colonies—Selfish policy of New York—Isolated policy of Transvaal—Quarrel between New York and Connecticut over duties—Similar tariff war between Cape and Transvaal—Closing of drifts—Feeling of Uitlander population—Dangers of this—Necessity for peaceful fusion of races—Fine qualities of Boers—English and Dutch traits complementary—Both necessary for development of South Africa.

THE period referred to in the history of America, opens with the signature of the preliminary articles of peace at Paris on the 20th January, 1783, which gave to the thirteen colonies of Great Britain the acknowledgment and guarantee of their independence after the revolutionary war. "When in the reign of George III. troubles arose between England and her North American colonists, there existed along the eastern coast of the Atlantic thirteen little communities, the largest of which (Virginia) had not more than half a million of free people, and the total population of which did not reach three millions. All owned allegiance to the British Crown, all, except Connecticut and Rhode Island (who elected their governors), received their governors from the Crown; in all, causes were carried by appeal from the colonial courts to the English Privy Council. Acts of the British Parliament ran there, as they now run in the British colonies, whenever expressed to have that effect, and could overrule such laws as the colonies might make. *But practically each colony was a self-governing commonwealth—left to manage its own affairs with scarcely any interference from home.* Each had its legislature, its own statutes adding to or modifying the English common law, its local corporate life and traditions, with no small local pride in its own history and institutions, superadded to the pride of forming part of the English race and the great free British realm. Between the various colonies there was no other political connection than that which arose from their all belonging to this race and realm, so that the inhabitants of each enjoyed in every one of the others the rights and privileges of British subjects." [1]

The means of travel were slow and expensive and dangerous, by reason of bad roads and unbridged rivers; people never undertook long journeys except for very important reasons. Most people lived and died without having seen any state but their own.

[1] Bryce's "American Commonwealth," p. 16.

And as the mails were irregular and uncertain, and the rates of postage very high, people heard from one another but seldom.

There were very limited commercial dealings between the different states. A few small cities were scattered along the immense line of coast, but they were isolated from each other. Agriculture was the chief occupation of the people, and this was carried on by small farmers who were naturally attached to old ideas and habits. Manufactures can hardly be said to have come into existence. Everywhere there was an extreme jealousy of outside interference or control. Indeed, the country was so thinly inhabited in many parts that there may be said to have been no government at all, and as in Africa, the outlying districts feared that in forming a government they might be "forging fetters for themselves."

"Under such circumstances the different parts of the country knew very little of each other, and local prejudices were intense. It was not simply free Massachusetts and slave-holding Carolina or English Connecticut and Dutch New York that misunderstood and ridiculed each other; but even between such neighbouring states as Connecticut and Massachusetts, both of them thoroughly English and Puritan, and in all their social conditions almost exactly alike, it used often to be said that there was no love lost."[1]

This description aids us in comprehending the difficulties which beset the path of those patriotic

[1] Fiske, "The Critical Period of American History," p. 62.

men in each state who saw that the time had come when such local feelings, unless properly directed, were likely to lead to a break up of the loose confederation which then existed, and to encourage the growth of a number of weakly states in place of the grand union of all in one united whole as we see it to-day. It has also an interest for our subject, inasmuch as it points to a state of affairs in many ways very similar to that in the South African States. The occupation of the people is chiefly agriculture cities are few and small; there are strong local prejudices, and little intercommunication between different districts, except in the quite recently constructed main lines of railway. The jealousies of states have their counterpart also—the rivalry between the Cape and Natal may be likened to that between Connecticut and Massachusetts, while the feeling between Natal and the Transvaal had its counterpart in that between English Connecticut and Dutch New York.

Commercial dealings are still very few between the South African States, the traffic to the Transvaal being chiefly in over-sea goods; and between Natal and the Cape there hardly exists any local traffic, if we except a little coal and less fruit. By reason, however, of the greater compactness of the territories of the South African States as a whole than those of America, and the smaller numbers, being practically five, if we include the Chartered Company's territories, as against thirteen in America, the difficulties in the way of bringing about a union are much lessened.

"At the time of the declaration of independence there were three forms of government in the Colonies. Connecticut and Rhode Island had always been true republics, with governors and legislative assemblies elected by the people. Pennsylvania and Maryland presented the appearance of limited hereditary monarchies. Their assemblies were chosen by the people, but the lords proprietary appointed their governors, or in some instances acted as governors themselves. In Maryland the office of lord proprietary was hereditary in the Calvert family; in Delaware and Pennsylvania, which though distinct commonwealths with separate legislatures had the same executive head, it was hereditary in the Penn family. The other eight colonies were viceroyalties, with governors appointed by the king, while in all alike the people elected the legislatures."[1] The states now made the necessary changes in order to provide for their separation from the home Government, and they all kept their House of Representatives, while in nearly all there was a senate as well, and the governor was elected for a short period with strictly limited prerogatives.

Each of these small states was now ready to assume a position as a sovereign state such as it had never occupied before, and all were thus beset by the danger we have noticed above, that they would form a set of petty states and not a grand confederation.

There had been some common action between the

[1] Fiske, "The Critical Period of American History," p. 64.

Colonies, as the war had been conducted by Congress, which had first met in 1777, but this Congress had made use of implied war powers rather than of any legal and constitutional power entrusted to it. It had no power to levy taxes or duties, and it had steadily declined in authority and respectability until eventually it was subjected to the indignity of being driven out of Philadelphia by some eighty recently disbanded soldiers. "These men broke from their camp at Lancaster, and marched down to Philadelphia, led by a sergeant or two. They drew up in line before the state house, where Congress was assembled, and after passing the grog, began throwing stones and pointing their muskets at the windows. They demanded pay, and threatened, if it were not forthcoming, to seize the members of Congress and hold them as hostages, or else break into the bank where the federal deposits were kept. The Executive Council of Pennsylvania sat in the same building, and so the federal Government appealed to the state Government for protection. The appeal was fruitless. President Dickinson had a few state militia at his disposal, but did not dare to summon them, for fear they should side with the rioters. The city government was equally listless, and the townsfolk went their way as if it were none of their business; and so Congress fled across the river and on to Princetown, where the college afforded it shelter. Thus in a city of thirty-two thousand inhabitants, the largest city in the country, the Government of the United States, the body which had just completed a treaty browbeating England

and France, was ignominiously turned out of doors by a handful of drunken mutineers."[1]

The incident was not very important in itself, but as an index of the feebleness of Congress, it brings before us the hopeless inefficiency of the body in discharging the functions of a supreme authority.

Washington saw all this clearly, and he, on June 8th, 1783, in view of the disbandonment of the army, had addressed to the governors and presidents of the several states a circular letter, which he wished to have regarded as his legacy to the American people. Among other points which he insisted upon as essential to the very existence of the United States of America as an independent power were "That there must be an indissoluble union of all the states under a single federal government, and that the people must be willing to sacrifice, if need be, some of their local interests to the common weal; they must discard some of their local prejudices, and regard one another as fellow-citizens of a common country with interests in the deepest and truest sense identical."

"But the time had not yet come, only through the discipline of perplexity and tribulation could the people be brought to realize the indispensable necessity of that indissoluble union of which Washington had spoken. Thomas Paine was sadly mistaken when, in the moment of exultation over the peace, he declared that the trying time was ended. The most trying time of all was just beginning. It is not too much to say that the period of five years

[1] Fiske, p. 112.

following the peace of 1783 was the most critical moment in all the history of the American people."[1]

The statesmen of Europe generally expected that the states would be split up into a set of little powerless republics. Josiah Tucker, Dean of Gloucester, far-sighted in many things, said, "As to the future grandeur of America, and its being a rising empire under one head, whether republican or monarchical, it is one of the idlest and most visionary notions that ever was conceived, even by writers of romance. The mutual antipathies and clashing interests of the Americans, their difference of governments, habitude, and manners indicate that they will have no centre of union and no common interest. They never can be united into one compact empire under any species of government whatever; a disunited people till the end of time, suspicious and distrustful of each other, they will be divided and subdivided into little commonwealths or principalities according to natural boundaries, by great bays of the sea, and by vast rivers, lakes, and ridges of mountains."

Such was the fate predicted for the states which had just won their independence, and there was really a great deal in the history of these five years to justify these forebodings. What then saved them from the fate predicted for them, and that with so much reason? The ability of the great men who were to be found in each state, men whose characters had been developed and brought out by the trying

[1] Fiske, p. 55.

times through which they had passed. But even more than the ability, the splendid patriotism of these men pulled their country through this crisis and set the foundations of future greatness. Delegates from twelve states met at Philadelphia in 1787, there were among them men of great political sagacity, men such as Randolph, Madison, Hamilton, and Benjamin Franklin, while Washington presided over their deliberations. They discussed the situation and agreed upon a new system of government, whereby the dangers of disunion might be once for all averted. Not only did they agree upon a scheme, but they succeeded in making the peoples of thirteen states adopt, defend, and cherish it. Thus by an act of splendid statesmanship they devised a constitution under which the United States of America have expanded and grown to the mighty power which we see them to-day.

We have seen, then, that at this time the sole bond between the now independent colonies was Congress. But, as we have already seen, this Congress was a merely revolutionary body which owed its existence to the war with England. It first assembled to meet what was thought to be only a temporary emergency. It is true that it declared the independence of the colonies, and in 1777 it assumed a legal character, when the Thirteen States, as they now called themselves, entered into a "firm league of friendship with each other," but at the same time declared that "Each state retains its sovereignty, freedom and independence, and every power, jurisdiction and right, which is not by this Confederation expressly delegated to the United States in Congress assembled."

It is to be carefully noted that this Confederation created no central authority. There was no federal executive, no central representation of the whole of the states, no power which came into direct relation with individuals in the states, it merely dealt with the states as states, making requisitions on them for such supplies as were necessary for carrying on the war, but it had no means of enforcing these requisitions, and, as a matter of fact, they were, in many instances, not complied with by the states.

"The power of levying the taxes was thus retained entirely by the states. They not only imposed direct taxes as they do to-day, but they laid duties on exports and imports, each according to its own narrow view of its local interests. . . . They shared likewise with Congress the powers of coining money, of emitting bills of credit, and of making their promissory notes a legal tender for debts."[1]

This was the constitution under which the states began to drift towards anarchy as soon as they were relieved from the pressure of foreign interference. To save their credit it was necessary that at least the interest on the public debt should be paid, and for this purpose Congress asked the powers to levy a five per cent. duty on imports. This was the signal for a year of angry discussion. It was said, "If taxes could thus be levied by any power outside the state, why had we ever opposed the Stamp Act or the tea duties?"

[1] Fiske, p. 98.

"For the current expenses of government in that same year $9,000,000 were needed. Of this it was proposed to raise $4,000,000 by loan, and the other $5,000,000 were demanded of the states. At the end of the year $422,000 had been collected, not a cent. of which came from Georgia, the Carolinas, or Delaware. Of the taxes assessed in 1783 only one fifth part had been paid by the middle of 1785."[1]

The army was without pay, and became unruly; matters went so far that Colonel Louis Nichola actually addressed a letter to Washington urging him to come forward as a saviour of society, and accept the crown at the hands of his faithful soldiers. Washington, of course, indignantly refused. Seditious meetings were called, and it needed all the influence and skill of Washington to prevent an outbreak. We have already seen how in 1781 Congress was driven out of Philadelphia by the mutinous soldiers.

The different states now began to make commercial war upon each other. "No sooner had the other three New England states virtually closed their ports to British shipping than Connecticut threw hers wide open, an act which she followed up by levying duties upon imports from Massachusetts. Pennsylvania discriminated against Delaware, and New Jersey —pillaged at once by both her greater neighbours— was compared to a cask tapped at both ends. The conduct of New York became equally selfish and blameworthy. After the departure of the British the revival of business went on with leaps and bounds. George Clinton had come to be the most powerful

---

[1] Fiske, p. 104.

man in New York. He had come to look upon the state almost as his own private manor, and his life was devoted to furthering its interests as he understood them. It was his first article of faith that New York must be the greatest state in the Union. But his conceptions of statesmanship were extremely narrow. He was the vigorous and steadfast advocate of every illiberal and exclusive measure, and the most uncompromising enemy of a closer union of the states. His great popular strength and the commercial importance of the community in which he held sway made him at this time the most dangerous man in America. Under his guidance the history of New York during the five years following the peace of 1783 was a shameful story of greedy monopoly and sectional hate." [1]

In South Africa we may compare the position of the Transvaal with that of New York. The same prosperity has come to the Transvaal after its independence was won, owing to the discovery of the gold mines; and its action has been in the direction of isolation from the neighbouring colonies.

What has been the cause of this policy? A fear that its independence may be endangered, and a feeling that the game was not being played quite fairly by the colonies. These latter are like spoilt children, constantly running to their mother England and complaining that the big bully, the Transvaal, has hurt them; as a proof of this we may instance the appeal to England when the "Drifts" were closed. This was a fair card for the Transvaal to

[1] Fiske, p. 145.

play in the interests of its own railway policy, and the game should have been left to the South African players, but one party prepared to call in the aid of England for its own purposes. The drifts would have been opened without this foreign pressure, for the domestic needs of the Transvaal were such that it would have been unable to maintain this obstruction for any length of time, and the same result, so far as the Cape Colony was concerned, would have been attained; but in this case without that bitter feeling which foreign interference must cause. These questions, which are entirely South African, should be settled between the South African Colonies and States without any foreign interference, and a far better feeling would prevail between them all when all are placed upon the same footing. This policy of isolation on the part of the Transvaal will be rendered unnecessary when a union is formed, such as we advocate, with complete autonomy in regard to all internal South African affairs.

We shall see that this tendency towards isolation has produced further results similar to those produced by similar action in America.

"The city of New York with its population of 30,000 souls, had long been supplied with firewood from Connecticut, and with butter and cheese, chickens and garden vegetables from the thrifty farms of New Jersey. This trade, it was observed, carried thousands of dollars out of the city, and into the pockets of detested Yankees and despised Jersey men. It was ruinous to domestic industry, said the men of New York. It must be stopped by those effective remedies of the Sangrado school of economic doctors, a navigation act and a protective tariff. Acts were accordingly passed, obliging every Yankee sloop which came down through Hell Gate, and every Jersey market boat which was rowed across from Paulus Hook to Cortlandt Street, to pay entrance fees and obtain clearances at the custom house, just as was done by ships from London or Hamburg; and not a cart-load of Connecticut firewood could be delivered at the back door of a country house in Beekman Street until it should have paid a heavy duty. Great and just was the wrath of the farmers and lumbermen. The New Jersey legislature made up its mind to retaliate. The city of New York had lately bought a small patch of ground on Sandy Hook, and had built a lighthouse there. This lighthouse was the one weak spot in the heel of Achilles where a hostile arrow could strike, and New Jersey gave vent to her indignation by laying a tax of $1800 a year on it. Connecticut was equally prompt. At a great meeting of business men, held at New London, it was unanimously agreed to suspend all commercial intercourse with New York. Every merchant signed an agreement, under penalty of $250 for the first offence, not to send any goods whatever into the hated state for a period of twelve months. By such retaliatory measures, it was hoped that New York might be compelled to rescind her odious enactment. But such meetings and such resolves bore an ominous likeness to the meetings and resolves which in the years before 1775 had heralded a state of war; and but for the good work done by the federal convention, another five years would scarcely have elapsed before shots would have been fired, and seeds of perennial hatred sown on the shores that look toward Manhattan Island."[1]

We can match these exclusive restrictions on the trade between New York and its neighbours when we remember the duties imposed by the Transvaal on vegetables and fruit coming from the Cape, and from that part of the Cape which had given that country most sympathy and support in its time of trial and tribulation—the districts of the Paarl, Stellenbosch, Wellington, and Worcester. These districts now saw the country which they had loved and cherished in its adversity, turn from them and spurn them in its day of prosperity, and this happened to coincide with the devastations of the Phylloxera in those very districts. A market for their other fruits would have been a godsend to them just then. The conduct of the Transvaal, however forcibly its action might be justified by a consideration of its own interests, was all the more painful to them.

Are we not in the presence of a real and increasing danger arising from these hostile measures in the great matter of commerce? For a very recent act of this kind we have only to refer to the closing of the " Drifts," an act of the most hostile character to the commerce of the Cape and Free State Railways. An act which has received the most severe condemnation at the hands of the public of all the South African States, and an act which gave rise to a very dangerous

[1] Fiske, p. 145.

state of feeling among the populations of the great gold centres of the Transvaal itself, who found their commerce and their industry paralyzed, and their supplies of food and provisions suddenly cut off. A timely concession on the part of the Government of the Transvaal averted any serious consequences at the moment, but it will leave a lasting impression on those populations that their vast interests may be sacrificed in a moment to the ill-advised action, as it appears to them, of an autocrat irresponsible so far as they are concerned.

The more shallow thinkers rather welcome the action of President Kruger on such occasions because they consider them favourable to an uprising of the large "Uitlander" population against the rule of the Boers at an earlier period than would otherwise be the case. But men who have the real interests of South Africa at heart, and know her best, realize the immense importance of a peaceful and natural solution to the great problem of the assimilation of the wealthy and populous communities, which have suddenly grown up around the gold areas, with the older population of the Transvaal and with the South African system generally. They realize that President Kruger has had to face one of the greatest difficulties which any statesman can be called upon to face, namely, the peaceful invasion of his state by foreigners who outnumber the original population. The problem presented by this condition of affairs is so difficult that it would try the powers of the ablest statesmen, and if a solution has not yet been attained, there is every reason why consideration and patience should be extended to the President's efforts to solve the difficulty.

The leading men among these communities have come from the Cape Colony, from Natal, and the Free State. They have brought with them their knowledge of the conditions of the colonies from which they have come; they have their circle of relatives and friends there and their many ties. In them, too, we find the most enterprising, the most active men who, at Kimberley and elsewhere, have shown their energy, and have mixed with the Europeans who have more recently arrived in South Africa, bringing with them their active ways and thoughts, and mode of action. These two different strains were in Cape Colony amalgamated into a society of men who have the qualities best suited to develop South Africa, and to solve the problem of the perfect union and fusion of European settlers with the more antiquated and conservative farmer, who still holds the larger part of the land of the Transvaal, the Cape Colony, and the Free State. This latter class of men are ready to follow the lead of those whom they perceive to be in sympathy with them, who understand the difficulties with which they have to cope in making the land yield an adequate return to their labours, and who appreciate the conditions of isolation under which they must exist and bring up their families. When they have once given a man of this kind their confidence they will follow him in the direction of progress far beyond the limit to which they can appreciate his motives or to which they can reason out affairs for themselves. Such men were

Sir George Grey, the late Mr. Porter and the late Sir John Molteno; the latter of these was able to carry the whole of the men of this character with him in his railway policy, when he brought in bills for the expenditure of five millions on railways in a country whose total revenue three or four years before was not 600,000*l.* per annum.

These yeomen farmers are now practically the backbone of South Africa, and splendid material they are. Physically they are grand men, and their moral qualities and their patriotism are capable of the highest development when opportunity offers. If treated unjustly, or with the rude hand of force, these lovers of liberty and peace are content first to fly from oppression to the wilderness, whenever this has been possible; but when brought to bay, as in the Transvaal in 1881, they are ready to face the might of England in following what they believe is "God and the right." It is, then, of supreme importance to South Africa that these men should not be set in antagonism to the new population before each has had time and opportunity to learn and appreciate the other's good qualities—which qualities are in a large measure complementary to each other—the one admirably adapted to work the soil under the rough conditions and in the isolation which must long remain characteristic of South African farming life, while the other naturally takes to the towns, and carries on the trade, the commerce, the mining and manufacturing industries, which are complementary to the pursuits of agriculture. Both are necessary for the solid and orderly development of South Africa.

CHAPTER III.

THE CRITICAL PERIODS—*Continued.*

Territorial troubles in America—Quarrel between Connecticut and Pennsylvania over Wyoming—Between New York and New Hampshire over Green Mountains—Territorial troubles in South Africa—Washington's remedy—Financial distress after war—Legislative attempts to remedy—Serious troubles in Rhode Island and Massachusetts—Armed risings—Attack on Federal arsenal—Army of 4000 men called out—Congress unable to restore order—Currency legislation at Cape—Trouble due to want of central power—Dangers of similar position in South Africa—America applied remedy—Will South African statesmen apply similar remedy—Danger of enmities if delayed—Common commercial interests brought states together in America—Similar operations of commercial interests in South Africa.

To the commercial troubles already described, there were also added territorial ones. "There was a chronic quarrel between Connecticut and Pennsylvania over the valley of the Wyoming in the Autumn of 1782. A special Federal Court had adjudged the prize to Pennsylvania, and the Government of Connecticut submitted. In 1784 a great flood overtook and overwhelmed this district. The people were starving with cold and hunger, but so strong was the feeling that the Pennsylvania Legislature refused to give any assistance; it was said it served the settlers right; they should have gone to Connecticut, to which they belonged, and a scheme was actually devised for driving out the settlers and partitioning their lands among a company of speculators. A force of militia was sent to Wyoming. They attacked the settlements, turned five hundred people out of doors, and burned their houses to the ground. Heartrending scenes ensued. Many died of exhaustion or furnished food for wolves. But this was more than the Pennsylvania Legislature intended. The leader of the expedition was recalled; he, however, disobeyed, then all the Connecticut men in the neighbouring country flew to arms. Men were killed on both sides. Great was the indignation in New England when all the proceedings were heard of. The matter had become very serious, and war between Connecticut and Pennsylvania might easily grow out of it."[1] The Pennsylvania Legislature now became ashamed of what had been done, and ordered full reparation to be made to the persecuted settlers of Wyoming.

It is with difficulty we can credit that such treatment could be accorded by people of the same blood and origin to one another, but a little anarchy soon gives rein to the evil and more brutal instincts of men.

"During the revolutionary war there was a fierce dispute between New York and New Hampshire for the possession of the Green Mountains; the Green Mountain Boys endeavoured to declare the district

[1] Fiske, p. 147.

of Vermont an independent state. Massachusetts now also laid claim to the disputed territory. New York sent troops to the threatened frontier; New Hampshire prepared to do likewise, and for a moment war seemed inevitable. Washington now appeared as peace-maker and managed to smooth matters down. Meanwhile, on the debatable frontier, between Vermont and New York, the embers of hatred smouldered; barns and houses were set on fire and belated wayfarers were found mysteriously murdered in the depths of the forest."[1]

South Africa, too, has had its territorial troubles, we can all recollect the strained state of feeling between the Chartered forces and those of the Transvaal on the Limpopo. Then there was the Stellaland and Goschen affair, when Sir Charles Warren's expedition was sent out to restore order. There can be no doubt that the Transvaal, Natal, and to some extent the Free State, have seen with feelings of some jealousy and keen regret the absorption of the large territory to the west and north of the Transvaal by the Chartered Company; we will return to this subject presently.

The state of affairs in America, which we have described above, was the subject of anxious thought on the part of the leading men of the country, the possibilities of serious results were all too evident. "It is clear to me as A B C," said Washington, "that an extension of federal powers would make us one of the most happy, wealthy, respectable, and powerful nations that ever inhabited the terrestrial globe;

[1] Fiske, p. 151.

without them we shall soon be everything that is the direct reverse. I predict the worst consequences from a half-starved, limping Government, always moving upon crutches and tottering at every step."

"There is no telling," says Fiske, "how long the state of affairs which followed the revolution might have continued had not the crisis been precipitated by the wild attempts of the several states to remedy the distress of the people by legislation."[1]

"The financial distress after the war was widespread and deep-seated. All trade had been dislocated, there was little else but specie with which to pay for imports, and the country was soon drained of what little specie there was. There was a reversion to the practice of barter, and the revival of business was further impeded. Whisky in North Carolina, tobacco in Virginia, did duty as the measures of value; and Isaiah Thomas, editor of the Worcester *Spy*, announced that he would receive subscriptions for his paper in salt pork."[2] All the states, with the exception of two, now began to issue paper money, and attempted to force it into circulation.

This gave rise to a very serious state of affairs. The merchants refused to take the paper money, acts were passed to force them, they then closed their shops, and all business in some of the states came to a standstill. In Rhode Island the troubles were worst. "The farmers determined to starve the city people into submission, and they entered into an agreement not to send any produce into the cities until the merchants should open their shops and

[1] Fiske, p. 162.   [2] Ibid. p. 165.

begin selling their goods at its face value. Not wishing to lose their pigs, butter, and grain, they tried to dispose of them in Boston and New York and in the coast towns of Connecticut. But in all these places their proceedings had awakened such lively disgust that they were disappointed in these quarters. They now threw away their milk, used their corn for fuel, and let their apples rot on the ground rather than supply the detested merchants."[1] Food grew scarcer, the farmers were threatened with armed violence. The paper dollar had been issued in May, in November it passed for 16 cents.

In Massachusetts there were serious risings, the courts were broken up by armed mobs. The Governor sent a force of 600 militia, under General Shepard, to protect the Supreme Court. They were met by 600 insurgents, under Daniel Shays, by whom they were forced to beat a retreat. Fresh riots followed at Worcester and Concord. A regiment of cavalry was sent out by the Governor, and, after a fight, captured Job Shattuch, an insurgent leader, who had succeeded in breaking up the courts with several hundred armed men. This only exasperated the insurgents, who assembled in Worcester to the number of 1200 or more. The Governor then called out an army of 4400 men, who were placed under General Lincoln. The rebels meanwhile marched upon Springfield, with intent to capture the federal arsenal there and provide themselves with muskets and cannons.

General Shepard held Springfield with 1200 men,

[1] Fiske, p. 175.

and Shays attacked him with 2000 insurgents, hoping to capture the place before Lincoln could arrive. The attack failed, and Shays withdrew. He was followed rapidly by General Lincoln, and eventually was taken prisoner and his men dispersed, but even then the rising was not quelled. Nearly a month later, one Captain Hamlin, with several hundred insurgents, plundered the town of Stockbridge and carried off the leading citizens as hostages; he was, however, defeated near Springfield, and this was the last of the insurrection in Massachusetts. There were other risings in the Northern States.[1]

Where was Congress during these troubles? Massachusetts would not hear of its troops setting foot on her territory, though Springfield was itself federal property. So weak was Congress that, when it was eventually decided to take some steps, owing to the alarm created in the whole country by the progress of the insurrection in Vermont, New Hampshire, Massachusetts, and Rhode Island, and when a call was made upon the states for a continental peace force, Congress did not dare to declare openly what it was to be used for, and the pretext put forward was that the troops were wanted for an expedition against the North-Western Indians. As Fiske has well said, National humiliation could go no further than such a confession on the part of the central Government, that it dared not use force in defence of those very articles of confederation to which it owed its existence. Thus, owing to all these various causes, "things had come to such a pass that people of all

[1] Fiske, p. 180.

shades of opinion were beginning to agree upon one thing—that something must be done and done quickly."[1]

In South Africa there have been few currency troubles, it is true ; paper money was resorted to in the Transvaal and Free State in early days, and strong attempts were made by the Government of the Cape which directly preceded responsible government to introduce a paper currency there, but though we have seen the prohibition of the use of English silver in the Transvaal, yet, so far as can at present be seen, no serious troubles are likely to arise there from this cause. The states and colonies are all too well off to make it necessary to resort to any extreme expedients of this kind. We have, however, drawn attention to these troubles in America, as they were in themselves very serious. They arose out of the unsettled and transitional state in which the thirteen states found themselves after their severance from Great Britain, and they will serve as a warning to South Africa to provide in time against similar dangers.

At such a time America had the extreme good fortune to have a large number of patriotic men who saw clearly that, however much such a condition of affairs might promote the interests of some of the larger states, and particularly those states which were so situated as to have an unlimited field for expansion in the almost unoccupied territories of the West, yet the great country as a whole would run the risk of being divided up into a number

[1] Fiske, p. 185.

of independent, petty, and hostile states constantly quarrelling among themselves, and eventually unable to present a united front to the world at large, whether in the way of commercial relations or in the more vital matter of self-defence. Already Europe regarded the states as hopelessly separated, and refused to make treaties of commerce; they "were bullied by England, insulted by Spain and France, and looked askance at in Holland," though the latter was the first to make a commercial treaty with them.

The statesmen of the infant republic were unselfish enough to sink their separate advantage in the benefit of the whole, and with what glorious results we now know, results which they in their most sanguine moments could never have anticipated.

The South African states have attained their independence happily in a peaceable manner in all instances save one, but this fact will not obviate the danger to which this power of independent action is liable. Has South Africa a sufficient number of statesmen who are able to appreciate the great future which may be hers if she is ready to form a strong union? Has she men able to see the serious dissensions which may arise out of actions such as the closing of the "drifts," and the imposition of duties on the produce of one part of South Africa against another? Has she men sufficiently unselfish to sink the aggrandizement of their own individual state or colony for the sake of the future greatness and prosperity of the whole of South Africa?

The population of each state will always support its own government in its action against any other state, however wrong that action may be; as Hamilton in the *Federalist* points out—and the italics which he uses are worthy of the importance of the statement, "*we should be ready to denominate injuries those things which were in reality the justifiable acts of independent sovereignties consulting a distinct interest.*" Hence the danger of setting the otherwise homogeneous populations of these South African states and colonies at enmity against one another if some plan of common union cannot be arranged.

A great future awaits South Africa, but the right moment must be seized for putting her on the road to consolidation of interests rather than to diversity. Wealth and population are pouring in with a rapidity unequalled almost in any country—great towns are springing up in Rhodesia, new states will be forming there. It is for South Africa's great men to come forward and sink all minor differences in a union which will, while recognizing the individuality of each state, yet combine all for the purposes common to all.

As commercial questions were responsible for much ill-feeling and trouble between the states of America, so commercial questions were those which eventually brought them together. The manner in which this was brought about is very instructive. In order to carry out a scheme suggested by Washington, to improve the navigation of the Potomac, it became necessary for two states—Virginia and Maryland—to act in concert, and eventually

Pennsylvania was also included. Washington suggested that while they were about it they might agree upon a common system of duties and other commercial regulations. Thereupon, Madison, in the Virginia legislature, prepared a motion that commissioners from all the states should hold a meeting to discuss the best method of securing a uniform treatment of commercial questions, but so jealous were the people of state rights that Madison, being the advocate of a closer union, did not dare to introduce it himself, but got John Tyler—a fierce zealot for state rights—to make the motion.[1] Maryland now suggested, in connection with the same matter, that while they were on the subject commissioners from all the states should meet to discuss a uniform system of duties.

Only five states met, so little was the interest in the matter, but on their presenting an address to all the states suggesting that a commission from all the states should consider a uniform system of commercial regulations, Congress approved the idea after long discussion, and eventually a convention, consisting of most of the best men in America, assembled in Independence Hall to amend the articles of confederation. All the states except Rhode Island were represented. As soon as the delegates met they chose George Washington as President, and after sitting for five months in secret conclave, they gave forth their constitution of the United States, which was eventually adopted by all the states.

In South Africa, too, we can see the germs of union

[1] Fiske, p. 214.

arising out of commercial questions. We see already the Cape Colony, the Free State, and the chartered territory in a Customs Union. We see also working arrangements for railways between the Cape and the Orange Free State, between the Transvaal and the Cape, between Natal and the Transvaal; and we have recently seen railway conferences sitting in which all the states and colonies of South Africa have been represented. We can, therefore, see a growing familiarity with the idea of common action and common policy, of mutual concessions and mutual considerations. A customs union and a railway union cannot be far off, and these will doubtless furnish effective stepping-stones to a closer political union.

CHAPTER IV.

CONDITIONS WHICH FAVOUR UNION IN SOUTH AFRICA.

One continuous territory—No great natural barriers—Healthy climate—Boundaries of South Africa defined—Republics populated from Cape Colony—European population uniformly dispersed—Assimilating power of Africander population—Similar distribution of English and Dutch languages throughout South Africa—Similar institutions—Same common law—Racial distinctions quickly disappear—Local patriotism supplants national antipathies—Distance from Europe favours freedom from European complications—Monroe Doctrine for South Africa.

WE have pointed out the reasons why this question of a federal union is a pressing one. We have seen that the newly-won freedom of the states in America led to anarchy until the machinery of union was devised. We have seen a similar freedom leading to similar results in South Africa. We have seen the dangers of delay and the invaluable lesson taught us by the great statesmen of America who took the proper steps to avert disaster. We will now proceed to consider whether and in what degree such a closer union is favoured by the circumstances of South Africa.

We may remark that South Africa is one continuous territory; there are no natural or impassable barriers between the various states and colonies. It is blessed with a variety of soils and productions, and, as a whole, it possesses as fine a climate as any in the world, a climate in which those of European origin are able to live and rear children, and not only able to maintain their physique, but to increase it, as is proved by the more than average height and physical development in those who have resided longest within its boundaries. It is true that it has no navigable rivers and lakes, but the advantage of railways for all practical purposes supplies the place of those natural waterways which in some countries so favourably affected their early development before the invention of steam.

When we speak of South Africa, we speak of the country bounded by the sea on all sides except the north, where the boundaries may roughly be said to be the Cunene towards the west and the Zambesi towards the east.

We have already pointed out incidentally how the populations of all the colonies and states have proceeded from a common origin in the Cape Colony. We have, therefore, a homogeneous element of population in all the states owing to this cause, while we have further the fact that a European population of most recent introduction has also spread itself over the several states in very similar proportions, and that a very rapid assimilation proceeds to identify these new streams of population wherever they are enabled to meet and, without interference from outside, learn to appreciate their mutual good qualities. The powerful absorbing and assimilating qualities of the Africander population is very remarkable when the absolute paucity of numbers is taken into account, and it may fitly be compared with the similar power shown by the relatively small number of America-born Americans, in absorbing and assimilating the gigantic streams of Europeans which have never ceased to pour into that continent during recent times. Each state has also its native population, but this is hardly to be looked at in the light of a connecting characteristic, as there is but little cohesion among this section of the people.

The languages of Dutch and English are distributed in a very similar manner in each colony or state, the towns being largely English-speaking, while the country populations all speak or understand Dutch.

The institutions of the colonies and states are very similar; each has its house of representatives and its governor or president at the head of its executive, while the system of laws is almost identical, the common law in all states or colonies being the old Roman-Dutch, with such additions as the legislature of each state has created by its statute law.

There are no racial differences or distinctions, wherever a knowledge of and sympathy with the older populations has had time to infuse the newer elements of the populations. All are ready to sink their differences of origin in their common efforts to advance the interests of the country in which they have made their homes and that of their children.

As Mr. Molteno, when supporting responsible government in 1871, said in reply to Mr. Eustace: "No feeling," said Mr. Molteno, "exists between Africanders and Englishmen as was represented by the last speaker (Mr. Eustace). As one knowing the country I can emphatically contradict that statement. (Cheers.) There are now not English, Dutch, French, or Germans, but colonists, desirous to do their best for their common country."

Removed from Europe by the ocean and by the deserts and swamps of Central Africa, South Africa need have feared no complications arising from the older and traditional enmities of the great European powers; but, unfortunately, South Africa had no common mouth-piece and no common voice to speak with authority at a critical time, and two European powers gained a footing and an increase of territory which has prevented the realization of the Monroe Doctrine [1] of South Africa for the South Africans becoming a fact, and which may yet embroil her in the quarrels of Europe. We will, however, return to this subject, and then point out the lesson of their loss and what hopes history holds out to us of the recovery of these lands for South Africa.

[1] This is based on President Monroe's Message to Congress in December, 1823:—

"We owe it, therefore, to candour and to the amicable relations between the United States and those powers to declare that we should consider any attempt on their part to extend their system to any portion of this hemisphere as dangerous to our peace and safety. With the existing colonies and dependencies of any European power we have not interfered, and shall not interfere."

CHAPTER V.

ADVANTAGES CONFERRED BY UNION.

>Preservation from evils of dissension—Arguments of *Federalist* applicable—Dangers from hostile duties and commercial rivalry—Territorial disputes—Loss of northern territories to South African system—Union would provide remedy—Northern territories compared with western territory of America—Surrender of claims of individual states to union—Precedent for South Africa—Necessity of dealing with the question—Success of American plan—Chartered Company's rule only temporary—Union would remove danger of hostile commercial action—Jealousies of South African states—Cost of collection of customs reduced by union—Abolition of internal customs' boundaries—Stimulus to commerce by internal free trade—Free interchange of products—Prosperity of each adds to prosperity of all—South Africa would present to world united front in matters of commerce.

HAVING seen, then, that nature has fitted South Africa to become one great and united whole, has favoured her in climate, has endowed her with vast mineral wealth, thus giving her the resources necessary for the establishment and maintenance of a powerful and united Government, we will proceed to examine what advantages are likely to accrue from a union of all her states and colonies.

And first among the advantages of such a union

will be the preservation of the young South African nation from the evils of dissension between the states themselves, and from domestic factions and convulsions. It may be said that while England remains the paramount power such dissensions would not be permitted, but we are taking a larger view of these matters, and it must be evident that the imperial factor in the local concerns of South Africa must, in the words of Sir H. Robinson, be gradually eliminated. We may here call to mind the fact that even while the American Colonies were under the British Government there were commercial rivalries and disputes over boundary lines. In 1756 Georgia and South Carolina even came to blows over the navigation of the Savannah River. Further, the union will be the founding. of a nation that is to be; hence the importance at this comparatively early stage of obviating the dangers of divided and hostile communities; we must, therefore, give this consideration its due weight. We may use the very words of Hamilton in the sixth number of the *Federalist*. "A man must be far gone in Utopian speculations who can seriously doubt that if these states should either be wholly disunited or only united in partial confederacies, the subdivisions into which they might be thrown would have frequent and violent contests with each other. To presume a want of motives for such contests as an argument against their existence, would be to forget that men are ambitious, vindictive, and rapacious. To look for a continuation of harmony among a number of independent and unconnected sovereignties in the same neighbourhood, would be to set at defiance the accumulated experiences of ages. The causes of hostility among nations are innumerable. There are some which have a general and almost constant 'operation upon the collective bodies of society. Of this description are the love of power or the desire of pre-eminence and dominion— the jealousy of power or the desire of equality and safety. There are others which have a more circumscribed, though an equally operative influence within their spheres. Such are the rivalships and competitions of commerce between commercial nations. And there are others not less numerous than either of the former, which take their origin entirely in private passions; in the attachments, enmities, interest, hopes and fears of leading individuals in the communities of which they are members. Men of this class, whether the favourites of a king or a people, have in too many instances abused the confidence they possessed, and assuming the pretext of some public motive, have not scrupled to sacrifice the national tranquillity to personal advantage or personal gratification."

We may say that this is theoretical and far-fetched, and that, as was even objected then and stated by Hamilton himself only to refute it, "the spirit of commerce has a tendency to soften men and to extinguish those inflammable humours which have so often kindled wars. Commercial republics like ours will never be disposed to waste themselves in ruinous contentions with each other. They will be governed by mutual interest, and will cultivate a spirit of mutual amity and concord." He replies,

ADVANTAGES CONFERRED BY UNION.

"Has commerce hitherto done anything more than charge the objects of war? Is not the love of wealth as domineering and enterprising a passion as that of power or glory? Have there not been as many wars founded upon commercial motives, since that has become the prevailing system of nations, as were before occasioned by the cupidity of territory or dominion? Has not the spirit of commerce, in many instances, administered new incentives to the appetite both for the one and for the other?" The experience of past history certainly proves this to be the case, and we have already seen the dangerous feeling produced by the duties placed upon Colonial produce in the Transvaal, and the excitement occasioned by the closing of the drifts; it would not be difficult to imagine circumstances in which less than these provocations might have led to serious trouble. We also see the keen rivalry for commercial advantages between Natal and the Cape Colony; these are, as it were, the merest cloud-specks which often herald an African storm. In South Africa, indeed, the clash of arms and the boom of cannon have not so far receded into the distance of the past as to seem altogether impossible in the future.

We have only to look at the continent of Europe to see that nations whose boundaries are contiguous are ready to fly at each other's throats, to realize the truth of the quotation from an intelligent writer quoted by Hamilton, who says, "Neighbouring nations are naturally enemies of each other, unless their common weakness forces them to league in a Confederative Republic, and their constitution prevents the differences that neighbourhood occasions, extinguishing that secret jealousy which disposes all states to aggrandize themselves at the expense of their neighbours." As Hamilton says, "This passage at the same time points out the evil and suggests the remedy" (*vide* "Principes des Negotiations par M. l'Abbe de Mably"). The Transvaal has, indeed, already separated herself from the South African comity of states by refusing citizenship to the children of the mother whence her own people sprung, viz. the Cape Colony.

Let us see in some further detail what occasions may arise for hostile feeling and action.

"Territorial disputes have at all times been found one of the most fertile sources of hostility among nations. Perhaps the greatest proportion of wars that have desolated the earth have sprung from this origin."[1]

We have seen something of these territorial disputes in South Africa, and we all know the evils occasioned by them. It is within our memory how the dispute with regard to the diamond fields embittered the feeling of the Free State, led to the calling out of commandos on its part, and to hostile movements of police on the part of the High Commissioner. We have also seen the Basuto war in the Free State, occasioned by disputes as to boundaries; we have seen the republics of Stellaland and Goschen set up and put down by armed interference, we have seen the free republic formed in Zululand, we have seen the troubles and embitterments of feeling over

[1] *Federalist*, vii.

the Swaziland settlement, but beyond all we have seen the hand of Great Britain come in to seize all that great territory to the north of the Cape, the Free State and the Transvaal. It is true that in our opinion, owing to the want of that union on which we are dwelling, the alternative to the Chartered Company's occupation would have been the occupation of a foreign power. But in whatever way the severance was brought about, this country had been looked upon as the heritage of the people of the Cape, Natal, Transvaal and Free State ; as the people had spread from the Cape into the wilderness, so were the people of these states gradually exploring, hunting in and trading in these great lands : no one knew anything of them but they, no one cared. It was a vast reserve to be gradually occupied, organized and assimilated in the South African system. But with the Berlin Conference on African affairs a sound principle was abandoned by England, namely, that effective occupation alone conferred a title to land in Africa, and paper protectorates were recognized as conferring a claim to possess land.

Immediately the European powers began to scramble for Africa, and no matter how distant or unexplored the land, it was greedily seized and declared to be the exclusive property of one or other of the competing powers. Hence the necessity of this northern territory being declared British territory, merely to possess it for South Africa until such time as it could be absorbed in the South African system. The home Government properly doubted whether it ought to commit the taxpayers of the United Kingdom to the almost unknown responsibilities which might be involved in such a declaration. Mr. Rhodes then came forward and said, "I will guarantee to take charge of and administer this territory without expense to the British taxpayers." In this respect he rendered an inestimable service to South Africa.

Still, the feeling exists that a heritage has been lost, and a union of the states would tend to remedy this state of affairs, for no settlement of the union would be satisfactory which did not deal with this territory from the standpoint of the interests of the whole of South Africa.

When the American colonies became independent there was to the westward a gigantic territory practically unoccupied, which became the common property of the United States of America, and out of this territory other states were gradually added to the union as the settlers grew sufficient in numbers and organization to take their proper position as members of that Union. This happy solution was not brought about without great difficulty. Some of the larger states had already established claims to portions of this domain, and refused to give up their rights, while in other cases the settlers—as in the case of Kentucky and Virginia—refused to be separated from their parent state. There was no middle course for them, it was a question of independence or of joining their mother state.

The existence of this great territory to the west in America and the northern territory of South

Africa present so many features of similarity that it will be instructive to dwell a little in detail on the manner in which the difficulty was adjusted, and it is an instance above all others of the self-sacrifice of individual states in order to obtain that union which it was believed would be beneficial to all. We may quote Fiske, who thus describes the condition of affairs.

"In that momentous war," he says, referring to the seven years' war between England, France and Spain, "the genius of the elder Pitt won the regions east of the Mississippi for men of English race, while the vast territory of Louisiana beyond passed under the control of Spain. During the revolutionary war, in a series of romantic expeditions, the state of Virginia took military possession of a great part of the wilderness east of the Mississippi, founding towns in the Ohio and Cumberland valleys, and occupying with garrisons of her state militia the posts at Cahokia, Kaskaskia, and Vincennes. We have seen how, through the skill of our commissioners at Paris, this noble country was secured for the Americans in the treaty of 1783, in spite of the reluctance of France and the hostility of Spain. Throughout the revolutionary war the Americans claimed the territory as part of the United States, but when once it passed from under the control of Great Britain, into whose hands did it go? To whom did it belong? To this question there were various and conflicting answers. North Carolina, indeed, had already taken possession of what was afterwards called Tennessee, and at the beginning of the war

Virginia had annexed Kentucky. As to these points there could be little or no dispute. But with the territory north of the Ohio River it was very different. Four states laid claim either to the whole or to parts of this territory, and these claims were not simply conflicting, but irreconcilable."[1] Massachusetts, Connecticut and New York laid claims to the land as far as the Mississippi River, but according to Virginia, "it made little difference what Massachusetts and Connecticut and New York thought about the matter, for every acre of land from the Ohio River up to Lake Superior belonged to her. Was not she the lordly 'Old Dominion' out of which every one of the states had been carved [another analogy to the position of the Cape Colony, or 'Old Colony' in regard to the other South African states] ? But besides all this, it was Virginia that had actually conquered the disputed territory, and held every military post in it, except those which the British had not surrendered. And who would doubt that possession was nine points of the law ?

"Of these conflicting claims those of New York and Virginia were the most grasping and the most formidable, because they concerned a region into which immigration was beginning rapidly to pour. They were regarded with strong disfavour by the small states of Rhode Island, New Jersey, Delaware and Maryland, which were so situated that they never could expand in any direction."[2]

Maryland now rose to the occasion, and when the articles of confederation were about to be presented

---

[1] Fiske, p. 188.   [2] Ibid., p. 190.

to the states for ratification, and the question arose how the conflicting western claims should be settled, a motion was made that "The United States in Congress assembled shall have the sole and exclusive right and power to ascertain and fix the western boundary of such states as claim to the Mississippi, ... and lay out the land beyond the boundary so ascertained into separate and independent states, from time to time, as the numbers and circumstances of the people may require." To carry out such a motion it would be necessary for the four claimant states to surrender their claims into the hands of the United States, and thus create a domain which would be owned by the confederacy in common.[1] Maryland held out, and in 1780 New York, partly through the influence of General Schuyler, set the example by deciding to cede all her claims to the western lands — Connecticut followed. In January, 1781, Virginia offered to cede all the territory north-west of the Ohio, provided Congress would guarantee her in the possession of Kentucky, but this gave rise to three years' discussion, when Virginia withdrew her proviso, and the cession was accepted in 1784. On the 19th April Massachusetts surrendered her claims; and the whole north-western territory—the area of the present great states of Michigan, Wisconsin, Illinois, Indiana and Ohio (excepting the Connecticut Reserve)—thus became the property of the United States.

"It was New York who set the praiseworthy example, but New York after all surrendered only a

[1] Fiske, p. 192.

shadowy claim, whereas Virginia gave up a magnificent and princely territory, of which she was actually in possession. She might have held back and made endless trouble, just as at the beginning of the revolution she might have refused to make common cause with Massachusetts, but in both instances her leading statesmen showed a far-sighted wisdom and a breadth of patriotism for which no words can be too strong."[1]

When the time is ripe in South Africa, this will afford useful precedent for the exercise of a similar magnanimity.

Although for the moment the question of the northern territories is settled, there is yet an urgent reason why some common arrangement should be made to provide for the ultimate absorption of this territory in the common South African system.

Events are there proceeding with enormous rapidity. Large towns are being built and a numerous population is daily being settled there. The administration of the Chartered Company is possible at present, but there can be no doubt that as soon as the number of these settlers has sufficiently increased, they will not be content to occupy their land on the tenure of lessees of the Chartered Company; they will demand a voice in the management of their own affairs, and this demand must eventually be acceded to. The nature of the state to be formed there is a matter of vast moment to the other colonies and states of South Africa, and one which admits of little delay in its solution.

[1] Fiske, p. 195.

Again we have to refer for a precedent to America to show how urgent the matter is. North Carolina, with praiseworthy generosity, surrendered her western territory, but the settlers were too numerous to be handed from one dominion to another without saying something about it themselves. The settlers did not wish to have their country made a national domain; they declared themselves an independent state under the name of Franklin, and asked for admission into the union as a state, but North Carolina now repealed her act of cession, and warned the backwoodsmen to return to their allegiance.

For the next two years there was something very like civil war until the secessionist party was defeated. It was the same with Kentucky; and Virginia kept her grasp upon that state until it was fully organized and ready for admission into the union.

"These troubles show how impracticable was the attempt to create a national domain in any part of the country which contained a considerable population. The instinct of self-government was too strong to allow it. Any such population could have refused to submit to ordinances of Congress. To obey the parent state or set up for one's self—these were the only alternatives which they could understand."[1]

The same difficulties will confront any attempt to deal with the northern territories of the Cape if the matter be not taken in hand before the population becomes too large. Is it desirable or in the interests of a united South Africa that an independent state should grow up there, laying claim probably to the

[1] Fiske, p. 201.

whole of the gigantic area now under the Chartered Company?

What did America do with its common land, which at that time comprised the magnificent territory north of the Ohio—an area as large as the German Empire with the Netherlands thrown in? The ordinances of Congress passed in 1787 provided that it should ultimately be carved into states not exceeding five in number, and any one of these might be admitted into the union as soon as its population should reach 60,000. In the meantime the whole territory was to be governed by officers appointed by Congress, and required to take an oath of allegiance to the United States.

The success of this scheme for gradually admitting new states has been perfect, and afforded a splendid precedent to the very similar state of affairs at the Cape; it was not seized upon when the time came to take possession of the northern territories. It is not, however, too late yet for a united South Africa to arrange for the government and gradual admission of this territory into the common union.

It must be as clear to the Chartered Company as it is to the impartial observer, that its mission can be but temporary so far as the actual government and administration of this vast territory is concerned. History has never yet, and probably never will, see a population of the sturdy stocks which have peopled Africa, submit to be transferred from the possession of one set of masters to another by the simple operation of a purchase of shares.

It will be clear, then, from the foregoing, how

important is the question of union, when we have regard to the future of this great northern possession of South Africa in its relation to the rest of South Africa.

Union would confer another advantage, it would remove the danger of collision from hostile and divergent commercial regulations. We have seen in South Africa one state holding the seaboard taxing the commodities of an inland state, and so causing dissatisfaction; this has, however, been remedied so far as the arrangement by which the Cape and Natal pay to the Free State the revenue derived from products which pass through their respective territories for consumption in that state. This is, however, a voluntary act, and might be withdrawn under stress of disagreement. Then we see the Transvaal chafing under its commercial dependence upon the southern colonies of Natal and the Cape, and desirous of having its own port; while the Cape and Natal are in strong rivalry for the trade of the Transvaal. We see them jealous of the aim of the Transvaal to have its own port independent of them. Here we may with advantage recall the principle stated by Hamilton: "We shall be ready to denominate injuries those things which were in reality the justifiable acts of independent sovereignties consulting a distinct interest." This jealousy would all vanish were the union to take place, for it would then be a matter of indifference to the whole of South Africa through which port its imports were carried. The union would have the control of the ports, and it could view with equanimity the acquisition of another port besides those which already belong to the colonies and states of South Africa. As was the case in America, so in South Africa, for many years to come the chief revenue must be derived from duties at the ports. It is collected with ease and certainty, and at a minimum of expense. As the *Federalist* said :—

"In America, it is evident that we must a long time depend for the means of revenue chiefly on such duties. In most parts of it excises must be confined within a narrow compass. The genius of the people will ill brook the inquisitive and peremptory spirit of excise laws. The pockets of the farmers, on the other hand, will reluctantly yield out scanty supplies, in the unwelcome shape of impositions on their houses and lands ; and personal property is too precarious and invisible a fund to be laid hold of in any other way than by the imperceptible agency of taxes on consumption.

"In France [at that time] there [was] an army of patrols (as they are called) constantly employed to secure their fiscal regulations against the inroads of the dealers in contraband trade. Mr. Neckar computed the number of these patrols at upwards of twenty thousand. This shows the immense difficulty in preventing that species of traffic where there is an inland communication, and places in a strong light the disadvantages with which the collection of duties in this country would be encumbered if by disunion the states should be placed in a situation with respect to each other resembling that of France with respect to her neighbours. The arbitrary and vexatious powers with which the patrols are necessarily armed would be intolerable in a free country.

"If, on the contrary, there be but one government pervading all the states, there will be, as to the principal part of our commerce, but one side to guard —the Atlantic coast."[1]

The feverish anxiety which now impels the Transvaal towards the coast in its independent career would diminish and disappear when it found itself a powerful member of a powerful union.

The monstrosity of internal customs-boundaries within South Africa would disappear. The cost of maintaining these customs-boundaries, with their officials, who must grow more and more numerous as the country becomes more thickly populated and opportunities for smuggling increase, will be saved to the inhabitants of South Africa.

"An unrestrained intercourse between the states themselves will advance the trade of each by an interchange of their respective productions, not only for the supply of reciprocal wants at home, but for exportation to foreign markets. The veins of commerce in every part will be replenished, and will acquire additional motion and vigour from a free circulation of the commodities of every part. Commercial enterprise will have much greater scope, from the diversity in the productions of different states. When the staple of one fails from a bad harvest or unproductive crop, it can call to its aid the staple of another.

"It may perhaps be replied to this, that whether

[1] *Federalist*, xii.

the states are united or disunited, there would still be an intimate intercourse between them, which would answer the same ends; but this intercourse would be fettered, interrupted, and narrowed by a multiplicity of causes, which in the course of these papers have been amply detailed. A unity of commercial, as well as political interests, can only result from a unity of government." [1]

In addition to these advantages of a negative character, there will be the benefit conferred upon the whole of South Africa by the free interchange of the various products of its different climates. In America there is absolute free trade between all the states, and it is hardly open to question that its prosperity has been in very large measure induced and maintained by this wise and liberal policy. The same result would follow in South Africa: we would see the sugar of Natal passing freely into the other states, and so benefiting all. The semi-tropical fruits of that country would also pass into the other states, while the temperate fruits of the Cape Colony, and particularly of its south-western districts, would be welcomed throughout the whole of the rest of South Africa; and as we see California supplying the greater part of America with its splendid fruits, so would the south-western districts of the Cape distribute the fruits, which it is equally well suited to produce, throughout the rest of South Africa, and this to the advantage of all. We have seen a small stream of produce just beginning to flow notwithstanding the serious obstructions imposed by the duties on

[1] *Federalist*, xi.

the borders of the Transvaal. Few men have any conception of the magnitude such a trade might assume if permitted to flow naturally and freely.

We should also see the sheep of the Cape Colony, whose uplands are so admirably suited to the raising of flocks and herds, supplying the markets of the mining towns of the Transvaal, whose territory is not adapted to the rearing of sheep.

The " conquered " territory of the Free State would become one of the granaries of South Africa, and supply the bread which must now come from all parts of the world to make up the deficiencies of the indigenous supply.

Thus the prosperity of each part would add to the prosperity of all, and with the interchange of products would come a knowledge of each other, and an intercourse which would give that coherence and unity necessary for the growth of one great and homogeneous nation. That isolation which has kept so many proportions of South Africa from participating in the advance of knowledge and progress, which has kept them poor and backward, this would become a thing of the past, a new life and a new vigour would be infused into the most distant extremities of the land. Such incidents as the closing of the "drifts," with all its attendant ill-feeling and recrimination, would be a thing of the past; men's minds and energies would be free to assist in advancing and developing their common country in such a manner that, while benefiting themselves, they would be conferring benefits on the whole of South Africa, in which they would then have a direct and common interest.

In addition South Africa would be able to present to the whole world a united front on all matters of commerce.

CHAPTER VI.

ADVANTAGES CONFERRED BY UNION—*Continued.*

Native question—Importance of combined action—Saving effected by one common administration instead of several—Form of government guaranteed to each colony and state—Law and order guaranteed—Security against native risings—Uitlander population in Transvaal—New population of Rhodesia—Importance of dealing with these questions in early stage—Objection that freedom of states would be destroyed met by *Federalist.*

WE have seen then some of the advantages which must accrue to South Africa in respect of common action in the unoccupied territories and in commerce. There is a further benefit to be derived from union. Each state in South Africa is confronted by the great problem presented by the low stage of development of its native population. It can hardly be doubted that common action on this great matter will tend to the safety and security of South Africa. It will be possible to pursue a policy of greater deliberation and care with these native populations when the force to be derived from common action is in reserve. While two peoples are about evenly balanced in strength, the advantage now on this side, now on that—as was the case with the white and the black populations of South Africa when Sir G. Grey arrived on its shores—there is naturally a feeling of strong antagonism and bitter hostility, resulting in fierce and sanguinary struggles for supremacy. There can be no calm consideration, no allowance for the lower stage of development of the native when he is in a position to attack you and put an end to your existence or your prosperity at the dictates of his uncertain passions. Sir George Grey, with that remarkable power of appreciating the new conditions of the countries to which he came—and which is so rare a faculty with Englishmen—saw that until the white man was unquestionably superior, there was no hope for the country, white or black. He therefore immediately set about developing the material resources of South Africa. He found that the leading public men at the Cape, such as Mr. Molteno and others, were ready to enter into his ideas, which, indeed, were largely theirs also, and that they were willing to aid him. He then set about establishing a port for South Africa in the inauguration of the Table Bay Harbour works. This policy, which was retarded and remained in abeyance after his departure owing to the character of his successor and the form of government, was taken up and pursued with a vigour such as never had been infused into it before when responsible government was granted to the Cape Colony. The late Sir John Molteno, as soon as the necessary surveys could be made, commenced the construction of railways and telegraphs, and set the note of a new era in South Africa. Since that time there could not be any question of the superiority of the white man over the black in the Cape Colony, however much it suited Sir Bartle Frere for other purposes to magnify the danger of the Colony during the Gaika and Galeka war. Mr. Molteno, who was then responsible for the safety of the Colony, and whose experience was unsurpassed, refused to permit the Governor to summon the aid of the Imperial troops, and desired nothing more than to be allowed to quell the rising with Colonial troops in accordance with Colonial experience; and so it would have been then as with the Matabele recently—a comparative handful of determined and active men would have soon settled the Gaikas and Galekas by their rapid movements.

Thus it will be with South Africa as a whole when unquestionably superior in force and resources to the natives, and ready and able to quell any rising; then will it have the leisure and security to do justice to the native populations, and to take measures for their advancement in the scale of civilization, thus turning them to the benefit of themselves and South Africa, in place of a menace and a danger. Have we not seen the same result in America, where at one time the natives threatened the very existence of the colonies, but are now cared for by native protectors, and treated with the utmost generosity and consideration?

Again, a further benefit to be derived by South Africa from a union would be the saving to be effected by the consolidation of a large part of the administration in one government for the whole of South Africa. Now each poor colony and state has its full and complete system of officials and departments for every detail of government. Under a union the central government would replace the separate administrations in those affairs which are of common concern to all the South African colonies and states; such affairs, for example, as the Federal revenue, the postal department, the railway administration, commerce both foreign and domestic, the currency, copyrights and patents, and the military and naval forces. The Federal Court would be applicable to the whole of South Africa, whether as a supreme court alone or with other Federal courts—the functions of which will be referred to again in the course of these pages. South African statesmen have from time to time drawn attention to the enormous cost to South Africa as a whole of the large number of separate administrations which at present carry on the government of so small an aggregate of people. An evil of unnatural growth inflicted upon South Africa by the mistaken policy of Great Britain.

The public are apt to forget that the more a government takes from them, whether by direct taxes such as income tax, or by the more insidious, because less easily perceived, indirect taxes of Customs duties, the less can they have for themselves, and the more difficult does it become to establish any industries in a country which is heavily taxed.

"It is evident," says the *Federalist*, referring to the condition of America in 1787, "from the state of the country, from the habits of the people, from the experience we have had on the point itself, that it is impracticable to raise any very considerable sums by direct taxation. Tax laws have in vain been multiplied; new methods to enforce the collection have in vain been tried; the public expectation has been uniformly disappointed, and the treasuries of the states have remained empty. The popular system of administration inherent in the nature of popular government, coinciding with the real scarcity of money incident to a languid and mutilated state of trade, has hitherto defeated every experiment for extensive collections, and has at length taught the different legislatures the folly of attempting them.

" No person acquainted with what happens in other countries will be surprised at this circumstance. In so opulent a nation as that of Britain, where direct taxes from superior wealth must be much more tolerable, and, from the vigour of the government, much more practicable than in America, far the greatest part of the national revenue is derived from taxes of the indirect kind, from imposts, and from excises. Duties on imported articles form a large branch of this latter description." This is equally true of South Africa.

We have to consider another advantage to be derived from the union of the states and colonies of South Africa. The union would naturally be such that, as in America, the form of government in each state would be guaranteed to it, and the preservation of law and order would be also guaranteed.

This is a matter of great importance, and it will only be necessary to indicate briefly the conditions which may give rise to troubles in the states of South Africa to realize that this will be a very valuable guarantee for the preservation of the tranquillity of the states.

We may still, unfortunately, see risings of natives in some of the states, particularly such a state as Natal, where there is a vast preponderance of the native over the European population. It would be the duty of the Federal Union to assist with Federal forces in quelling such a rising, should the state itself be unable to cope with the outbreak. So serious has this liability been considered by the leading statesmen of South Africa, that they have hitherto refused, as far as the Cape Colony is concerned, to undertake such a liability, hence their preference for the plan of annexation, or the unification of South Africa by gradually adding to the existing state, the Cape Colony, these outlying and less settled territories as they become suited in their conditions thus to be absorbed. This was the plan of the late Sir John Molteno, as opposed to confederation on equal terms. We have seen this carried on as the natural consolidation of South Africa. We have seen by this process the Transkei and Griqualand West absorbed, then Pondoland, then Bechuanaland. But circumstances have now somewhat changed; the sudden accession of wealth, and the development of the resources of the Free State and the Transvaal and the grant of responsible government to Natal, have made it impossible now to apply that principle to the whole of South Africa. Had there not been that unwise attempt to force confederation which led to the occupation of the Transvaal and the subsequent retrocession, this natural consolidation would have followed in South Africa on the grant of responsible government and the experience of its unfettered working in the Cape Colony.

As already stated, the great development of the material resources of all the colonies and states will gradually remove this objection to a union.

There are, however, more important questions with which this article would deal. We see in the Transvaal a large alien, or Uitlander, population growing up, as far outnumbering the original inhabitants in mere numbers as in wealth, energy, and enterprise they differ from them. Here is a danger not only to the Transvaal itself, but to South Africa as a whole. Should any unwise treatment or sudden difficulty arise, here are the materials for a revolution in that state, and possibly a civil war. Nothing could be more disastrous for the development of the whole of South Africa than such a calamity. It is of the utmost importance that the peaceful continuity of development should be preserved, that the necessary time should be allowed for the fusion of the two elements, for the appreciation by the new-comers of what is best in the views of the older portion of the community, and for the progressive influence of the former to gradually leaven the older and more conservative tendencies in the state. As confidence was established between these two elements, so would the more restrictive and illiberal measures, which we have seen enacted from a spirit of distrust, be abrogated, and a mutual respect would lead to a mutual confidence. The government of the Transvaal, being assured of the support of the Union in maintaining domestic tranquillity, would be ready to act in this more liberal spirit.

Again we see in the rapidly growing communities of Rhodesia, Salisbury, and Buluwayo other centres whence trouble may arise, if they are allowed to develop in a manner out of harmony with, and out of touch with, the South African system. We may quote Madison in the *Federalist*—" The influence of faction leaders," he says, " may kindle a flame within their particular States, but will be unable to spread a general conflagration through the other States. A religious sect may degenerate into a political faction in a part of the confederacy ; but the variety of sects dispersed over the entire face of it must secure the national councils against any danger from that source. A rage for paper money, for an abolition of debts, for an equal division of property, or for any other improper or wicked project, will be less apt to pervade the whole body of the union than a particular member of it ; in the same proportion as such a malady is more likely to taint a particular county or district, than an entire state." This indicates both the nature of the trouble and the remedy which union offers.

In South Africa the early tendencies and inclinations in these newly settled territories would be towards union. The homogeneity of feeling derived from the admixture of a large number of persons from the old states with those who are arriving from Europe, would be made use of to the full, before it has time to disappear in an exclusive attachment to purely local institutions. The natural authority possessed by such persons with new-comers, owing to their larger acquaintance with the country and its conditions, an authority out of all proportion greater than that given by their mere numbers, would be enlisted in favour of unity at the time best suited for its operation. Thus it is for the present inhabitants of South Africa to consider, and to settle on a sound basis of national union, the lines on which the future development of the states is to take place. Let them follow the precedent set them by the great statesmen of America, who, seizing the fateful moment, sank all petty aspirations, jealousies, and separate advantages in the fabric of a splendid union, the greatness of which grows and increases yearly and even daily, and the future of which no man can foresee.

"A firm union," says Hamilton, "will be of the utmost moment to the peace and liberty of the states, as a barrier against domestic faction and insurrection. It is impossible to read the history of the petty republics of Greece and Italy without feeling sensations of horror and disgust at the distractions with which they were continually agitated, and at the rapid succession of revolutions by which they were kept in a state of perpetual vibration between the extremes of tyranny and anarchy. If they exhibit occasional calms, these only serve as short-lived contrasts to the furious storms that are to succeed. If now and then intervals of felicity open to view, we behold them with a mixture of regret, arising from the real reflection that the pleasing scenes before us are soon to be overwhelmed by the tempestuous waves of sedition and party rage. If momentary rays of glory break forth from the gloom, while they dazzle us with a transient and fleeting brilliancy, they at the same time admonish us to lament that the vices of government should pervert the direction, and tarnish the lustre, of those bright talents and exalted endowments for which the favoured soils that produced them have been so justly celebrated.

"From the disorders that disfigure the annals of those republics the advocates of despotism have drawn arguments, not only against the forms of republican government, but against the very principles of civil liberty. They have decried all free government as inconsistent with the order of society, and have indulged themselves in malicious exultation over its friends and partisans. Happily for mankind, stupendous fabrics reared on the basis of liberty, which have flourished for ages, have, in a few glorious instances, refuted their gloomy sophisms. And, I trust, America will be the broad and solid foundation of other edifices, not less magnificent, which will be equally permanent monuments of their errors."

This was indeed prophetic! Has South Africa an equal ambition? has it the men who can put it in the way of realizing that ambition? namely, that it too may lay the broad and solid foundation of another edifice, not less magnificent, which will be an equally permanent monument.

Hamilton proceeds to meet an objection offered to union that it would diminish the freedom of the states and tend to destroy their individuality. As this objection would have some force in Africa, we quote his words:—

"The inordinate pride of state importance has suggested to some minds an objection to the principle of a guaranty in the Federal Government, as involving an officious interference in the domestic concerns of the members. A scruple of this kind would deprive us of one of the principal advantages to be expected from union, and can only flow from a misapprehension of the nature of the provision itself. It could be no impediment to reforms of the state constitutions by a majority of the people in a legal and peaceable mode. This right would remain undiminished. The guaranty could only operate against changes to be effected by violence. Towards the preventions of calamities of this kind, too many checks cannot be provided. The peace of society and the stability of government depend absolutely on the efficacy of the precautions adopted on this head. Where the whole power of the government is in the hands of the people, there is the less pretence for the use of violent remedies in partial or occasional distempers of the state. The natural cure for an ill-administration, in a popular or representative constitution, is a change of men. A guaranty by the national authority would be as much levelled against the usurpations of rulers as against the ferments and outrages of faction and sedition in the community."

CHAPTER VII.

THE EXCLUSION OF FOREIGN INTERFERENCE.

Danger of foreign interference—Arguments of *Federalist*—Interference of Germany—Deliberate plan—German annexations—Danger of adding interference of another power in South Africa—Estrangement of Transvaal—Territory necessary for South African system—Similar question in America in 1787—Successful solution in America—Loss of valuable territories owing to supineness of British Government—Walwich Bay—Delagoa Bay—Union necessary to enforce claims—Failure of English statesmen to understand South Africa—Mr. Gladstone's opinion—Complication of many factors—Difficulty of discovering true South African opinion—A neglected warning—Sir Owen Lanyon's military rule—Disastrous results—The late Sir John Molteno's views on exclusion of foreign interference.

WE have now examined the necessity for union and the advantages to be derived from it, in securing the domestic peace of the component parts and preserving an amicable spirit in their interstate relations, while preserving for each its special form of government, and guaranteeing it against internal disturbances. We have now to pursue our investigations from a different aspect, namely, the preservation of the union from outside foreign interference. This subject divides itself naturally into two branches; the present dangers of foreign interference, and the exclusion in the future of any such interference in the territories which should be ultimately a portion of the United States of South Africa.

It must be borne in mind that we are dealing with the future, and not alone with the present, in South Africa.

Taking, then, these subjects in their order, we may quote from a general point of view the arguments of Jay in the *Federalist*, v. If the Cape States remain isolated, then, as he there predicts, "Whenever, and from whatever causes, it might happen, and happen it would, that any one of these nations or confederacies should rise on the scale of political importance much above the degree of her neighbours, that moment would those neighbours behold her with envy and with fear.

"Both these passions would lead them to countenance, if not to promote, whatever might promise to diminish her importance; and would also restrain them from measures calculated to advance or even to secure her prosperity. Much time would not be necessary to enable her to discern these unfriendly dispositions. She would soon begin, not only to lose confidence in her neighbours, but also to feel a disposition equally unfavourable to them. Distrust naturally creates distrust, and by nothing is goodwill and kind conduct more speedily changed than by invidious jealousies and uncandid imputations, whether expressed or implied.

"They who well consider the history of similar

divisions and confederacies will find abundant reason to apprehend that those in contemplation would in no other sense be neighbours than as they would be borderers; that they would neither love nor trust one another, but on the contrary would be a prey to discord, jealousy, and mutual injuries; in short, that they would place us exactly in the situations in which some nations doubtless wish to see us, viz. formidable only to each other.

"From these considerations it appears that those gentlemen are greatly mistaken who suppose that alliances offensive and defensive might be formed between these confederacies, and would produce that combination and union of wills, of arms, and of resources, which would be necessary to put and keep them in a formidable state of defence against foreign enemies.

"When did the independent states, into which Britain and Spain were formerly divided, combine in such alliance, or unite their forces against a foreign enemy? The proposed confederacies will be distinct nations. Each of them would have its commerce with foreigners to regulate by distinct treaties; and as their productions and commodities are different and proper for different markets, so would those treaties be essentially different. Different commercial concerns must create different interests, and of course different degrees of political attachment to and connection with different foreign nations. Hence it might, and probably would happen, that the foreign nation with whom the Southern confederacy might be at war would be the one with whom the Northern confederacy would be the most desirous of preserving peace and friendship. An alliance so contrary to their immediate interest would not, therefore, be easy to form, nor, if formed, would it be observed and fulfilled with perfect good faith.

"Nay, it is far more probable that in America, as in Europe, neighbouring nations, acting under the impulse of opposite interests and unfriendly passions, would frequently be found taking different sides. Considering our distance from Europe, it would be more natural for these confederacies to apprehend danger from one another than from distant nations, and therefore that each of them should be more desirous to guard against the others by the aid of foreign alliances, than to guard against foreign dangers by alliances between themselves."

Do we not see very clear signs that in South Africa these ever acting principles are at work? Have we not seen the Transvaal practically appealing to Germany? Have we not seen its President telling the public that it was ready to make use of the jealousies of the great powers of Europe for its own purposes, and that it dearly desired to pit Germany against England in South Africa? This is indeed a sad spectacle to all who love South Africa, and let us remember, in the words of the *Federalist*, " How much more easy it is to receive foreign fleets into our ports, and foreign armies into our country, than it is to persuade or compel them to depart. How many conquests did the Romans and others make in the character of allies, and what innovations did they, under the same character, introduce into the governments of those whom they pretended to protect?" If the unwise interference of one European power has led to serious evils, how much more serious will be the evils which will flow from the complications due to the interference, in the internal affairs of South Africa, of a second European power!

The acts and intentions of Germany in South Africa, however isolated they may appear, have been based on a well concerted and well considered plan. A certain German, named Ernst von Weber, drew up a scheme, which, in a brilliant and most forcible argument, he placed before Prince Bismarck and the German Government. This fact is known to few in Africa, but it is well worth bearing in mind. In this he sketched out a scheme for the acquisition of the whole of South Africa by Germany, and his ambition did not stop even here: German South Africa was to be made the basis of an empire to stretch from the Cape to Cairo. These vast objects were to be accomplished by taking advantage of the fact that the two republics of the Transvaal and Free State were Dutch, or really Low German, and, as England's policy had estranged them, it would be easy to bring them under German influence. With their aid, and with the aid of the kindred populations of the Cape and Natal, the two latter were also to be secured, while every unoccupied piece of territory was to be seized, and a belt of German territory was to be drawn across South Africa to make all doubly secure. We will give his own words:—

"What could not such a country [the Transvaal], full of such inexhaustible natural treasures, become, if in course of time it is filled with German immigrants? *A constant mass of German immigrants would gradually bring about a decided numerical preponderance of Germans over the Dutch population, and, of itself, would by degrees effect the Germanization of the country in a peaceful manner.* Besides all its own natural and subterraneous treasures, the Transvaal offers to the European power which possesses it an easy access to the immensely rich tracts of country which lie between the Limpopo, the Central African lakes and the Congo.

" It was this free unlimited room for annexation in the north, this open access to the heart of Africa, which principally impressed me with the idea, not more than four years ago, that Germany should try, *by the acquisition of Delagoa Bay and the subsequent continual influx of German immigrants to the Transvaal, to secure the future dominion over this conntry, and so pave the way for a German African Empire of the future.* I gave expression to this idea in a memorial which I sent in March, 1875, from South Africa to his Majesty the Emperor and H.S.H. Prince Bismarck.

" There is at the same time the most assured prospect that the European power who would bring these territories under its rule will found one of the largest and most valuable empires of the globe; and it is, therefore, on this account truly to be regretted that Germany should have, quietly and without protest, allowed the annexation of the Transvaal Republic to England, because the splendid country, *taken possession of and cultivated by a German race*, ought to be entirely won for Germany, and would, moreover, have been so easily acquired, and thereby the beginning made and foundation laid of a mighty and, ultimately, rich Germany in the Southern Hemisphere. Germany ought, at any price, to get possession of some points on the East as well as the West Coast of Africa." The italics are ours. Thus it was no love for the Transvaal, but a base treachery upon its simple inhabitants, which was to be practised by Germany.

At another place he makes the significant remark : "I know of no race [referring to the Boers] in the world which offer such splendid material for Grenadier Guards and Cuirassiers."[1]

In pursuance of this policy, South-West Africa was seized on the one side of Africa and gunboats were despatched to St. Lucia Bay on the other. The seizure of this port was only prevented by the urgent private representations which induced Mr. Gladstone to send a British gunboat to forestall the German war vessel already on its way ; at the same time agents were sent to make treaties with all the native chiefs north of the Cape Colony and Transvaal. Things have not gone quite as the Germans have expected and wished, but it is clear that they have never yet abandoned their design of securing

[1] Geographische Nachrichten, November, 1879, quoted in Parliamentary Papers, C. 4190, p. 1.

THE EXCLUSION OF FOREIGN INTERFERENCE.

the two republics.[1] England, the nation of liberty, has given many proofs that she will not endeavour, in any way, to thwart or injure the development of the young nation. It is true that, owing to her ignorance of the difficulties of South Africa, she has unwittingly done immense wrong and injury, but whenever her people have been appealed to she has endeavoured to undo these wrongs and make reparation. Woe betide South Africa if it ever passes into the grip of Germany; verily it will feel, as did the Hebrews of old, that Germany's little finger is thicker than England's thigh, and a chastisement of whips will be replaced by one of scorpions.[2]

We see further that the Transvaal has preferred

[1] A recent number of the German newspaper *Das Vaterland* says: "For German politicians the Transvaal is the Archimedian fulcrum from which they wish to form a German Imperial Empire in South Africa. To this end the Republic must first be persuaded to place itself under a German protectorate, and after a reasonable interval, the Transvaal would be converted politically into a military centre. Officers of the German army would be sent there in ever-increasing numbers, German capitalists, heads of German commercial ventures, and German agriculturists would, as it were, flood the country, and at length South Africa would become German instead of English."

[2] As an illustration of the harsh and stringent methods of the Germans in their colonies, we quote the following extract from a recent traveller, who, in describing the capital of German East Africa, Dar es Salaam, says:—

"We concluded that it was really an open-air court of justice, and that either the Germans were very strict or the natives extremely lax in their ideas of law and order, for the place was crammed with culprits, and we did not see one of them let off. It was also a shock to our English ideas to see numbers of native women working on the roads, and driven to their work allying herself with the Portuguese at Delagoa Bay, to making friendly arrangements with the southern colony of the Cape and the sister colony of Natal. When union has rendered the interference of the English Government unnecessary in the domestic affairs of South Africa, this repugnance to a closer union must cease on the part of the people of the various colonies and states, but while England acts as the champion of the colonies, it is inevitable that the Republics will seek a champion to set against the champion of the colonies. Thus we see that there have come into active operation in South Africa those dangers which the statesmen of America foresaw, and against which they made provision in good time by

by a white man carrying a raw hide whip. I became daily more astonished at the number of convicts and prisoners.

"Everywhere you came upon gangs of four to eight—often women—chained together by their necks, and hounded along by a black policeman."—"Twelve Hundred Miles in a Waggon," by Blanche Balfour, 1895.

We may call to mind that the Germans have, immediately on taking possession of their new colonies, had, in every instance, to fight the natives, and we see by the above extract why this has been so. We may further call to mind the serious outbreak at the Cameroons a year or two ago, because of the flogging of native women. Yet England assisted the Germans in East Africa in subduing their newly acquired subjects; what an outcry would have been raised if South Africa had acted as the Germans have done! In the case of the Germans Exeter Hall and the British public were silent.

This harsh policy is not confined to the blacks—the whites are subject to the same arbitrary and severe regulations—and we can easily understand that, apart from all other causes, no large white population could attain prosperity or develop under such conditions.

The Exclusion of Foreign Interference.

drawing up a constitution which has been perfectly successful in obviating their occurrence in America. We will be wise to adopt for South Africa the remedy which was provided, with so much prescience and wisdom, for America.

We must now point out the necessity for union in dealing with the question of eliminating foreign power and foreign interference in the future of South Africa.

If we look at the accompanying map of America, representing the political divisions of the continent at the time when the union took place, we cannot but be struck with the great similarity of conditions to those of South Africa at the present day. It will be seen that the colonies occupied a mere fringe on the Atlantic coast. The common territory stretched westward as far as the Mississippi, but no further; and towards the south, not even thus far. The greater part of what is now the United States of America did not then form any part of their territory. Spain possessed the province of Florida and the mouth of the Mississippi, and went so far as to close its navigation to the United States of America; Spain also possessed the gigantic province of Louisiana, west of the Mississippi, which soon passed into French hands; so that the United States of America had Spain, England, and France for its neighbours, the most powerful nations of Europe. Looking at the map of South Africa, we see a similar state of affairs. We have on the west, German South-West Africa; and on the east, Portuguese territory, both of which are indispensable to the future united South Africa.

But is it not clear that if the thirteen states of America had remained separate and disunited, there would have been no chance of securing those great foreign possessions to them? Each would have put forward its own claims to as much as possible of the common territory, and in their divisions would have been the opportunity of the European powers. They would have been unequal to effecting and carrying out such vast operations as the purchase of Louisiana in 1803 from Napoleon, and the cession of Florida in 1819, which freed the continent of America of French and Spanish rule. So in South Africa it will be necessary for the colonies and states to unite if they wish to possess the requisite prestige and resources for eventually realizing the aspirations of South Africa in this respect.

The loss of South-West Africa and Delagoa Bay would have been impossible had there been a united South Africa, ready and able to enforce its rights and its interests with adequate firmness and insistence. The history of this loss is so instructive and has so many lessons for the future, that we will enter upon it in some further detail.

Very shortly after responsible government had been brought into operation at the Cape, the attention of the Government was directed to the possibility of foreign influence being allowed to operate in the country bounded by the Cunene and the Orange River, the ports of which are Angra Pequena and Walwich Bay. With a view to setting at rest this danger, which a wise and careful prescience saw as a reality, the Ministry of Mr. Molteno introduced a resolution

THE EXCLUSION OF FOREIGN INTERFERENCE.

into the House of Assembly for annexing Walwich Bay and so much of the surrounding territory as might be found desirable. This resolution was passed and communicated to the Secretary of State, who immediately made objections to it, for his mind was full of his South African Federation; indeed, this resolution was passed in 1875—the very year of his famous Confederation dispatch. With that ignorance of local conditions, and that assurance which have so often characterized the actions of those who have controlled the destinies of South Africa from afar, Lord Carnarvon at once took objection. The Governor's remarks on the proposals of the Ministry to issue a Commission and introduce a Bill for actual annexation are to the effect that he " could not refer so confidently as is proposed to the introduction of a Bill by this Government for the purpose (of annexation of Walwich Bay), and still more so to give the Commissioner authority to perfect arrangements either for taking over the country or anything else. The utmost I can do is by virtue of the approval signified by his Lordship's dispatch, No. 68 of October 26th, 1874, which has not yet been revoked, to issue a Commission something in the form indicated." A Commissioner was sent, but in the meantime Lord Carnarvon said he would allow no annexation to the Cape; the port would form an excellent harbour for Kimberley! Such was his ignorance of its position. Notwithstanding the worry and excitement of the Confederation dispatches and the special session of the Cape Parliament summoned to deal with Mr. Froude's unconstitutional agitation, the Ministry still kept the object in view and pressed for its accomplishment, but to show who opposed them, we quote what the Governor wrote under date June 12th, 1876, to Mr. Palgrave, the Commissioner: "I do not suppose that I shall get any positive authority to annex the west coast until Mr. Molteno has seen Lord Carnarvon, which cannot be till late next month." When Mr. Molteno arrived in Europe he lost no time in pressing upon Lord Carnarvon the importance and urgency of annexing Walwich Bay, but Lord Carnarvon now thought he had a lever with which to urge Mr. Molteno to abandon his opposition to confederation, and resorted to the petty expedient of refusing to sanction it unless Mr. Molteno would fall in with his views. Sir Bartle Frere, Lord Carnarvon's specially chosen instrument, on his arrival at the Cape, lost no time in urging upon Lord Carnarvon the importance of the annexation being carried out without delay; thereupon Lord Carnarvon consented merely to the British Flag being hoisted at Walwich Bay, but "he did not at the moment feel in a position to sanction Sir Bartle Frere's larger proposals,"[1] which were for the annexation originally desired by the Cape Ministry up to the Cunene, the Portuguese boundary. Within a few days, the man who had hindered this great work out of petty ignorance and resentment at the unfavourable reception accorded to his ill-advised schemes, and who had lit a conflagration which was to involve South Africa in war and bloodshed, quitted office voluntarily, and so escaped the

[1] Parliamentary Papers, C. 2144, p. 7.

THE EXCLUSION OF FOREIGN INTERFERENCE. 85

responsibility of coping with the ruin which he had been instrumental in bringing down upon the unfortunate country committed to his charge.

The subsequent history of the treatment of the British Government of this question may shortly be traced. The troubles brought about by Lord Carnarvon's policy followed in rapid succession; all had to give way. The Cape Ministry was dismissed, the Transvaal having been treacherously seized a short time before. Then followed war in Zululand and war in the Transvaal, and the question of the annexation of the Walwich Bay territory had to remain over until time could be found, and when this time came, the Colonial Secretary was heartily sickened and terrified by the whirlwind raised by Lord Carnarvon's policy, and replied that "the Orange River should be maintained as the northwestern boundary of the Cape Colony, and that Her Majesty's Government would give no encouragement to schemes for the retention of British jurisdiction over Great Namaqualand and Damaraland."[1] In 1884, while Lord Derby was declaring that England would not allow Germany a footing there, the instructions were already on their way which irrevocably declared the German possession. In 1892, notwithstanding the protest of the Cape, this territory was actually increased by giving a further strip to Germany as far as the Zambesi.

Well might Bismarck declare, as he did before the Reichstag Committee on June 24th, 1884, that the

[1] Parliamentary Papers, C. 2754, p. 8, referred to by Count Munster, C. 4190.

British Government was sufficiently complacent in yielding up territories in which her colonies were interested. He used these significant words:—" No opposition is apprehended from the British Government, and the machinations of Colonial authorities must be prevented." Thus the only defenders of British colonial rights and interests were to be foiled in their opposition to parting with these rights and interests to foreign powers by the joint action of the mother country and those powers. We are not surprised to learn that a fear was expressed that Lord Salisbury had suggested to, and indeed pressed upon, the Cape Government his desire to hand over Walwich Bay to Germany. It is true that when this question was put in Parliament, to Mr. W. H. Smith, the then leader of the House of Commons, it was officially denied, but the extension of German territory in this very portion of Africa against the urgent representations made by the Cape, lends probability to the suggestion that the proposition was made to the Cape.

With regard to Delagoa Bay, the sole guardian of South African interests was, at that time, the High Commissioner. His opinion was neither sought by Her Majesty's Secretary of State, nor when proffered was it followed.

When, in 1872, the High Commissioner learned from the public prints that Her Majesty's Government were likely to go to arbitration over their rights at Delagoa Bay and Inyack Island, which commands the entrance to that port, he pointed out to Lord Kimberley the enormous importance of this harbour to the commerce of the South African colonies, and

THE EXCLUSION OF FOREIGN INTERFERENCE. 87

said that he feared that a reference to arbitration would result in the loss to Great Britain of another island over which the British flag was floating, and the transference of the military command of a British colony to a foreign power.

It is stated that so little did Portugal value her claims at this time that she offered them to England for the sum of 12,000l. without having recourse to arbitration, but this sum was not forthcoming in the interests of South Africa, and Her Majesty's Government preferred to run the risks of arbitration, the results of which amply justified the High Commissioner's forebodings.

Thus were the most vital interests of South Africa treated by a Colonial Secretary ignorant of the conditions of the country with which he was called upon to deal. Surely had there been a union of the states, the demand for the exclusion of Germany would have had its due weight, and would have been effective. Surely it is high time that the Cape Colony should realize this fact; indeed, South Africa as a whole should realize what each state was long convinced of, and has now realized for its own government, namely, that no one could so well manage its affairs from a distance as could the persons who were on the spot, and who were conversant with all the details of the large and difficult questions which have from time to time come up for settlement.

The failure of English statesmen to understand South Africa has been confessed in the following words of Mr. Gladstone, who, in addressing the House of Commons in 1883, said :—

"It [South Africa] has been the one standing difficulty of our Colonial policy which we have never been able to set right. In other parts of the world difficulties have arisen—in India, in Canada, in New Zealand—and every one has been dealt with and satisfactorily disposed of, but never in South Africa. It was my lot in the latter part of the administration of Sir R. Peel to be Secretary of State, and I then told Lord Grey that the case of South Africa presented a problem of which I, for one, could not see the solution, and so it has continued from that day to this—difficulties always recurring, never healed."

The problems of South Africa are largely complicated by factors which are absent in the case of colonies like Australia, where the population is homogeneous though under different Colonial Governments. In South Africa there are the two Colonies of the Cape and Natal, the independent Republics of the Free State and the Transvaal, and the independent and semi-independent native jurisdictions; there is the old Dutch and rural population—conservative and independent—the progressive town populations, the populations of Dutch extraction and those of English, and the problem of the native populations in each state in their relations to the white population. All these factors complicate the problem of Government enormously.

For any new-comers or strangers the problems are almost insoluble, for there is no public press which adequately represents the feelings and the deep-set determinations of the rural population, and oftentimes

THE EXCLUSION OF FOREIGN INTERFERENCE. 89

has this feeling been set at nought with disastrous results; witness the seizure of the Transvaal, and the events which led to its retrocession. Mr. Gladstone has recently stated, with all that fiery indignation and righteous wrath which are peculiarly his own, that he was deceived by all who professed to know the feelings of the people of the Transvaal; that high and low, whether official by position or officious strangers who claimed acquaintance with the country by reason of a few months' knowledge of it, all combined to give a false picture of the actual state of feeling, and that had he known what that feeling was—as it was subsequently proved to be—he would immediately on the resumption of office in 1880 have handed back the Transvaal to the Government of its own people.

At the time when in the Cape Colony the question of responsible government or despotic rule was in the balance, Mr. Molteno, than whom no man had a better knowledge of the rural population who really hold the land of the Cape, solemnly warned the Government of the day from his place in Parliament, "that this population was a quiet and long-suffering one, but if taxes and contributions were to be wrung from it by a Government with whom the people were not in sympathy, they would not endure it, and only overwhelming force could compel them." These were indeed prophetic words, amply fulfilled when the myrmidons of that military autocrat, Sir Owen Lanyon, wrung from the people of the Transvaal the taxes at the point of the bayonet, and seized the beloved ox-waggon—the symbol of their very life—by an armed force of soldiery for forced sale. The ox-waggon, which has been to the African pioneer his refuge and his strength, which has held all he most cherished, his wife and children, his Bible and household belongings, and has shielded it from the perils of the desert and the greater perils of the rushing hordes of savages, when, with horrid yells, they swept down upon him ; which has been his home for many days, which has been his last resort and refuge to carry him away into the desert when tyranny has followed him into the wild home which he has rescued from the savage and murderous bands of Moselikatze and Dingaan. When this was wrenched from him by armed force to pay tax to the hated foreigner who had done him such wrong, was it wonderful, was it blameworthy, if the spirit of his ancestors rose within him and, feeling as they felt when Spain forced its hated Inquisition into their very homes, and their very thoughts were under its hated rule, he took up arms for that liberty which he valued more than life ? It was intolerable, and to England's eternal glory, be it said, there was a man at the head of her affairs who could appreciate this, and who could withstand the pagan cry of vengeance which rose against these long-suffering men, and who could say, "We have sinned against you; we will not add to the wrong by shedding more blood before we acknowledge our error. Liberty is our life and our love ; it will be yours too so far as we can give it you "—so spoke Gladstone.

Bitter have been the wrongs done, with best intent and desire of South Africa's welfare, because of the ignorance on the part of those controlling its destiny from afar of the conditions of the problems which it presents.[1] Surely we may extend the words of Mr. Molteno's speech in 1871 on responsible government:—" I believe that in desiring the colonists to take responsible government, they (English statesmen) wish to strengthen the bonds that unite the dependencies to England (cheers) ; that the bond is for the future to be one of more intense sympathy (cheers), and not intermeddling with our local affairs (cheers). As the home Government withdraws from the control of our business, it knows that that business stands a better chance of being done well by those who, living on the spot and knowing all the circumstances, can better understand it. . . . Are we ever to be like weak children requiring a nurse from Downing Street to guide our steps ? . . . I maintain, living as we do in the country and knowing its people thoroughly, we are in a much better position to act wisely for ourselves than any man, however wise he may be, who lives at a distance. (Hear, hear.) We cannot throw up the responsibilities devolving upon us unless we abrogate our rights and privileges. Even if we did that, our difficulties would be greater than they are now. But, sir, the people of this Colony are not going to do anything so

[1] England's troubles in South Africa have arisen almost entirely from the failure of its statesmen to utilize the experience of the statesmen on the spot, who have devoted their lives to the service of their country, and who have gained the requisite experience by a lifetime spent in studying the local difficulties.

degrading and so debasing as to give up those privileges which they received as their rights, and which they hope to hand down to their children. (Cheers.) If I know the people of this Colony, sir —and I venture to think that I ought to have some knowledge of them—they will never accept such degradation." . . . Referring to the management of natives, he said :—" I think, sir, that we who live in this country, and who know its various native races, are much better qualified to know how to deal with them than a man, however great his ability and however high his position, who is sent out as an amateur to this country. (Hear, hear.) It is utterly impossible to expect that gentlemen by putting their feet on the shores (of Table Bay) can know more of these questions than those familiar with the country and its people. (Hear, hear.) The opinion of the country on this, as on other subjects, ought to be given by the legitimate representatives of the people."

These words are wise words, and capable of extension with advantage to the questions which ought to be dealt with by South Africa as a whole. But only by union can we speak with that authority and with that moral force which is necessary in order that these questions may be solved in accordance with the true interests of South Africa.

CHAPTER VIII.

THE FORM OF FEDERAL UNION.

Maintenance of present governments—Attachment to governments—Feeling at Cape—Feeling in America—How far present governments must part with rights—Two forms of Federation—Essentials of Federation—Independence in matters of local concern—Dependence in matters of common concern—Examples from history—Relation of states to Federal government—One class of Federation represents only several members of Union—Viciousness of this form—Example of America before present union formed—Evil results—Analysis of causes of weakness—These of universal operation—Other class of Federation operates on governments and on citizens as well—Latter good form of Federation—America since union formed on this principle has prospered—Importance of subject—Argument of Federalist—*If operation of central government be on separate states, only force can compel obedience to Federal mandate—Evils of resort to force—Remedy, operation of central government on individuals—If opposition to central government, offending party must take aggressive action—Impossibility of providing for every contingency—Application of* Federalist *argument to Africa.*

WE have now dealt with the disadvantages of disunion, with the dangers of internal discord and domestic strife, with the dangers of external interference and foreign intermeddling, and with the advantages of union, to preserve that orderly development which is the best guarantee of future prosperity, and to establish and to forward the realization of those legitimate aspirations which a united South Africa must cherish.

We must now deal with the question of the means and method by which such a union can be achieved. It is not with us as it was with the famous Federalist—we have no constitution drawn by the wisest and best men in the land, the acceptance of which we can advocate ; we can but indicate the advantages of such a constitution, and deal with some of the difficulties which are obvious at present, and for the solution of which we can hope to derive much aid and assistance from the valuable precedents established in America.

And first among these is the question of the preservation of those State Governments to which the people are naturally attached, and their relation to a Federal Government.

We have already seen how the parent colony of the Cape of Good Hope was forcibly deprived of her offspring by the policy of Her Majesty's Government. It was in 1852 that the Transvaal Republic was recognized; and in 1854 the Orange River sovereignty was abandoned by England, whether the inhabitants wished it or no.

Thus it is not yet half a century since the peoples of the two republics in South Africa were compelled to organize such a system of government as would preserve law and order for them, and maintain civilization in the wild and isolated regions in which they were just settled down. Bravely have they conducted the struggle against great odds. With but few sources of revenue open to them, they have faced the task of administering a country of vast extent and occupied by a mere handful of people spread over wide areas; they have been on the verge of seeing all their limited number of officials unpaid altogether; they were compelled to see paper money issued and its depreciation. They have struggled for bare existence with the neighbouring hordes of savages; and not with these alone, but with the might and power and prestige of Great Britain, both with arms in their hands and in the field of diplomacy. All these sources of respect and veneration have been added to the more ordinary causes which tend to move men's minds to loyalty and regard for their Government. As the *Federalist* has it, "It is a known fact in human nature, that its affections are commonly weak in proportion to the distance or diffusiveness of the object. Upon the same principle that a man is more attached to his family than to his neighbourhood, to his neighbourhood than to the community at large, the people of each state would be apt to feel a stronger bias towards their local governments than towards the government of the Union, unless the force of that principle should be destroyed by a much better administration of the latter.

"This strong propensity of the human heart would find powerful auxiliaries in the objects of state regulation.

"The variety of more minute interests, which will necessarily fall under the superintendence of the local administrations, and which will form so many rivulets of influence, running through every part of the society, cannot be particularized without involving a detail too tedious and uninteresting to compensate for the instruction it might afford.

"There is one transcendent advantage belonging to the province of the state governments, which alone suffices to place the matter in a clear and satisfactory light—I mean the ordinary administration of criminal and civil justice. This, of all others, is the most powerful, most universal, and most attractive source of popular obedience and attachment. It is that which, being the immediate and visible guardian of life and property, having its benefits and its terrors in constant activity before the public eye, regulating all those personal interests and familiar concerns to which the sensibility of individuals is more immediately awake, contributes, more than any other circumstance, to impressing upon the minds of the people, affection, esteem and reverence towards the government. This great cement of society, which will diffuse itself almost wholly through the channels of the particular governments, independent of all other causes of influence, would insure them so decided an empire over their respective citizens as to render them at all times a complete counterpoise, and, not unfrequently, dangerous rivals to the power of the union."[1]

Owing then to all these various causes, we find that a strong feeling of attachment to their prospective governments prevails among the peoples of the Free

[1] *Federalist*, xvii.

State, Transvaal and Natal, and this feeling must be considered in any plan of a confederation of all these peoples into a United States of Africa. The same feeling existed in America. The feeling of loyalty and respect for the separate governments was so strong and so powerful that it may be said to have been the most serious obstacle with which the Union had to contend. A vast amount of argument is devoted by the *Federalist* to overcoming the reluctance of the people of the states to seeing the establishment of any authority of a superior order to that of their own state. We think then, that very serious difficulty, indeed more, that certain failure will attend any attempt to set aside these separate state governments, and to absorb them in one large and extended government, which would take their place entirely and for all purposes.

Is it possible then to establish an effective and coherent federation without sacrificing those separate governments of the colonies and states of South Africa, to which the respective peoples have become accustomed and attached? What does history say on this question? "Two requisites," says Freeman, "seem necessary to constitute a federal government in this its most perfect form. On the one hand, each of the members of the Union must be wholly independent in those matters which concern each member only. On the other hand, all must be subject to a common power in those matters which concern the whole body of members collectively. Thus each member will fix for itself the laws of its criminal jurisprudence, and even the details of its political constitution. And it will do this, not as a matter of privilege or concession from any higher power, but as a matter of absolute right, by virtue of its inherent powers as an independent commonwealth. But in all matters which concern the general body, the sovereignty of the several members will cease. Each member is perfectly independent within its own sphere; but there is another sphere in which its independence, or rather its separate existence, vanishes. It is invested with every right of sovereignty on one class of subjects, but there is another class of subjects on which it is as incapable of separate political action as any province or city of a monarchy or of an indivisible republic. The making of peace and war, the sending and receiving of ambassadors, generally all that comes within the department of international law, will be reserved wholly to the central power. Indeed, the very existence of the several members of the Union will be diplomatically unknown to foreign nations, which will never be called upon to deal with any power except the central government. A federal union, in short, will form one state in relation to other powers, but many states as regards its internal administration."[1]

"A federal commonwealth, then, in its perfect form, is one which forms a single state in its relations to other nations, but which consists of many states with regard to its internal government. Thus the city of Megalopolis in old times, the State of New

---

[1] Freeman, "Federal Government," p. 2.

York or the Canton of Zurich now, has absolutely no separate existence in the face of other powers ; it cannot make war or peace, or maintain ambassadors or consuls. The common Federal Government of Achaia, America, or Switzerland, is the only body with which foreign nations can have any intercourse. But the internal laws, the law of real property, the criminal law, even the electoral law, may be utterly different at Megalopolis and at Sikyon, at New York and in Illinois, at Zurich and at Geneva. Nor is there any power in the Assembly at Aigion, the Congress at Washington, or the Federal Council at Berne, to bring their diversities into harmony. In one point of view there is only a single commonwealth, as truly a national whole as France or Spain ; in another point of view, there is a collection of sovereign commonwealths as independent of one another as France and Spain can be."[1] We see from these clear expositions of the essentials of a federal government that it is not necessary for the allied states to lose their autonomy, and abandon altogether the attributes of sovereignty, but merely those which, for common purposes, must be wielded by the supreme federal government. But in order to efficiently carry out its functions, the federal government must have some relation to the states which compose the federation. The proper arrangement of this relation is a matter of supreme importance for the smooth working of the machinery of the federation. The peoples of each state are so attached

---

[1] Freeman, " Federal Government," p. 7.

to their own government, that in any dispute with the federal government they would invariably tend to side with their own government, and defy the federal authority. There must then be devised such machinery as will obviate or minimize this danger, and here we arrive at a fundamental distinction between the two classes of confederacies which history presents to us. "In the one class," says Freeman, "the federal power represents only the several members of the Union; its immediate action is confined to these governments; its powers consist simply in issuing requisitions to the state governments, which, when within the proper limits of the federal authority, it is the duty of those governments to carry out. If men or money be needed for federal purposes, the federal power will demand them of the several state governments, which will raise them in such ways as each may think best."[1]

This was the class of confederation which was formed in 1778 by the States of America, and under which they were rapidly drifting towards anarchy; the condition of the country under it is thus summarized by the *Federalist :*—

"We may indeed with propriety be said to have reached almost the last stage of national humiliation. There is scarcely any thing that can wound the pride or degrade the character of an independent nation which we do not experience. Are there engagements to the performance of which we are held by every tie respectable among men? These are the subjects of constant and unblushing violation.

[1] Freeman, "Federal Government," p. 8.

Do we owe debts to foreigners and to our own citizens contracted in a time of imminent peril for the preservation of our political existence? These remain without any proper or satisfactory provision for their discharge. Have we valuable territories and important posts in the possession of a foreign power which, by express stipulations, ought long since to have been surrendered? These are still retained, to the prejudice of our interests, not less than of our rights. Are we in a condition to resent or to repel the aggression? We have neither troops, nor treasury, nor government. Are we even in a condition to remonstrate with dignity? The just imputations on our own faith, in respect to the same treaty, ought first to be removed. Are we entitled by nature and compact to a free participation in the navigation of the Mississippi? Spain excludes us from it. Is public credit an indispensable resource in time of public danger? We seem to have abandoned its cause as desperate and irretrievable. Is commerce of importance to national wealth? Ours is at the lowest point of declension. Is respectability in the eyes of foreign powers a safeguard against foreign encroachments? The imbecility of our government even forbids them to treat with us. Our ambassadors abroad are the mere pageants of mimic sovereignty. To shorten an enumeration of particulars which can afford neither pleasure nor instruction, it may in general be demanded what indication is there of national disorder, poverty, and insignificance that could befall a community so peculiarly blessed with natural advantages as we are, which does not form a part of the dark catalogue of our public misfortunes."[1]

The cause of this weakness is described very clearly:—

"Government implies the power of making laws. It is essential to the idea of a law, that it be attended with a sanction; or, in other words, a penalty or punishment for disobedience. If there be no penalty annexed to disobedience, the resolutions or commands which pretend to be laws will, in fact, amount to nothing more than advice or recommendation. This penalty, whatever it may be, can only be inflicted in two ways: by the agency of the courts and ministers of justice, or by military force: by the coercion of the magistracy, or by the coercion of arms. The first kind can evidently apply only to men; the last kind must of necessity be employed against bodies politic or communities or states. It is evident that there is no process of a court by which the observance of the laws can, in the last resort, be enforced. Sentences may be denounced against them for violations of their duty; but these sentences can only be carried into execution by the sword. In an association where the general authority is confined to the collective bodies of the communities that compose it, every breach of the laws must involve a state of war; and military execution must become the only instrument of civil obedience. Such a state of things can certainly not deserve the name of government, nor would any prudent man choose to commit his happiness to it.

"There was a time when we were told that

[1] *Federalist*, xv.

breaches, by the states, of the regulations of the federal authority were not to be expected; that a sense of common interest would preside over the conduct of the respective members, and would beget a full compliance with all the constitutional requisitions of the Union. This language, at the present day, would appear as wild as a great part of what we now hear from the same quarter will be thought, when we shall have received further lessons from that best oracle of wisdom, experience. It at all times betrayed an ignorance of the true springs by which human conduct is actuated, and belied the original inducements to the establishment of civil power. Why has government been instituted at all? Because the passions of men will not conform to the dictates of reason and justice, without constraint. Has it been found that bodies of men act with more rectitude or greater disinterestedness than individuals? The contrary of this has been inferred by all accurate observers of the conduct of mankind; and the inference is founded upon obvious reasons. Regard to reputation has a less active influence, when the infamy of a bad action is to be divided among a number, than when it is to fall singly upon one. A spirit of faction, which is apt to mingle its poison in the deliberations of all bodies of men, will often hurry the persons of whom they are composed into improprieties and excesses, for which they would blush in a private capacity." [1]

"In our case, the concurrence of thirteen distinct sovereign wills is requisite, under the confederation,

[1] *Federalist*, xv.

to the complete execution of every important measure that proceeds from the Union. It has happened, as was to have been foreseen, the measures of the Union have not been executed; the delinquencies of the states have, step by step, matured themselves to an extreme, which has at length arrested all the wheels of the national government, and brought them to an awful stand. Congress, at this time, scarcely possesses the means of keeping up the forms of administration, till the states can have time to agree upon a more substantial substitute for the present shadow of a federal government. Things did not come to this desperate extremity at once. The causes which have been specified produced at first only unequal and disproportionate degrees of compliance with the requisitions of the Union. The greater deficiencies of some states furnished the pretext of example, and the temptation of interest to the complying, or to the least delinquent states. Why should we do more in proportion than those who are embarked with us in the same political voyage? Why should we consent to bear more than our proper share of the common burden? These were suggestions which human selfishness could not withstand, and which even speculative men, who looked forward to remote consequences, could not, without hesitation, combat. Each state, yielding to the persuasive voice of immediate interest or convenience, has successively withdrawn its support, till the frail and tottering edifice seems ready to fall upon our heads, and to crush us beneath its ruins."[1]

[1] *Federalist*, xv.

In the above lucid exposition we see the analysis of those forces which operated in America, and which are of general application, and would operate whenever the relationship of the states to the Federal Government was the same. As the *Federalist* points out, the remedy for this state of things is to be found in the operation of the Federal Government on the individuals of the states, and not on the states themselves.

"The great and radical vice in the construction of the existing Confederation is in the principle of legislation for states or governments, in their corporate or collective capacities, and as contradistinguished from the individuals of which they consist. Though this principle does not run through all the powers delegated to the Union, yet it pervades and governs those on which the efficiency of the rest depends. Except as to the rule of appointment, the United States has indefinite discretion to make requisitions for men and money; but they have no authority to raise either by regulations extending to the individual citizens of America. The consequence of this is, that, though in theory the resolutions concerning those objects are laws, constitutionally binding on the members of the Union, yet in practice they are mere recommendations which the states observe or disregard at their option."[1]

This introduces us to the second, or perfect form of Federal Government, as it has been termed.

"In the other class, the Federal powers will be, in the strictest sense, a government, which in the other

[1] *Federalist,* xv.

class it can hardly be called. It will act, not only on the governments of the several states, but directly on every citizen of those states. It will be, in short, a government co-ordinate with the state governments, sovereign in its own sphere, as they are sovereign in their sphere. It will be a government with the usual branches, legislative, executive, and judicial; with the direct power of taxation, and the other usual powers of a government; with its army, its navy, its civil service, and all the usual apparatus of a government, all bearing directly upon every citizen of the Union, without any reference to the governments of the several states. The state administration, within its own range, will be carried on as freely as if there were no such thing as an Union; the Federal administration, within its own range, will be carried on as freely as if there were no such thing as a separate state. This last class is what writers on international law call a composite state, or supreme federal government. The former class they commonly remand to the heads of mere confederacies, or, at most, systems of confederate states."[1]

"The real difference between the two classes seems to be that the one is a good, the other a bad, way of compassing the same objects. Both America and Switzerland found by experience that, without the direct action of the Federal power upon individuals, the objects of the Federal Union could not be carried out. The several state governments are, indeed, under the other system, constitutionally bound to carry out all requisitions which do not

[1] Freeman's "Federal Government," p. 9.

transcend the limits of the Federal authority. But we may be sure that the state government will always lie under a strong temptation to disobey such requisitions, not only when they really transcend the limits of the Federal authority, but also when they are simply displeasing to local interests or wishes. Such a compact, in short, may constitutionally be a Federal Union, but practically it will amount to little more than a precarious alliance."[1]

We now clearly see the difference between the two kinds of Federal Government, and we can hardly hesitate to choose between them.[2]

America, the latest and greatest example of Federal Government the world has ever seen, tried the first and found it an egregious failure. The causes of failure we have indicated above, and they were thus epitomized by Randolph in his opening speech in the great Convention which drafted the Constitution. "The Confederation," he said, "was made in the infancy of the science of constitutions, when the inefficiency of requisitions was unknown; when no commercial discord had arisen among states; when no rebellion like that in Massachusetts had broken out; when foreign debts were not urgent; when the havoc of paper money had not been foreseen; when treaties had not been violated; and when nothing

---

[1] Freeman's "Federal Government," p. 10.
[2] The second form of Federal Government has John Stuart Mill's approval; see his "Representative Government," p. 300. For a further discussion of the objects and purposes to be attained by a Federal Government, and the different forms of it, see H. Sidgwick, "Elements of Politics," chap. xxvi.

better could have been conceded by states jealous of their sovereignty. But it offered no security against foreign invasion, for Congress could neither prevent nor conduct a war, nor punish infractions of treaties or of the law of nations, nor control particular states from provoking war. The Federal Government has no constitutional power to check a quarrel between separate states; nor to suppress a rebellion in any one of them; nor to establish a productive impost; nor to counteract the commercial regulations of other nations; nor to defend itself against the encroachments of the states. From the manner in which it has been ratified in many of the states, it cannot claim to be paramount to the state constitutions; so that there is a prospect of anarchy from the inherent laxity of the government."[1]

America has tried the second form of federal government, and for more than one hundred years this form has continued to answer more and more the expectations of those who devised and set it in operation. Switzerland has also made trial of both forms. Until the year 1842 the first form prevailed, but in that year it was abandoned for the second or perfect form which now prevails.[2] The extreme importance of this subject must be our apology for going more minutely into it, and we quote here the whole of No. XVI. of the *Federalist*.

"The tendency of the principle of legislation for states, or communities, in their political capacities,

[1] Fiske, "A Critical Period of American History," p. 235.
[2] For a comparison of the two forms of federation, see Mill's "Representative Government," p. 301.

as it has been exemplified by the experiment we have made of it, is equally attested by the events which have befallen all other governments of the confederate kind, of which we have any account, in exact proportion to its prevalence in those systems. The confirmation of this fact will be worthy of a distinct and particular examination. I shall content myself with barely observing here, that of all the confederacies of antiquity which history has handed down to us, the Lycian and Achæan leagues, as far as there remain vestiges of them, appear to have been most free from the fetters of that mistaken principle, and were accordingly those which have best deserved, and have most liberally received, the applauding suffrages of political writers.

" This exceptionable principle may, as truly as emphatically, be styled the parent of anarchy: it has been seen that delinquencies in the members of the Union are its natural and necessary offspring; and that whenever they happen, the only constitutional remedy is force, and the immediate effect of the use of it, civil war.

" It remains to inquire how far so odious an engine of government, in its application to us, would even be capable of answering its end. If there should not be a large army constantly at the disposal of the national government, it would either not be able to employ force at all, or when this could be done, it would amount to a war between parts of the Confederacy concerning the infractions of a league, in which the strongest combination would be most likely to prevail, whether it consisted of those who supported or of those who resisted the general authority. It would rarely happen that the delinquency to be redressed would be confined to a single member, and if there were more than one who had neglected their duty, similarity of situation would induce them to unite for common defence. Independent of this motive of sympathy, if a large and influential state should happen to be the aggressive member, it would commonly have weight enough with its neighbours to win over some of them as associates to its cause. Specious arguments of danger to the common liberty could easily be contrived, plausible excuses for the deficiencies of the party could, without difficulty, be invented to alarm the apprehensions, inflame the passions, and conciliate the good-will, even of those states which were not chargeable with any violation or omission of duty. This would be the more likely to take place, as the delinquencies of the larger members might be expected sometimes to proceed from an ambitious premeditation in their rulers, with a view to getting rid of all external control upon their designs of personal aggrandisement; the better to effect which it is presumable they would tamper beforehand with leading individuals in the adjacent states. If associates could not be found at home, recourse would be had to the aid of foreign powers, who would seldom be disinclined to encouraging the dissensions of a confederacy, from the firm union of which they had so much to fear. When the sword is once drawn, the passions of men observe no bounds of moderation. The suggestions of wounded pride, the instigations of irritated resentment, would be apt to carry the states against which the arms of the Union were exerted, to any extremes necessary to avenge the affront or to avoid the disgrace of submission. The first war of this kind would probably terminate in a dissolution of the Union.

"This may be considered as the violent death of the confederacy. Its more natural death is what we now seem to be on the point of experiencing, if the federal system be not speedily renovated in a more substantial form. It is not probable, considering the genius of this country, that the complying states would often be inclined to support the authority of the Union by engaging in a war against the non-complying states. They would always be more ready to pursue the milder course of putting themselves upon an equal footing with the delinquent members by an imitation of their example. And the guilt of all would thus become the security of all. Our past experience has exhibited the operation of this spirit in its full light. There would, in fact, be an insuperable difficulty in ascertaining when force could with propriety be employed. In the article of pecuniary contribution, which would be the most usual source of delinquency, it would often be impossible to decide whether it had proceeded from disinclination or inability. The pretence of the latter would always be at hand. And the case must be very flagrant in which its fallacy could be detected with sufficient certainty to justify the harsh expedient of compulsion. It is easy to see that this problem alone, as often as it should occur, would open a wide field for the exercise of factious views, of partiality, and of oppression, in the majority that happened to prevail in the national council.

"It seems to require no pains to prove that the states ought not to prefer a national Constitution which could only be kept in motion by the instrumentality of a large army continually on foot to execute the ordinary requisitions or decrees of the government. And yet this is the plain alternative involved by those who wish to deny it the power of extending its operations to individuals. Such a scheme, if practicable at all, would instantly degenerate into a military despotism; but it will be found in every light impracticable. The resources of the Union would not be equal to the maintenance of an army considerable enough to confine the larger states within the limits of their duty; nor would the means ever be furnished of forming such an army in the first instance. Whoever considers the populousness and strength of several of these states singly at the present juncture, and looks forward to what they will become, even at the distance of half a century, will at once dismiss as idle and visionary any scheme which aims at regulating their movements by laws to operate upon them in their collective capacities, and to be executed by a coercion applicable to them in the same capacities. A project of this kind is little less romantic than the monster-taming spirit which is attributed to the fabulous heroes and demi-gods of antiquity.

"Even in those confederacies which have been composed of members smaller than many of our counties, the principle of legislation for sovereign states, supported by military coercion, has never been found effectual. It has rarely been attempted to be employed but against the weaker members; and in most instances attempts to coerce the refractory and disobedient have been the signals of bloody wars, in which one half of the confederacy has displayed its banners against the other half.

"The result of these observations to an intelligent mind must be clearly this, that if it be possible at any rate to construct a federal government capable of regulating the common concerns and preserving the general tranquillity, it must be founded, as to the objects committed to its care, upon the reverse of the principle contended for by the opponents of the proposed constitution. It must carry its agency to the persons of the citizens. It must stand in need of no intermediate legislation, but must itself be empowered to employ the arm of the ordinary magistrate to execute its own resolutions. The majesty of the national authority must be manifested through the medium of the courts of justice. The government of the Union, like that of each state, must be able to address itself immediately to the hopes and fears of individuals, and to attract to its support those passions which have the strongest influence upon the human heart. It must, in short, possess all the means, and have a right to resort to all the methods of executing the powers with which it is entrusted, that are possessed and exercised by the governments of the particular states.

"To this reasoning it may perhaps be objected that if any state should be disaffected to the authority of the Union, it could at any time obstruct the execution of its laws, and bring the matter to the same issue of force, with the necessity of which the opposite scheme is reproached.

"The plausibility of this objection will vanish the moment we advert to the essential difference between a mere non-compliance and a direct and active resistance. If the interposition of the State legislatures be necessary to give effect to a measure of the Union, they have only not to act, or to act evasively, and the measure is defeated. This neglect of duty may be disguised under affected but unsubstantial provisions, so as not to appear, and of course not to excite any alarm in the people for the safety of the Constitution. The State leaders may even make a merit of their surreptitious invasions of it on the ground of some temporary convenience, exemption or advantage.

"But if the execution of the laws of the national government should not require the intervention of the State legislatures, if they were to pass into immediate operation upon the citizens themselves, the particular governments could not interrupt their progress without an open and violent exertion of an unconstitutional power. No omissions nor evasions would answer the end. They would be obliged to act, and in such a manner as would leave no doubt that they had encroached on the national rights. An experiment of this nature would always be hazardous in the face of a constitution in any degree competent to its own defence, and of a people enlightened enough to distinguish between a legal exercise and an illegal usurpation of authority. The success of it would require not merely a factious majority in the legislature, but the concurrence of the courts of justice and of the body of the people. If the judges were not embarked in a conspiracy with the legislature, they would pronounce the resolutions of such a majority to be contrary to the supreme law of the land, unconstitutional, and void. If the people were not tainted with the spirit of their State representatives, they, as the natural guardians of the Constitution, would throw their weight into the national scale and give it a decided preponderancy in the contest. Attempts of this kind would not often be made with levity or rashness, because they could seldom be made without danger to the authors, unless in cases of a tyrannical exercise of the federal authority.

"If opposition to the national government should arise from the disorderly conduct of refractory or seditious individuals, it could be overcome by the same means which are daily employed against the same evil under the State governments. The magistracy, being equally the ministers of the law of the land, from whatever source it might emanate, would doubtless be as ready to guard the national as the local regulations from the inroads of private licentiousness. As to those partial commotions and insurrections, which sometimes disquiet society, from the intrigues of an inconsiderable faction, or from sudden or occasional ill-humours that do not infect the great body of the community, the general government could command more extensive resources for the suppression of disturbances of that kind than would be in the power of any single member. And as to those mortal feuds which, in certain conjunctures, spread a conflagration through a whole nation, or through a very large proportion of it, proceeding either from weighty causes of discontent given by the government or from the contagion of some violent popular paroxysm, they do not fall within any ordinary rules of calculation. When they happen, they commonly amount to revolutions and dismemberments of empire. No form of government can always either avoid or control them. It is in vain to hope to guard against events too mighty for human foresight or precaution, and it would be idle to object to a government because it could not perform impossibilities."

We see that under this second and successful system of Federation there would be accorded to the several states of South Africa a large measure of autonomy, and this would harmonize with those feelings of regard which have been described as having grown up in them for their respective Governments, endeared to them more than ever as they have been by reason of the vicissitudes and struggles through which they have guided the states into the calmer atmosphere which now surrounds their existence. But combined with this autonomy there must be a Federal authority in direct relation with the individuals of the states. We shall deal later on with the machinery by which this Federal power should be exercised on individuals.

CHAPTER IX.

FEDERAL OBJECTS AND FEDERAL MACHINERY.

Objects described as federal by United States Constitution—By Constitution of Dominion of Canada—Constitution written—Not subject to legislature—Supreme over all authorities—Contrast to flexible constitution of England—Historical origin of American Constitution—Similar written and supreme constitution for South African Federation—Idea familiar owing to existence of constitution ordinances in colonies and grondwets in republics—Provision in constitution for discharge of duties by federal government—President—Mode of election and powers—Administration by cabinet preferable—Principles of cabinet government—Senate—Powers and functions—Has succeeded—Desirable in South Africa—House of Representatives—Powers and duties—Desirable in South African Federation.

WHAT, then, are those purposes of government which may be said to be of common concern to the whole of the states composing the Federation? And what is the character of the Federal machinery? We shall best get an idea of these matters by enumerating the subjects which, by the constitution of the United States of America, have been reserved for the Federal Government.

" The administrative, legislative, and judicial functions for which the Federal Constitution provides are those relating to matters which must be deemed common to the whole nation, either because all the parts of the nation are alike interested in them, or because it is only by the nation as a whole that they can be satisfactorily undertaken. The chief of these common or national matters are :—

> War and peace: treaties and foreign relations generally.
> Army and navy.
> Federal courts of justice.
> Commerce, foreign and domestic.
> Currency.
> Copyright and patents.
> The post-office and post roads.
> Taxation for the foregoing purposes, and for the general support of the Government.
> The protection of citizens against unjust or discriminating legislation by any state.

"This list includes the subjects upon which the national legislature has the right to legislate, the national executive to enforce the Federal laws and generally to act in defence of national interests, the national judiciary to adjudicate. All other legislation and administration is left to the several states, without power of interference by the Federal legislature or Federal executive."[1]

In the case of Canada, the distinction between the civil matters within the province of the Dominion Parliament and the Provincial Legislatures bears a general resemblance to that which prevails in the case of the United States of America, while criminal

---

[1] Bryce's "American Commonwealth," p. 30.

law is reserved for the Dominion Parliament, and no province has a right to maintain a military force.¹

There is, then, a tolerable consensus of authority as to the objects which would be reserved for the Federal Government, and which would apply in South Africa as well as elsewhere, with some modifications to suit the special circumstances. Thus it would be a question whether the subject of natives should be reserved for the Federal Government to deal with or for the separate action of each state. We do not desire to lay down any hard-and-fast line on these questions, but to raise the questions in a general form, so that they may be thought over and gradually a matured opinion may be formed upon them. If we know and appreciate the manner in which this great question has been dealt with by others, we are more likely to arrive at a correct conclusion in our case.

Before we proceed to examine the machinery by which the American Constitution provided for the discharge of the duties of the Federal Government, we must draw attention to the character of that Constitution itself. We will subsequently examine in further detail some of its principal provisions, but we now desire to draw attention to one most important characteristic. The United States Constitution is a written Constitution, and its authority stands above every other authority in the United States; its provisions override all acts, whether of the President or

¹ For some account of the Canadian Constitution see article "Federal States of the World," 19 cent., July, 1884, by J. N. Dalton.

Congress, or of the legislatures of the several states composing the Federation. The acts of any of these authorities, whenever they transgress the rules laid down by the Constitution, limiting their functions, and prescribing their spheres of action, are absolutely void, and may be set aside by the private citizen. Now, in England this distinction between its Constitution and its Parliament does not exist. The Parliament represents the whole nation, it is not in theory merely an organ of the community, but it represents the community itself. It is a sovereign assembly, and there are no limits prescribed to its powers by any superior authority; each separate Parliament, when once elected, is in theory the whole people, and it may make or unmake any law, it may fundamentally alter the whole political fabric of the country if it is so minded. The late Sir Henry Maine, in his work on "Popular Government," has drawn attention to this feature of the British Constitution in contrast with the system of the United States of America, and has pointed out the serious dangers to which it is open by reason of this extreme facility for bringing about change, and he inclines to some provision for a check upon this absolute power of change.[1]

It is true that the Constitution itself may be amended in the proper manner by the people of the

---

[1] Sir Henry Maine, "Popular Government," p. 240: "But of all the infirmities of our Constitution in its decay, there is none more serious than the absence of any special precautions to be observed in passing laws which touch the very foundation of our political system."

United States, and that they are ultimately the sovereign power who can effect whatever change they may desire, provided that they give effect to their will in the manner prescribed by the Constitution.

We see, then, that the American Congress by no means corresponds to the Parliament of England, but it must exercise all its powers within the lines prescribed by the Constitution. We must, however, regard the Constitution from another point of view. It is the mode selected by the people of America when, as states, they joined together to form a great union to define and secure the respective spheres of action of the supreme Federal authority and the states governments.[1] We have already seen what a strong fear existed that the supreme authority would encroach too far upon the powers of the individual states, and nothing less than a very clear and exact definition of the respective spheres would have satisfied the men of 1787.

Even while the English connection remained we have seen that the colonies enjoyed a large share of freedom of action, and were for many purposes autonomous. England was far off, and could exercise but a shadowy influence on the colonies, and now that they had rid themselves of even this remnant of a controlling power, they were more than ever fearful of a controlling authority being erected, not to exercise its powers from a distance, but in their very midst. It was only experience of the dire

[1] See Mill, "Representative Government," p. 303; also A. V. Dicey, "Federal Government," in *Law Quarterly Review*, Jan., 1885, p. 83.

distress and calamities caused by their want of cohesion which compelled them to surrender their freedom, and naturally the extent of such a surrender must be very clearly laid down. There was likewise the desire to define certain leading principles of liberty and of government, which were held to be irrefragably established and never to be questioned. This idea of defining fundamental principles would seem to be derived from the English charters of liberty, such as Magna Charta, the Petition of Right, and the Bill of Rights.[1]

"This fundamental divergence," says Bryce, "from the British system is commonly said to have been forced upon the men of 1787 by the necessity, in order to safeguard the rights of the several states, of limiting the competence of the national government. But even without this necessity, even supposing there had been no states to be protected, the jealousy which the American people felt of those whom they chose to govern them, their fear lest one power in the government should absorb the rest, their anxiety to secure the primordial rights of the citizens from attack, either by magistrate or by legislature, would doubtless have led, as happened with the earlier constitutions of revolutionary France, to the creation of a supreme constitution or fundamental instrument of government, placed above and controlling the national legislature itself. They had already such fundamental instrument in the charters of the colonies, which had passed into the constitutions of the several

[1] See A. V. Dicey's article, "Federal Government," *Law Quarterly Review*, Jan., 1885, p. 80.

States; and they would certainly have followed, in creating their national constitution, a precedent which they deemed so precious.

"The subjection of all the ordinary authorities and organs of government to a supreme instrument expressing the will of the sovereign people, and capable of being altered by them only, has been usually deemed the most remarkable novelty of the American system. But it is merely an application to the wider sphere of the nation, of a plan approved by the experience of the several states. And the plan had, in these states, been the outcome, rather, of a slow course of historical development than of conscious determination taken at any one point of their progress from petty settlements to powerful republics."[1]

The same desire on the part of the states of South Africa to have definitely laid down whatever portion of their sovereign attributes they may consent to surrender for the purpose of forming the Federal union, will render it absolutely certain that this method must be adopted in the constitution of the South African Federation, while their own Grondwets or fundamental constitutions in the Republics have familiarized them with the idea, as did the constitutions of the American colonies in their case, and as do the constitution ordinances of the colonies in South Africa.[2]

[1] Bryce, p. 33.
[2] As to necessity of the constitution being "written," see A. V. Dicey's article above quoted. He says: "The supremacy of the constitution is due to the fact that the state derives its ery existence as a federal state from the constitution."
This, he says, involves three consequences. The constitution

It is interesting in this connection to observe that the Constitution of the Dominion of Canada was drafted by a kind of convention, and was enacted as a whole by the British Parliament, and can be altered only by that Parliament, except on certain specified points, with which the Dominion legislature can deal. There is no power possessed by the provinces to amend their constitutions similar to that possessed by the peoples of the several states in America.

There are, however, differences between the circumstances attending the formation of that Constitution, both in regard to the character of the colonies which combined to form the Union, and in the time at which it was completed.

There exists a more liberal and wiser view of the relations of the colonies to the mother country to-day than existed when the Dominion Constitution was enacted, while the almost complete autonomy of the Transvaal and Free State constitute a very important difference in the circumstances of South Africa, and it is to the American model, rather than to the newer and less tried constitution of the Dominion of Canada, that we should look for a precedent for South Africa.[1]

---

must be a written constitution. It must be inflexible or inexpansive. It must be capable of being changed only by some authority above and beyond the ordinary legislative bodies, whether Federal or State legislatures, existing under the constitution.

[1] As Mr. Dicey points out, the Dominion Constitution is really drawn on the model of the United States Constitution, though

How, then, did the American Constitution provide for the discharge of the duties of the Federal Government? As already stated, each state had its two Houses of Parliament; thus it was natural that the Federal Constitution should be based upon a similar principle. The founders of the American Constitution "preferred, as far as circumstances permitted, to walk in the old paths, to follow methods which experience had tested. Accordingly they started from the system on which their own Colonial Governments, and afterwards their State Governments, had been conducted. . . . They created an executive magistrate, the President, on the model of the State Governor and of the British Crown. They created a legislature of two houses—Congress—on the model of the two houses of their State legislature and of the British Parliament, and they created a judiciary appointed for life, and irremovable save by an impeachment. In these great matters they copied not so much the constitution of England as the constitution of their several states, in which, as was natural, many features of the English Constitution had been embodied."[1]

In the Cape, we have already pointed out, there are two Houses in each state—except the Free State, which has one, and which resembles Pennsylvania in this respect—and their constitutions resemble those of the American colonies, so that we may naturally expect a similar constitution for the

untruly said in the preamble to be on the model of the constitution of the United Kingdom. See article above quoted.

[1] Bryce, p. 31. See also Maine, "Popular Government," chapter on the constitution of the United States.

Federal Government of the United States of South Africa.

We must now briefly examine the functions of the respective members of the Federal Government, beginning with the President. Now in founding their constitution the Americans had in view four objects as essential to its excellence:—

"Its vigour and efficiency.

The independence of each of its departments (as being essential to the permanency of its form).

Its dependence on the people.

The security under it of the freedom of the individual.

"The first of these objects they sought by creating a strong executive, the second by separating the legislative, executive, and judicial powers from one another, and by the contrivance of various checks and balances, the third by making all authorities elective, and elections frequent, the fourth both by the checks and balances aforesaid, so arranged as to restrain any one department from tyranny, and by placing certain rights of the citizen under the protection of the written Constitution."[1]

In order to secure this system of checks and balances the President was to be chosen, not by the Congress, but by a means entirely free from the influence of Congress, so that he might act and draw his power and authority in a manner quite independent of Congress. He is therefore elected as follows:—

[1] Bryce, p. 31.

According to the Constitution each state chooses a number of persons as electors equal to the number of representatives of such state in Congress. These persons assemble in their own state, and there vote for some fit person as President, the voting taking place on a day fixed by law. This provision of a double election was looked upon as one of the most successful provisions of the Constitution, and it is specially praised by Hamilton as a security against tumult and disorder, while giving the people a direct voice in the election, yet the interposition of the electors is likely to make the choice more certain to fall upon a man who possesses the requisite qualifications. A different answer would probably be given now to the question of its success or non-success.

The powers and duties of the President are enumerated by the Constitution. "The President shall be commander-in-chief of the army and navy of the United States; and of the militia of the several states, when called into the actual service of the United States; he may require the opinion, in writing, of the principal officer in each of the executive departments upon any subject relating to the duties of their respective offices; and he shall have power to grant reprieves and pardons for offences against the United States, except in cases of impeachment.

"He shall have power, by and with the advice and consent of the Senate, to make treaties, provided two-thirds of the senators present concur; and he shall nominate, and, by and with the advice and consent of the Senate, shall appoint ambassadors, other public ministers and consuls, judges of the

Supreme Court, and all other officers of the United States, whose appointments are not herein otherwise provided for, and which shall be established by law. But the Congress may by law vest the appointment of such inferior officers, as they think proper, in the President alone, in the courts of law, or in the heads of departments.

"The President shall have power to fill up all vacancies that may happen during the recess of the Senate, by granting commissions which shall expire at the end of their next session.

"He shall from time to time give to the Congress information of the state of the Union, and recommend to their consideration such measures as he shall judge necessary and expedient; he may, on extraordinary occasions, convene both houses, or either of them, and in case of disagreement between them, with respect to the time of adjournment, he may adjourn them to such time as he shall think proper; he shall receive ambassadors and other public ministers, he shall take care that the laws be faithfully executed, and shall commission all the officers of the United States."

As the President is charged with the whole Federal administration, and responsible for its due conduct, he chooses his executive subordinates; and here we arrive at a fundamental distinction between the administration of the United States of America and a British colony or the British Constitution. There is no Prime Minister and no Cabinet in America; the ministers and chief secretaries are responsible to the President, not to the people as represented in Congress. When the Americans thought it necessary to appoint a President, they were not acquainted with the method of government by Cabinet, with a Prime Minister who really rules the country. They were really looking to the old Governor of the colony, who subsequently became President of the state, and to the British Constitution, which was the freest which they could find at that time.[1]

"The fact that in every one of their commonwealths there existed an officer in whom the State Constitution vested executive authority, balancing him against the State legislature, made the establishment of a Federal chief magistrate seem the obvious course."[2]

The examples of the ancient Republics of Greece showed that a single head was not necessary to a republic; and the experience of modern Switzerland also points in this direction. It is, then, very probable that it would be undesirable in any South African Federal Government to introduce the American President—if there be any head at all, it would rather be a nominal representative of the authority of the state, but without those administrative and other powers possessed by a President of the American type. The real Government would be administered by a cabinet on the principle in vogue in the colonies under responsible government. The

[1] Maine, "Popular Government," p. 212, says the President was really copied from the English king as he then appeared to the Americans.
[2] Bryce, p. 36.

principles of this system, as seen in the Parliamentary systems of England, Belgium, Italy and the self-governing colonies, are four.

"The head of the executive (be he king or governor) is irresponsible. Responsibility attaches to the cabinet, i.e. to the body of ministers who advise him, so that if he errs, it is through their fault; they suffer and he escapes. The ministers cannot allege, as a defence for any act of theirs, the command of the Crown. If the Crown gives them an order of which they disapprove, they ought to resign.

"The ministers sit in the legislature, practically forming in England, as has been observed by the most acute of English constitutional writers, a committee of the legislature, chosen by the majority for the time being.

"The ministers are accountable to the legislature and must resign office as soon as they lose its confidence.

"The ministers are jointly as well as severally liable for their acts: i.e. the blame of an act done by any of them falls on the whole cabinet, unless one of them chooses to take it entirely on himself and retire from office. Their responsibility is collective."[1]

"In America the administration resembles not so much the cabinets of England and France as the group of ministers who surround the czar, or the sultan, or who executed the bidding of a Roman emperor like Constantine or Justinian; such ministers are severally responsible to their masters, and are severally called in to counsel him, but they have not

[1] Bryce, p. 88.

necessarily any relations with one another, nor any duty of collective action." [1]

In the Republics of South Africa, compelled suddenly and under stress of extreme danger to form a constitution, no time could be devoted to weighing the various considerations as to the exact form of Republican Government which ought to be adopted, and the American model, with such modifications as were inevitable to fit it to altered conditions, coming handiest was followed. But when adequate time is available to weigh all the pros and cons, a careful consideration discloses that the true cabinet system is more in accord with modern ideas, and with a genuine confidence and trust in the people.

We must now examine the National Legislature of the United States of America, called Congress; it consists of two bodies—the Senate, and the House of Representatives.

The Senate is composed of two senators from each state chosen by the legislature of that state. Each senator must be at least thirty years of age and a citizen of the United States of nine years' standing and an inhabitant of the state for which he is elected. No senator can hold any office under the United States. They are chosen for six years, but one-third must retire every two years; thus the whole Senate must be re-elected every six years, though the senators are eligible for re-election. The original number of senators was twenty-six, as there were thirteen states, but it is now eighty-eight,

[1] Bryce, p. 90.

there being forty-four states. The Vice-President of the United States of America is *ex-officio* President of the Senate.

The Senate has legislative, executive and judicial powers. Its legislative function is to pass with the House of Representatives, in the same manner as the Upper Chambers of other legislatures, the Bills which on the assent of the President become the acts of Congress. If the President's assent be withheld, the bills, if passed by a two-thirds majority of each house, become law.

Its executive functions comprise the approval or disapproval of the President's nomination of judges, ministers of State, ambassadors and other Federal officers. There is likewise the duty of approving the treaties made by the President, but this must be done by a two-thirds majority of those present, and if this be not done the treaty falls to the ground.

Its judicial function is to act as a court to hear impeachments at the instance of the House of Representatives.

It is important to observe that the Senate represents the country as composed of separate commonwealths. Every state sends two senators, such unlike states as Maine, Louisiana and California, New York, and Rhode Island have the same number of representatives in this branch of Congress. This arrangement was the subject of long and anxious debate in the Federal Convention. The representatives of the larger states long resisted it on the ground that it would go far to preserve the distinction between the states and so prevent an amalgamation of the population into one homogeneous whole. But nothing less than this would satisfy the smaller states. This arrangement was known as the "Connecticut compromise." The concession of equal representation to each of the states in the Senate turned out to have been a very wise act, and went a long way to smoothe the further difficulties with which the convention had to deal. The smaller states being assured of an equal voice in one of the branches of the Congress, were ready to entrust Congress with much wider powers. This principle of the constitution is now very difficult to alter as "no state can be deprived of its equal suffrage in the Senate without its consent." No difficulties have arisen between the large states and the small ones, as their interests have really been the same.

"The plan," says Bryce, "of giving representatives to the states as commonwealths has had several useful results. It has provided a basis for the Senate unlike that on which the other House of Congress is chosen. Every nation which has formed a legislature with two houses has experienced the difficulty of devising methods of choice sufficiently different to give a distinct character to each house. Italy has a Senate composed of persons nominated by the Crown. The Prussian House of Lords is partly nominated, partly hereditary, partly elective. The Spanish senators are partly hereditary, partly official, partly elective. In the Germanic Empire the Federal Council consists of delegates of the several kingdoms and principalities. France appoints her senators by indirect election. In England the members of the House of

Lords now sit by hereditary right; and those who propose to reconstruct that ancient body are at their wits' end to discover some plan by which it may be strengthened, and made practically useful, without such a direct election as that by which members are chosen to the House of Commons. The American plan, which is older than any of those in use on the European continent, is also better, because it is not only simple, but natural—i.e. grounded on and consonant with the political conditions of America. It produces a body which is both strong in itself, and different in its collective character from the more popular house."[1]

The senators are elected by the legislatures of each state to represent that state. As we see, this method of representing the states in the Federal Government has worked well in America, and is well worthy of the careful attention of the statesmen of South Africa in any consideration of a Federal Senate. The number of the states in South Africa being more limited, a larger number of members than two from each colony or state might be sent to compose the Federal Senate.[2] It only remains to add that members of the Senate vote as individuals, and not by states. It is not so in the present Federal Council of the German Empire, in which each state votes as a whole, though the number of her votes is proportioned to her population. With

---

[1] Bryce, p. 94.
[2] Switzerland, in 1874, adopted the plan of two representatives for each state, irrespective of the population of the state. There are forty-four senators.

regard to the objects for which the Senate was created, and the manner it which it has worked, "The Americans consider," says Bryce, "the Senate one of the successes of their Constitution, a worthy monument of the wisdom and foresight of its founders. Foreign observers have repeated this praise, and have perhaps, in their less perfect knowledge, sounded it even more loudly.

"The aims with which the Senate was created, the purposes it was to fulfil, are set forth, under the form of answers to objections, in five letters (lxi.-lxv.), all by Alexander Hamilton, in the *Federalist*. These aims were the five following :—

" To conciliate the spirit of independence in the several states, by giving each, however small, equal representation with every other, however large, in one branch of the national government.

" To create a council qualified, by its moderate size and the experience of its members, to advise and check the President in the exercise of his powers of appointing to office and concluding treaties.

" To restrain the impetuosity and fickleness of the popular House, and so guard against the effects of gusts of passion or sudden changes of opinion in the people.

"To provide a body of men whose greater experience, longer term of membership, and comparative independence of popular election, would make them an element of stability in the government of the nation, enabling it to maintain its character in the eyes of foreign states, and to preserve a continuity of policy at home and abroad.

"To establish a court proper for the trial of impeachments, a remedy deemed necessary to prevent abuse of power by the executive.

"All of these five objects have been more or less perfectly attained; and the Senate has acquired a position in the government of the nation which Hamilton scarcely ventured to hope for. In 1788 he wrote: 'Against the force of the immediate representatives of the people nothing will be able to maintain even the constitutional authority of the Senate, but such a display of enlightened policy, and attachment to the public good as will divide with the House of Representatives the affections and support of the entire body of the people themselves.'

"It may be doubted whether the Senate has excelled the House in attachment to the public good; but it has certainly shown greater capacity for managing the public business, and has won the respect, if not the affections, of the people, by its sustained intellectual power."[1]

We come now to the House of Representatives. This House represents the nation on the basis of population, as the Senate represents it on the basis of states. The Constitution provides that representatives and direct taxes shall be apportioned among the several States according to their respective numbers, and under this provision Congress allots so many members of the House to each state in proportion to its population at the last preceding decennial census, leaving the state to determine the districts within its own area, for, and by which, the members shall be

[1] Bryce, p. 198.

chosen. The original House which met in 1789 contained only sixty-five members, the idea being that there should be one member for every 30,000 persons. At present the number is 356, being, according to the census of 1890, one member to 173,901 persons. The electoral franchise on which the House is elected is, for each state, the same as that by which the members of the more numerous branch of the state legislature are chosen. Each state has the right to regulate its own franchise, so that there is no uniformity in this respect. Members are elected for two years, and the election always takes place in even years : 1892, 1894, 1896. The powers of the House are in theory purely legislative. The House has no share in the executive function of the Senate, on the other hand it has the exclusive right of initiating revenue bills, and of impeaching officials, and of choosing a President in case there should be no absolute majority of presidential electors for any one candidate.

The House of Representatives is so similar in character and constitution to the House of Representatives both in the colonies and states of South Africa, that there can be no question as to the establishment of such a body being part of the Federal legislature to be devised for South Africa.

CHAPTER X.

THE FEDERAL COURTS.

Necessity for federal courts—Established by constitution—Jurisdiction of courts—Courts have worked well—Provide means of operation of federal government on individuals—Civil process for securing authority of state against infringement—Success of these provisions—Further function of federal courts—Maintain the supremacy of the constitution—Give effect to relative validity of federal constitution, of federal statutes, of state constitutions and state statutes—Court acts as international arbiter between states—Has preserved peace among states—Unanimous verdict in favour of success of courts—Valuable precedent for South African Federation.

WE must now describe a very important authority directly constituted by the constitution of the United States of America, we refer to the Federal courts. "When in 1788," says Bryce, "the loosely confederated states of North America united themselves into a nation, national tribunals were felt to be a necessary part of the national government. Under the Confederation there had existed no means of enforcing the treaties made or orders issued by the Congress, because the courts of the several states owed no duty to that feeble body, and had little will to aid it. Now that a Federal legislature had been established, whose laws were to bind directly the individual citizen, a Federal judicature was evidently needed to interpret and apply these laws, and to compel obedience to them. The alternative would have been to entrust the enforcement of the laws to state courts. But state courts were not fitted to deal with matters of a quasi-international character, such as admiralty jurisdiction and rights arising under treaties. They supply no means for deciding questions between different states. They could not be trusted to do complete justice between their own citizens and those of another state. Being under the control of their own state governments, they might be forced to disregard any Federal law which the state disapproved; or even if they admitted its authority, might fail in the zeal or the power to give due effect to it. And being authorities co-ordinate with and independent of one another, with no common court of appeal placed over them to correct their errors or harmonize their views, they would be likely to interpret the Federal Constitution and statutes in different senses, and make the law uncertain by the variety of their decisions. These reasons pointed imperatively to the establishment of a new tribunal or set of tribunals, altogether detached from the states, as part of the machinery of the new government. Side by side of the thirteen (now forty-two) different sets of state courts, whose jurisdiction under state laws and between their own citizens was left untouched, there arose a new and complex system of Federal courts. The Constitution drew the outlines of the system. Congress perfected it by statutes; and as the details rest upon these statutes, Congress retains the power of altering them. Few American institutions are better worth studying than this intricate judicial machinery; few deserve more admiration for the smoothness of their working; few have more contributed to the peace and well-being of the country."[1]

There are three kinds of courts—the Supreme court, the Circuit courts, and the District courts. The Supreme court is established as such by the constitution. It consisted originally of six judges, and these have now been increased to nine. They are nominated by the President and confirmed by the Senate, holding office during good behaviour, and removable by impeachment. This provision was regarded by the founders of the constitution as of great importance for securing the independence of the judges, for they were to be independent in their actions both of Congress and the President, and acting as a check on them if necessary. Competent authorities affirm that the judges have acted with independence, uninfluenced by Congress or by party feeling, and that their secure position has not been abused by them.

The Circuit and District courts have been created by Congress under the provisions in the Constitution for the erection of inferior courts. The jurisdiction of the Federal courts extends to the following, any other cases being left to the state courts:—

1. Cases in law and equity arising under the Constitution, the laws of the United States, and treaties made under their authority.

[1] Bryce, p. 225.

By this provision the National Constitution is assured its supremacy over the state laws, and by this clause any case in which either party bases his claim upon any Federal act is brought before a Federal court.

2. Cases affecting ambassadors.

3. Cases of admiralty and maritime jurisdiction.

4. Controversies to which the United States shall be a party.

5. Controversies between two or more states, between a state and citizens of another state, between citizens of different states, between citizens of the same state claiming lands under grants of different states, and between a state, or the citizens thereof, and foreign states, citizens, or subjects.

The Supreme court has original jurisdiction where a state is a party and in cases affecting ambassadors, and appellate jurisdiction in cases from inferior Federal courts and state courts ; and it has exclusive jurisdiction in some cases, while in others it is concurrent with that of the state courts.

" The French or English reader may ask how it is possible to work a system so extremely complex, under which every yard of ground in the Union is covered by two jurisdictions, with two sets of judges and two sets of officers, responsible to different superiors, their spheres of action divided only by an ideal line, and their action liable in practice to clash. The answer is that the system does work, and now, after a hundred years of experience, works smoothly. It is more costly than the simpler systems of France, Prussia, or England, though, owing to the small salaries paid, the expense falls rather on litigants than on the public treasury. But it leads to few conflicts or heart-burnings, because the key to all difficulties is found in the principle that wherever Federal law is applicable Federal law must prevail, and that every suitor who contends that Federal law is applicable is entitled to have the point determined by a Federal court."[1]

We have seen the stress which the Federalist laid on the importance of the Federal government being constituted so as to operate not on the states composing the Federation, but on the individuals which compose those states; and we have just seen that the requisite machinery entrusted with this object in view has answered its purpose, and has ensured the harmonious working of the Federal laws throughout the Union.

Indeed we may say that this system of Federal courts has stood in the place of any armed coercion for enforcing the Federal statutes, it has been a civil process similar to that of which we have experience daily in the enforcement of domestic legislation in our civil courts.[2]

---

[1] Bryce, "American Commonwealth," 234.

[2] Sir H. Maine points out that "the federal court is the unique creation of the founders of the constitution. . . . The success of this experiment has blinded men to its novelty. There is no exact precedent for it either in the ancient or the modern world," and he goes on to point out the most important fact that previous remedies for the infringement of the authority of the state had been by criminal process of impeachment of the offender, the American plan supplied its place by a civil remedy.—" Popular Government," p. 217.

We may conclude this portion of our subject by describing the powers of the Federal courts to enforce their decisions.

An officer called the United States Marshal carries out the writs, judgments, and orders of each Federal court. He may, in case of resistance, call on all good citizens for assistance, and in case of extreme need he refers to Washington for the aid of Federal troops.

There is also a Federal public prosecutor, who institutes proceedings against parties who transgress Federal laws or against whom the Federal Treasury desires to proceed. These officers are independent of the state courts and of the state public prosecutor.

The success which has attended all these provisions in regard to Federal courts and the necessity for them, which was foreseen by the men who drew up the Constitution, all tend to point to the importance of a similar provision being secured in the future Constitution of the United States of South Africa.

Before we leave the courts, we must refer to a function of the utmost importance to the Federation which is discharged by them. To make this quite clear, we must again refer to the difference between countries which have a Constitution which stands above every authority in the state, and those which have a legislative body which can alter every principle of the Constitution at its pleasure.

"In England and many other modern states there is no difference in authority between one statute and another. All are made by the legislature; all can be changed by the legislature. What are called in England constitutional statutes, such as Magna

Charta, the Bill of Rights, the Act of Settlement, the Acts of Union with Scotland and Ireland, are merely ordinary laws, which could be repealed by Parliament at any moment in exactly the same way as it can repeal a highway act or lower the duty on tobacco. The habit has grown up of talking of the British Constitution as if it were a fixed and definite thing. But there is in England no such thing as a Constituion apart from the rest of the law; there is merely a mass of law, consisting partly of statutes and partly of decided cases and accepted usages, in conformity with which the government of the country is carried on from day to day, but which is being constantly modified by fresh statutes and cases. The same thing existed in ancient Rome, and everywhere in Europe a century ago. It is, so to speak, the 'natural,' and used to be the normal, condition of things in all countries, free or despotic.

"The condition of America is wholy different. There the name Constitution designates a particular instrument adopted in 1788, amended in some points since, which is the foundation of the national government. This Constitution was ratified and made binding, not by Congress, but by the people acting through conventions assembled in the thirteen states which then composed the Confederation. It created a legislature of two houses; but that legislature, which we call Congress, has no power to alter it in the smallest particular. That which the people have enacted, the people only can alter or repeal."[1]

[1] Bryce, p. 237; see also A. V. Dicey "Federal Government" in *Law Quarterly Review*, Jan., 1885, p. 83.

Thus we see that in America Congress must confine itself to the limits laid down by the Constitution. It must legislate in accordance with these provisions; but in the event of its transgressing these limits—as it may do, whether with the intention of so doing or, as is more likely, by mere inadvertence—what authority is there to set it right, and so secure the paramount control of the Constitution? In this case, the validity or invalidity of a statute must be determined by the Federal courts, who compare the statute with the Constitution, and wherever there is any conflict between them, the Constitution must prevail. There is a further field for the operation of the Federal courts. The Federal Constitution, being paramount in authority, must prevail over the provisions of the state constitutions, should any such be found to conflict with its provisions. And further, it prevails over any statutes which the state legislatures may enact, and which may be found to be in any way at variance with its provisions.

Thus we see that there are to be found in the American system no less than four kinds of law—the Federal constitution, the Federal statutes, the state constitutions, and the state statutes. There may be a conflict between these different kinds of law, but their relative precedence has been clearly settled by the Constitution, and the only question left to the courts is whether, in any particular case, such a conflict arises, and in the event of such a conflict being established, the weaker law is void on this particular point; and in this manner we see that there is no conflict between the courts and the legislature, but merely between the different kinds of law.

Of the working of this provision we may again quote the distinguished writer to whom we have had occasion so frequently to refer :—

"There is no part of the American system," says Bryce, "which reflects more credit on its authors, or has worked better in practice. It has had the advantage of relegating questions, not only intricate and delicate, but peculiarly liable to excite political passions, to the cool, dry atmosphere of judicial determination. The relations of the central Federal power to the states, and the amount of authority which Congress and the President are respectively entitled to exercise, have been the most permanently grave questions in American history, with which nearly every other political problem has become entangled. If they had been left to be settled by Congress, itself an interested party, or by any dealings between Congress and the state legislatures, the dangers of a conflict would have been extreme, and instead of one civil war there might have been several. But the universal respect felt for the Constitution, a respect which grows the longer it stands, had disposed men to defer to any decision which seems honestly and logically to unfold the meaning of its terms. In obeying such a decision they are obeying, not the judges, but the people who enacted the Constitution. To have foreseen that the power of interpreting the Federal constitution and statutes, and of determining whether or no state constitutions and statutes transgress Federal provisions, would be sufficient to prevent struggles between the national government and the state governments, required great insight and great faith in the soundness and power of a principle. While the Constitution was being framed the suggestion was made, and for a time seemed likely to be adopted, that a veto on the acts of state legislatures should be conferred on the Federal Congress. Discussion revealed the objections to such a plan. Its introduction would have offended the sentiment of the states, always jealous of their autonomy; its exercise would have provoked collisions with them. The disallowance of a state statute, even if it did really offend against the Federal Constitution, would have seemed a political move, to be resented by a political counter-move. And the veto would often have been pronounced before it could have been ascertained exactly how the state statute would work, sometimes, perhaps, pronounced in cases where the statute was neither pernicious in itself, nor opposed to the Federal constitution. But, by the action of the courts the self-love of the states is not wounded, and the decision annulling their laws is nothing but a tribute to the superior authority of that supreme enactment to which they were themselves parties and which they may themselves desire to see enforced against another state on some not remote occasion." [1]

[1] Bryce, p. 250; see also what John Stuart Mill says :—" The tribunals which act as umpires between the federal and the state governments, naturally also decide all disputes between the citizen of one state and the Government of another. The

"The men of 1787, feeling the cardinal importance of anticipating and avoiding occasions of collision, sought to accomplish their object by the concurrent application of two devices. One was to restrict the functions of the national government to the irreducible minimum of functions absolutely needed for the national welfare, so that everything else should be left to the states. The other was to give that government, so far as those functions extended, a direct and immediate relation to the citizens, so that it should act on them, not through the states, but of its own authority and by its own officers. These are fundamental principles whose soundness experience has approved, and which will deserve to be considered by those who in time to come may have in other countries to frame Federal or quasi-Federal constitutions. They were studied, and to a large extent, though in no slavish spirit, adopted by the founders of the present constitution of the Swiss Confederation, a constitution whose success bears further witness to the soundness of the American doctrines."[1]

It is difficult to exaggerate the importance of the functions which these Federal courts have discharged in preserving the peace and harmony of

usual remedies between nations, war and diplomacy, being precluded by the federal union, it is necessary that a judicial remedy should supply its place. The Supreme Court of the federation dispenses international law, and is the first great example of what is now one of the most prominent wants of civilized society, a real International Tribunal."—" Representative Government," p. 305.

[1] Bryce, p. 318.

co-operation among the states, and maintaining the homogeneity of the whole country. The action of these courts is quiet and unobtrusive, they are called into activity only by "cases" or actual controversies to which individuals or states or the United States are parties. Unanimous praise has been awarded them by all authorities who have examined their working. There is every reason to believe that the adoption of this principle in the constitution of the United States of South Africa would have equally satisfactory results.

CHAPTER XI.

GENERAL PROVISIONS OF THE AMERICAN CONSTITUTION.

Preface—No export taxes—No preferential commercial regulations—No titles of nobility—Importance of excluding titles from South Africa—No state shall make law impairing the obligation of contract—Importance of this provision—No state can impose duties on exports or imports—Value of this article for securing internal free trade—No state may make war or make engagements with foreign powers—Recognition of judicial records of courts throughout Union—Citizens of each state entitled to all privileges of citizens in any other state—Mutual extradition—Congress to have power to legislate for common territory—Guarantee of form of government and internal order in each state—Mode of amending constitutions—No religious tests—Freedom of speech, of press, of assembly and petition—Security from unlawful arrest or search—Adoption of these principles in Federal Constitution for South Africa.

WE may now, with advantage, briefly examine some of the principal features which are to be found in the American constitution, and which are worthy of consideration, and possibly of imitation, in any similar constitution to be drawn up for the United States of South Africa. We have, incidentally, while describing the various authorities created by the constitution, described many of its provisions, but we now desire to refer to the more general principles therein enumerated, and which are of wide application.[1]

The Constitution prefaces its provisions by these noble words, "We, the people of the United States, in order to form a more perfect union, establish justice, insure domestic tranquility, provide for the common defence, promote the general welfare, and secure the blessings of liberty to ourselves and our posterity, do ordain and establish this Constitution for the United States of America."

After defining the President and Congress, it continues to define the powers which Congress may exercise, and with which we have already dealt. It then proceeds to enact that:—

"No Bill of attainder or ex post facto law shall be passed.

"No tax or duty shall be laid on articles exported from any state.

"No preference shall be given by any regulation of commerce or revenue to the ports of one state over those of another; nor shall vessels bound to, or from, one state be obliged to enter, clear, or pay duties in another.

"No title of nobility shall be granted by the United States; and no person holding any office of profit or trust under them shall, without the consent of the Congress, accept of any present, emolument,

---

[1] For the explanation of the inclusion of these articles in the Constitution, see A. V. Dicey, "Federal Government," *Law Quarterly Review*, January, 1885.

office or title, of any kind whatever, from any king, prince, or foreign state.

"No state shall enter into any treaty, alliance, or confederation; grant letters of marque or reprisal; coin money; emit bills of credit; make anything but gold and silver coin a tender in payment of debts; pass any bill of attainder, ex post facto law, or law impairing the obligation of contracts, or grant any title of nobility.

"No state shall, without the consent of the Congress, lay any imposts or duties on imports or exports except what may be absolutely necessary for executing its inspection laws; and the net produce of all duties and imposts, laid by any state on imports or exports, shall be for the use of the treasury of the United States; and all such laws shall be subject to the revision and control of the Congress.

"No state shall, without the consent of the Congress, lay any duty of tonnage, keep troops or ships of war in time of peace, enter into any agreement or compact with another state, or with a foreign power, or engage in war, unless actually invaded, or in such imminent danger as will not admit of delay."[1]

Articles of the above nature might with advantage be applied to the constitution of the United States of South Africa. They would secure internal free trade

---

[1] For the value and importance of these provisions see Maine, "Popular Government," p. 247. With reference to the rule that no state make any law impairing the obligation of contracts, Sir H. Maine says, "There is no more important provision in the whole constitution;" see also Dicey, *Law Quarterly Review*, Jan. 1885, on the far-reaching effects of this provision.

between the colonies and states, and the absence of foreign interference in the affairs of the Federation.

The self-denying ordinance with regard to titles of nobility would be particularly worthy of imitation in South Africa. The existence of titles of nobility or artificial caste among the peoples of Europe is a disadvantage inherited from their past. It has given rise to great evils in most European states, and at the present time gives a false standard of merit.

It is in every way desirable that the men who compose the state should be unfettered by any artificial distinction in rising to and filling those posts which their merits may fit them to hold. The well-being of the community as well as of its individuals, depend in large measure upon its power to avail itself of its best men for those posts for which they are best suited, and the happiness of the individuals of the state is largely dependent upon their being able to rise to those positions for which their qualities or their abilities best fit them. We have now attained a sufficient degree of enlightenment and liberal feeling to perceive that men are not to be estimated according to the titles their fathers, or they themselves, have obtained, but by their own good qualities and their own merits.

A false standard is created by such distinctions, a bad example set to all, the prevalence of "snobbishness" becomes established and tends to undermine that sturdy self-respect and manly independence which is one of the most valuable traits of a free people. The older countries of Europe are gradually emancipating themselves from this undesirable feature. Why then should it be introduced into a new country where no tradition and no past has made it a necessary survival? As Herbert Spencer says in describing the evolution of the industrial type of society of the future as opposed to the military type which existed in the past and survives to our own day :—" So long as corporate action is necessitated for national self-preservation—so long as, to effect combined defence or offence, there is maintained that graduated subordination which ties all inferiors to superiors, as the soldier is tied to his officer—so long as there is maintained the relation of status, which tends to fix men in the positions they are severally born to; there is insured a comparative rigidity of social organization. But with the cessation of those needs which initiate and preserve the militant type of structure, and with the establishment of contract as the universal relation under which efforts are combined for mutual advantage, social organization loses its rigidity. No longer determined by the principle of inheritance, places and occupations are now determined by the principle of efficiency; and changes of structure follow when men, not bound to prescribed functions, acquire the functions for which they have proved themselves most fit" (*Spencer's Principles of Sociology*, vol. i. p. 613).

"Full faith and credit shall be given in each state to the public acts, records and judicial proceedings of every other state. And the Congress may by general laws prescribe the manner in which such acts, records, and proceedings shall be proved, and the effect thereof.

"The citizens of each state shall be entitled to all privileges and immunities of citizens in the several states.

"A person charged in any state with treason, felony, or other crime, who shall flee from justice and be found in another state, shall, on demand of the executive authority of the state from which he fled, be delivered up, to be removed to the state having jurisdiction of the crime."

These are very necessary articles for securing the homogeneity of the Federation.

"New states may be admitted by the Congress into this union, but no new state shall be formed or erected within the jurisdiction of any other state; nor any state be formed by the junction of two or more states, or parts of states, without the consent of the legislatures of the states concerned as well as of the Congress.

"The Congress shall have power to dispose of and make all needful rules and regulations respecting the territory or other property belonging to the United States, and nothing in this constitution shall be so construed as to prejudice any claims of the United States, or of any particular state."

An article of this character would be necessary in order that the United States of South Africa might deal with the settlement and orderly admission into the union of the states which are destined to be formed in the northern territories.

"The United States shall guarantee to every state in this union a republican form of government, and shall protect each of them against invasion; and on application of the legislature, or of the executive (when the legislature cannot be convened) against domestic violence."

We have already pointed out the value of this provision to the States of South Africa.

The next provision provides the mode of amending the constitution.

"The Congress, whenever two-thirds of both houses shall deem it necessary, shall propose amendments to this constitution, or on the application of the legislatures of two-thirds of the several states, shall call a convention for proposing amendments, which, in either case, shall be valid, to all intents and purposes, as part of this constitution, when ratified by the legislatures of three-fourths of the several states, or by conventions in three-fourths thereof, as the one or the other mode of ratification may be proposed by the Congress ; provided that no amendments which may be made prior to the year one thousand eight hundred and eight shall in any manner affect the first and fourth clauses in the ninth section of the first article ; and that no state, without its consent, shall be deprived of its equal suffrage in the senate.

" No religious test shall ever be required as a qualification to any office or public trust under the United States."

This should certainly be embodied in the constitution of the United States of South Africa.

"Congress shall make no law respecting an establishment of religion, or prohibiting the free exercise thereof ; or abridging the freedom of speech or of the press; or the right of the people peaceably to assemble, and to petition the government for a redress of grievances."

This is a most important article; we have seen its principles denied and violated in recent times in South Africa.

"The right of the people to be secure in their persons, houses, papers, and effects, against unreasonable searches and seizures, shall not be violated, and no warrants shall issue, but upon probable cause, supported by oath or affirmation, and particularly describing the place to be searched, and the person or things to be seized.

"All persons born or naturalized in the United States, and subject to the jurisdiction thereof, are citizens of the United States and of the states wherein they reside. No state shall make or enforce any law which shall abridge the privileges or immunities of citizens of the United States; nor shall any state deprive any person of life, liberty, or property, without due process of law; nor deny to any person within its jurisdiction the equal protection of the laws.

"The right of citizens of the United States to vote shall not be denied or abridged by the United States or any state on account of race, colour, or previous condition of servitude.

"The Congress shall have power to enforce this article by appropriate legislation."

These are the provisions of the constitution which have a more than local application, and which are worthy of the careful consideration of those upon whom it may devolve to devise the machinery for a closer union of the states of South Africa.[1]

[1] The reader may consult for an elucidation of the provisions of the constitution the splendid "Commentaries on the Constitution" of Story and of Kent. Also the works of Fiske and Bryce to which reference has been so frequently made, and in addition Bancroft's works. Sir Henry Maine's chapter on the American constitution in his "Popular Government" is most valuable—in it he traces the historical principles on which the provisions of the constitution are founded, and discusses the results of the test to which they have been put by the lapse of time. See also A. V. Dicey's article "Federal Government," *Law Quarterly Review*, Jan. 1885, p. 80, to which reference has already been made. The full text of the constitution will be found set out in the appendix.

CHAPTER XII.

THE PROVED ADVANTAGES OF FEDERAL GOVERNMENT.

Arguments for federation used in case of America—Provides union for national purposes—Separate state government for state purposes—Federalism best means for developing new countries—Sir John Seeley's opinion—Self-government stimulates political life—Secures good administration of local affairs—Diminishes difficulty of governing great areas—Relieves central legislature of much work better dealt with by local legislation—All above advantages hold good for South Africa—Sir George Grey's opinion—Only road to safety and success in South Africa—Bryce's opinion on success of federalism in America—Fiske's opinion—Freeman's eulogy—Federal success in case of Switzerland—Value of Swiss precedent for South Africa—Sir Henry Maine's tribute to success—Lesson plain to South Africa—Rapid movement of questions in South Africa—Direction of development towards powerful union—Importance of seizing right moment—Value of federation to enable South Africa to occupy proper position in regard to Europe—To realize its legitimate aspirations.

WE have now had in review the causes which, in America, compelled the States to form a strong federal government while retaining their own individuality and independence. We have seen the machinery which they devised for this purpose. We have reviewed and described the office of president, the constitution and powers of Congress, and the functions of the federal courts. We have also enumerated the most important clauses of the constitution, which is of higher authority than any of these. We have incidentally pointed out how similar evils in South Africa point to a similar remedy, and have indicated the advantages which would flow from the establishment of a federal government.

Let us then once more recapitulate the proved advantages of the federal system so far as they have a bearing on the present condition of affairs in South Africa.

"There are two lines of argument by which the federal system was recommended to the framers of the constitution of America, and by which it is still put forward as worthy of imitation by other countries.

"1. That federalism furnishes the means of uniting commonwealths into one nation under one national government without extinguishing their separate administrations, legislatures, and local patriotisms. As the Americans of 1787 would probably have preferred complete state independence to the fusion of their states into a unified government, federalism was the only resource. So when the new Germanic Empire, which is really a federation, was established in 1871, Bavaria and Wurtemburg could not have been brought under a national government save by a federal scheme."[1]

We see in South Africa also a strong local attach-

[1] Bryce, p. 342.

ment to the separate governments, and a desire to retain them as separate governments, as far as may be consistent with the formation of a Federal government.

"2. That Federalism supplies the best means of developing a new and vast country. It permits an expansion, whose extent and whose rate and manner of progress cannot be foreseen, to proceed with more variety of methods, more adaptation of laws and administration to the circumstances of each part of the territory, and altogether in a more truly natural and spontaneous way than can be expected under a centralized government, which is disposed to apply its settled system through all its dominions. Thus the special needs of a new region are met by the inhabitants in the way they find best; its special evils are met by special remedies, perhaps more drastic than an old country demands, perhaps more lax than an old country would tolerate; while at the same time the spirit of self-reliance among those who build up these new communities is stimulated and respected."[1]

This applies to South Africa where the northern territories are now being settled, and the question of the manner of their absorption in the South African system is an immediate and pressing one. Sir John Seeley says: "The United States have solved the problem substantially similar to that which our old colonial system could not solve, by showing how a state may throw off a constant stream of emigration, how from a fringe of settlement on the Atlantic a whole continent as far as the Pacific may be peopled,

[1] Bryce, "American Commonwealth," p. 343.

and yet the doubt never arise whether those remote settlements will not soon claim their independence, or whether they will bear to be taxed for the whole."
—" The Expansion of England," p. 74.

" 3. That it prevents the rise of a despotic central government, absorbing other powers, and menacing the private liberties of the citizen."[1]

This is not so much a fear in South Africa except as regards the independence of the states.

The second set of arguments are as follows :—

" 1. Self-government stimulates the interest of the people in the affairs of their neighbourhood, sustains local political life, educates the citizen in his daily round of civic duty, teaches him that perpetual vigilance and the sacrifice of his own time and labour must be paid for individual liberty and collective prosperity."[2]

This is of general application to South Africa as well as other countries.

"2. Self-government secures the good administration of local affairs by giving the inhabitants of each locality due means of overseeing the conduct of their business."

" 3. Federalism, if it diminishes the collective force of a nation, diminishes also the risks to which its size and the diversities of its parts expose it. A nation so divided is like a ship built with water-tight compartments. When a leak is sprung in one compartment, the cargo stowed there may be damaged but other compartments remain dry and keep the

[1] Bryce, "American Commonwealth," p. 347.
[2] Ibid. p. 343.

ship afloat. So if social discord or an economic crisis has produced disorders or foolish legislation in one member of the Federal body, the mischief may stop at the state frontier, instead of spreading through and tainting the nation at large."

"4. Federalism, by creating many local legislatures with wide powers, relieves the national legislature of a part of that large mass of functions which might otherwise prove too heavy for it. Thus business is more promptly despatched, and the great central council of the nation has time to deliberate on those questions which most nearly touch the whole country."[1]

All these arguments recommending Federalism have proved valid in American experience, they would no doubt prove equally valid if Federation were tried in South Africa. Of America it is said, "To create a nation while preserving the states was the main reason for the grant of powers which the national government received ; an all-sufficient reason, and one which holds good to-day. The several states have changed greatly since 1789, but they are still commonwealths, whose wide authority and jurisdiction practical men are agreed in desiring to maintain."[2] This must surely be the object also in view in uniting the South African states.

We may quote Sir George Grey's opinion. Writing to the Secretary of State in 1858, he advised that the several legislatures of the Cape of Good Hope, Natal, and the Orange Free State should be empowered to

---

[1] Bryce, "American Commonwealth," p. 345.
[2] Ibid. p. 345.

found a Federal union, and with authority to adopt into the Union all states which might wish to join them. In 1859, in his opening speech to the Cape Parliament, he brought before the latter the resolutions of the Orange Free State Volksraad in favour of union, and said, "You would, in my belief, confer a lasting benefit upon Great Britain, and upon the inhabitants of this country, if you could succeed in devising a form of Federal union, under which the several provinces composing it should have full and free scope of action left to them, through their own local governments and legislatures, upon all subjects relating to their individual prosperity or happiness; whilst they should act under a general Federal Government in relation to all points which concern the general safety or weal." He further continued to point out that in Federation of the different South African colonies and states alone lay safety and success. He was dismissed for this suggestion, but his advice was sound and true, and remains so to this day.

To sum up in the words of Bryce:—

"The problem which all federalized nations have to solve is how to secure an efficient central government and preserve national unity, while allowing free scope for the diversities, and free play to the authorities, of the members of the Federation. It is, to adopt the favourite astronomical metaphor which no American panegyrist of the constitution omits, to keep the centrifugal and centripetal forces in equilibrium, so that neither the planet states shall fly off into space, nor the sun of the central government draw them into its consuming fires. The characteristic merit of the American Constitution lies in the method by which it has solved this problem. It has given the national government a direct authority over all citizens, irrespective of the state governments, and has, therefore, been able safely to leave wide powers in the hands of those governments. And by placing the constitution above both the national and the state governments it has referred the arbitrament of disputes between them to an independent body, charged with the interpretation of the constitution, a body which is to be deemed not so much a third authority in the government as the living voice of the constitution, the unfolder of the mind of the people whose will stands expressed in that supreme instrument.

"The application of these two principles, unknown to, or at any rate little used by any previous Federation, has contributed more than anything else to the stability of the American system, and to the reverence which its citizens feel for it, a reverence which is the best security for its permanence." [1]

We may also add the opinion of an American author who has made the origin and birth of the American Constitution his special study.

"Thus at length," says Fiske, "was realized the sublime conception of a nation in which every citizen lives under two complete and well-rounded systems of laws—the state law and the Federal law—each with its legislature, its executive, and its judiciary moving one within the other, noiselessly and without friction.

[1] Bryce, "American Commonwealth," p. 348.

It was one of the longest reaches of constructive statesmanship ever known in the world. There was never anything quite like it before, and in Europe it needs much explanation to-day even for educated statesmen who have never seen its workings. Yet to Americans it has become so much a matter of course that they, too, sometimes need to be told how much it signifies. In 1787 it was the substitution of law for violence between states that were partly sovereign. In some future still grander convention, we trust the same thing will be done between states that have been wholly sovereign, whereby peace may gain and violence be diminished over other lands than this which has set the example."[1]

We may take another testimony: "At all events," says Freeman, "the American Union has actually secured, for what is really a long period of time, a greater amount of combined peace and freedom than was ever before enjoyed by so large a portion of the earth's surface. There have been, and still are, vaster despotic empires, but never before has so large an inhabited territory remained for more than seventy years in the enjoyment at once of internal freedom and of exemption from the scourge of internal war. Now this is the direct result of the Federal system. Either entire independence or closer union would have brought with it evils which the Federal relation has prevented. Had the thirteen states remained wholly independent commonwealths, had new states, equally independent, grown up to the west of them, we cannot doubt that the American continent would

[1] Fiske, "The Critical Period of American History," p. 301.

before this time, have become the theatre of constant wars between so many independent and rival powers."[1] Let us leave America for a moment and see what Federation has done for a country where conditions are very different, and in some respects far less favourable. "The territory of the Swiss Conferation is, both in a military and political point of view, one of the most important in Europe. Lying between the two great despotisms of France and Austria, it is above all things needful that it should be held by a free and an united people. But disunion seems stamped upon the soil by the very hand of nature, no less than on the soil of Hellas itself. Every valley seems to ask for its own separate commonwealth. The land, small as it is, is inhabited by men of different races, different languages, different religions, different stages of society. Four languages are spoken within the narrow compass of the League. Religious and political dissensions have been so strong as more than once to have led to civil war. How are such a people to be kept united among themselves, so as to guard their mountains and valleys against all invaders? I need hardly stop to show that the citadel of Europe could not be safely entrusted to twenty-two wholly independent republics or to twenty-two wholly independent princes. But would consolidation answer the purpose? Shall we give them the stereotyped blessing of a hereditary king, a responsible ministry, an elected and a nominated House of Parliament? Or shall we, by way of variety, give them some neatly planned

---

[1] Freeman, "Federal Government," p. 86.

scheme of a republic one and indivisible? Such a kingdom, such a republic, would but present, on a smaller scale, much such a spectacle as the empire of Austria and Turkey. The Burgundian and the Italian provinces would rebel against a dominant German government, and would fly for support to their neighbours of kindred speech beyond the limits of the kingdom. France would soon become to Vaud what Piedmont has been to the Italian provinces of Austria, what Russia has been to the Slavonic provinces of Turkey. The Federal relation has solved the problem. Under the Federal system, the Catholic and Protestant, the aristocrat and the democrat, the citizen of Bern and the mountaineer of Uri, the Swabian of Zurich, the Lombard of Ticino, the Burgundian of Geneva, the speakers of the unknown tongues of the Rhaetian valleys—all can meet side by side as free and equal confederates. They can retain their local independence, their local diversities, nay, if they will, their local jealousies and hatreds, and yet they can stand forth, in all external matters, as one united nation, all of whose members are at once ready to man their mountain rampart the moment that the slightest foreign aggression is committed on any one of their brethren. The Federal system, in short, has here, out of the most discordant ethnological, political and religious elements, raised up an artificial nation, full of as true and heroic national feeling as ever animated any people of the most unmixed blood."

What a valuable lesson for South Africa! We see that in the case of Switzerland the problem of uniting

ADVANTAGES OF FEDERAL GOVERNMENT.

peoples who speak different languages, and are of different race, has been solved successfully, a far more difficult problem than that at the Cape, owing to the fact of there being not two languages, but four.

For the enormous and vital benefits conferred upon America by her constitution, and as indicating the similar benefits which a similar constitution would confer on South Africa, we quote what that most acute and able thinker, the late Sir Henry Maine, says: " The powers and disabilities attached to the United States and the several states by the Federal Constitution, and placed under the protection of the deliberately contrived securities we have described, have determined the whole course of American history. That history began, as all its records abundantly show, in a condition of society produced by war and revolution, which might have condemned the great Northern Republic to a fate not unlike that of her disorderly sisters in South America. But the provisions of the constitution have acted on her like those dams and dykes which strike the eye of the traveller along the Rhine, controlling the course of a mighty river, which begins amid mountain torrents, and turning it into one of the most equable waterways in the world." [1]

To South Africa the lesson is plain, " he who runs may read." The time has come when her statesman must face and solve the problem of the constitution of a central centripetal force to counteract the centrifugal force which is constantly tending to separate the communities and states. Events are

[1] " Popular Government," p. 245.

moving fast. The balance of population is being upset in the Transvaal, and troubles must arise unless its tranquility is to be guaranteed by the conservative forces of the whole of South Africa. Rhodesia is receiving a population whose numbers grow by leaps and bounds; already we have seen public meetings organized there to protest against being administered or controlled from Cape Town. Surely it will be wise to lose no time in arranging the machinery of those new territories in such a manner that they may automatically become members of the South African system, as and when their conditions fit them to be so, in the same way as the states which are formed from time to time in the great western territory become part of the United States of America.

The question of the introduction of an Indian population into South Africa is a serious one, and can only be dealt with by a United South Africa; it is a pressing question, an open sore, the larger it will grow, the more difficult will it be to deal with, the longer it is left. The dangers from hostile commercial action on the part of the different states, the dangers from territorial difficulties, the dangers from a want of union in the treatment of the native questions, have all been dwelt upon. All signs point to the fact that South Africa is on the eve of great developments of a commercial and industrial character, which must be controlled in such a manner that the forces derived from them shall be directed to the establishment of a powerful union, and not to the aggrandizement of one or other of the states, so as to enable it to pursue a selfish policy out of harmony with the interests of South Africa as a whole.

We have missed our aim if we have failed to convey the idea that the men of America saw the critical point at which they had arrived in 1787, seized the opportunity and founded a great nation. We will add a further testimony on this point:—

"The Convention met at the most fortunate moment in American history. Between two storms there is often a perfectly still and bright day. It was in such an interval of calm that this work was carried through. Had it been attempted four years earlier or four years later, at both which times the waves of democracy were running high, it must have failed. In 1783 the people, flushed with their victory over England, were full of confidence in themselves and in liberty, persuaded that the world was at their feet, disposed to think all authority tyranny. In 1791 their fervid sympathy with the Revolution in France had not yet been damped by the excesses of the Terror, nor alienated by the insolence of the French Government and its diplomatic agents in America. But in 1787 the first reaction from the War of Independence had set in. Wise men had come to discern the weak side of popular government; and the people themselves were in a comparatively humble and teachable mind. Before the next wave of democratic enthusiasm swept over the country the organization of a national government under the Constitution was in all its main features complete. It was seen that liberty was still safe, and men began ere long to appreciate the larger and fuller national life which the Federal Government opened before them. History sees so many golden opportunities lost that she gladly notes those which the patriotic foresight of such men as Washington and Franklin, Hamilton and Madison and Roger Sherman seized and used." [1]

Is another golden opportunity to be lost in South Africa? Are we not at the parting of the ways? one to disunion and feebleness, the other to union, to power, to self-respect, to the respect of other nations, to the vindication of our proper rights and desires and the adequate care of our vast interests.

England will protect our seaboard. No power can do it so effectively, no power will do it so generously. She will have her reward, our gratitude, the honour of founding and protecting the infancy of a great nation, and in a material point of view the value of our great trade carried on chiefly with her. But for all internal questions between the colonies and states, and in all the territories which may justly be claimed as belonging properly to the South African system, there we must be absolutely and entirely independent. While we see large tracts of South Africa in foreign hands we cannot feel safe or content, we must, as did America under similar circumstances, wait and seize our opportunities of recovering and restoring these territories to South Africa; this can only be done by a United South

---

[1] Bryce, "American Commonwealth," p. 639.

Africa. It can hardly be doubted that opportunities will occur for the peaceful acquisition of these lands, as they did with the great western possessions of America. We shall be ready to avail ourselves of any such opportunity so soon as it arrives.

CHAPTER XIII.

OUR CONNECTION WITH EUROPE.

Must be connected with some European power—Which power —Spanish, French, and English systems tried in America— England's colonies self-governing—French and Spanish despotically ruled—Victory of English system—Collapse of French Canada when attacked by English colonies— Despotic rule—Cause of collapse—Same despotic rule in Portuguese and German colonies in South Africa—Consequent stagnation—English colonies in America resist England when she coerces—America after independence adopts English system—Special mechanism by which England has avoided despotism—Develops principle of representation and local self-government—Origin of principle—Territorial as opposed to Græco-Roman city system —Failure of Græco-Roman system—Goths introduce free institutions to Europe—Loss of this freedom on Continent, save in Holland and Switzerland—Cause of loss—Necessity for military organization—Insular position of England— Permits development of freedom—Contact with sea increases tendency to freedom—Importance of principle of self-government—Attempt by Sir Philip Woodehouse to destroy at Cape—Instances of safety of England due to insular position—Expansion of English institutions in America—Revolt against arbitrary rule in America— Similar revolt at Cape—Anti-convict agitation—Constitutional struggle—Sir Bartle Frere—Despotism—War of Independence—Dangers of interference in internal affairs of South Africa—Importance of using great principles of self-government and Federation at Cape—For above reasons connection must be with England.

IN the early days of our national life we must derive force and strength from a connection with some one of the great powers of Europe, otherwise we would fall a prey to their jealousies, their greed of territory and their dissensions. Why should we, in the interest of our young nation, prefer to see England the paramount power in South Africa?

This question is well worthy of our careful thought; let us, then, devote a few lines to its consideration.

In the sixteenth century the great political question lay between Protestantism, or individualism, and Catholicism, or despotism; Holland and England supported the one, while Spain and the Pope supported the other. The struggle mainly went on in Europe, but the discovery of America at this time opened up a vast field for the operation of political principles. Spain, the greatest power in Europe, was first in the field, then France and England.

These three powers contended for the dominion of that vast and almost uninhabited region, which was so admirably suited for colonists of European descent. England planted its sturdy communities, who immediately put in operation the principles of self-government,[1] whilst Spain and France governed their

---

[1] Sir John Seely says :—" In the old colonial system there was no such thing as a Crown Colony in which Englishmen are governed administratively without representative assemblies. In the old system assemblies were not formally instituted, but grew up of themselves because it was the nature of Englishmen

colonies from home, and for the benefit of the parent states.

The result of this great trial was to prove which kind of civilization was the sturdiest and best adapted for wide empire. Let us briefly record the facts and the results in two contiguous and adjacent portions of America which belonged to England and France respectively, and this contrast will serve to bring out the great superiority in respect of national vitality possessed by a freely-governed country over one that is governed by a centralized despotism.

"When we consider," says Fiske, "the declared rivalry between France and England in their plans for colonizing the barbarous regions of the earth; when we consider that the military power of the two countries has been not far from equal, and that France has at times shown herself a maritime power by no means to be despised, it seems to me that her overwhelming and irretrievable defeat by England in the struggle for colonial empire is one of the most striking and one of the most instructive facts in all modern history. In the struggle for the possession of North America, where the victory of England was so decisive as to settle the question for all coming time, the causes of the French failure are very plainly to be seen. The French colony in Canada was one of the most complete examples of a despotic government that the world has ever seen. All the autocratic and bureaucratic ideas of Louis XIV. were here

to assemble. Thus the old historian of the colonies, Hutchinson, writes under the year 1619, 'This year a house of Burgesses broke out in Virginia.'"—" Expansion of England," p. 67.

carried out without let or hindrance. It would be incredible, were it not attested by such abundant evidence, that the affairs of any people could be subjected to such minute and sleepless supervision as were the affairs of the French colonists in Canada. A man could not even build his own house, or rear his own cattle, or sow his own seed, or reap his own grain, save under the supervision of prefects acting under instructions from the home government. No one was allowed to enter or leave the colony without permission, not from the colonists, but from the king. No farmer could visit Montreal or Quebec without permission. No Huguenot could set his foot on Canadian soil. No public meetings of any kind were tolerated, nor were there any means of giving expression to one's opinions on any subject. Never was a colony, moreover, so loaded with bounties, so fostered, petted, and protected. The result was absolute paralysis, political and social. When, after a century of irritation and skirmishing, the French in Canada came to a life and death struggle with the self-governing colonists of New England, New York, and Virginia, the result for the French power in America was instant and irretrievable annihilation. The town meeting pitted against the bureaucracy was like a Titan overthrowing a cripple. The historic lesson owes its value to the fact that this ruin of the French scheme of colonial empire was due to no accidental circumstances, but was involved in the very nature of the French political system. Obviously it is impossible for a people to plant beyond sea a colony which shall be self-suppporting, unless it has retained intact the power of self-government at home. It is to the self-government of England, and to no lesser cause, that we are to look for the secret of that boundless vitality which has given to men of English speech the uttermost parts of the earth for an inheritance."[1]

But in South Africa we need scarcely go so far back to history, or so far off to other shores, for examples of the fatal effects of this centralized policy. Do we not see at our very doors the lifeless and stagnant colonies of Portugal, governed by officials sent from Lisbon? These colonies possess no free assemblies or means of representation, such as we see flourishing in our midst. It may be said in answer that the Portuguese are an effete people, in a bad climate which deprives all men of energy. This argument is met when we look to the other coast and see the vigorous and aggressive German power settled in a healthy country; we see, however, in the German colony of South West Africa the same stagnation. The Germans have possessed that colony for thirteen years, but owing to the restrictions placed by the officials on every kind of movement or enterprise, and the paternal control exercised over the affairs of each individual, no progress or development has been possible; and we see the European population a mere handful, not more than six or seven hundred, of which perhaps between five and six hundred are soldiers and officials in the direct service and pay of the mother country. The same fatal centralization and absence of self-govern-

[1] Fiske, "American Political Ideas," p. 54.

ment, as we have seen in the case of French Canada, must result in a similar want of self-reliance and independence in the German colonies. We shall see later on in these pages that, owing to Germany's extreme militancy, despotic rule must prevail at home, and she can only extend the arbitrary rule which prevails at home to any colonial dependencies. It is only a free country that can found free colonies.

We have seen above how, when the inferior French civilization in Canada became troublesome, it was struck down by the sturdy self-governing English communities at a blow. But further, " When the mother country, under the guidance of an ignorant king and short-sighted ministers, undertook to act upon the antiquated theory that the new communities were merely groups of trading-stations, the political bond of connection was severed; yet the war which ensued was not like the war which had but just now been so gloriously ended by the victory of Wolfe. It was not a struggle between two different peoples, like the French of the old *régime* and the English, each representing antagonistic theories of how political life ought to be conducted. But, like the Barons' war of the thirteenth century and the Parliament's war of the seventeenth, it was a struggle sustained by a part of the English people in behalf of principles that time has shown to be equally dear to all. And so the issue only made it apparent to an astonished world that instead of one there were now two Englands, alike prepared to work with might and main towards the political regeneration of mankind."[1]

[1] Fiske, "American Political Ideas," p. 129.

In what direction did the American colonies look when they had just thrown off their allegiance to the English king? Not to France, Spain, or Italy, but to free England; because here was the freest constitution which the world has ever seen. Having experienced evils from their connection with England, they would have gone elsewhere for their constitutional principles could they have found a better set of precedents.

But in what manner has England secured this freedom, by what special mechanism has she contrived to avoid the despotism which was supreme in every country of continental Europe except Holland and Switzerland, at the end of the last century, and which still prevails in the greater part of Europe to-day?

She maintained it by carefully preserving and developing the principles of the Teutonic peoples whose policy was based on a system of shires or land districts, and opposed to the Græco-Roman system of town units. This became in English hands the great principle of representation which enables a whole country to be combined for common purposes.

"But as for the principle of representation," says Fiske, "that seems to have been an invention of the Teutonic mind; no statesman of antiquity, either in Greece or at Rome, seems to have conceived the idea of a city sending delegates armed with plenary powers to represent its interests in a general legislative assembly."[1]

This is perhaps rather sweeping in its generality,

---

[1] "American Political Ideas," p. 59.

for according to Durvy " Each Roman province had its general assembly .... and the Lycians possessed a true legislative body formed by deputies of their twenty-three towns " (Durvy, " Histoire des Romains," iii. 376, quoted by H. Spencer), but these examples of representation were never developed so as to become of any historical importance.

When the Roman Empire began to crumble away under the successive attacks of the Gothic nations, whether of its Teutonic or Scandinavian branch, its centralized system was superseded by the freer forms of rule which prevailed among these invading peoples. Among the primitive Germans there were the assemblies of " principes," described by Tacitus as being general assemblies of the people in which all important affairs of state were discussed ; and there was also the system of local self-government among them based upon territorial divisions known as " hundreds."

So with Danes, the " Ting," or popular assembly, was such that every freeman, capable of bearing arms, had a right to attend and had also an equal voice, and there were similar divisions of the country into hundreds for the purpose of local self-government.

In all the kingdoms formed by these peoples out of the conquered provinces of Rome, there existed some form of council or assembly which the king or leader was bound to consult, and whose consent was necessary for important matters affecting the State. Among the Anglo-Saxons there was the great council or Witenagemote, and among the Normans, the great council of barons which the Norman Duke used to summon and consult on all important occasions, and this system was followed when the Norman Duke became the English king.

Thus we see in all these cases the representation was not a town one, but was based on the territorial divisions, whether as represented by great barons, or in local matters by inferior representatives, in this manner contrasting strongly with the Græco-Roman system which hardly recognized the country in any way.

These councils and this system of local self-government were not yet developed into a system of representation such as we know it. In the reign of William the Conqueror, the earliest case of true representation is said to have occurred; and, again, another case is referred to in the reign of King John; but it was not until the reign of Henry III. that the true system of representation, as we know it, became clearly established. From this time until the present day, its growth has been almost continuous.

The evolution of this system of representation is regarded by Mr. Fiske as of the utmost importance, when we have regard to the future stability of the political system devised by the English. "In the four discreet men, sent out to speak for their township in the old Anglo-Saxon county assembly, we have the germs of institutions that have ripened into the House of Commons, and into the legislature of modern kingdoms and republics. In the system of representation thus inaugurated lay the future possibility of such gigantic political aggregates as the United

States of America" (Fiske, "American Political Ideas," p. 70) The Greek and Roman systems had failed to give peace to large areas, or to establish a system which would preserve its vitality, however far from the central head the outlying country, to which it was applied, might be situated.

The Greek city system bound its own citizens together very closely, but its patriotism was too limited. As a number of neighbouring cities grew up, they were involved in constant war with each other, and the causes of hostility, which we have dealt with so fully in other parts of this work, were in operation and maintained a continual series of wars between these small and jealous communities. It is true that, for a time, and over certain areas, there were federations, such as the Achæan and Ætolian leagues which, by means of the principles of federation, were able to give peace and solidarity to somewhat larger areas, and thus confer one of the most important benefits upon their members, a state of relative internal peace; but their federations were very imperfect, and came to an untimely end owing to various external causes, as well as to the internal defect which made the federation in its corporate capacity act upon the states as units, and not upon the individuals who composed the states.

Another principle which extended the area of peace was to be seen in the method of "conquest with incorporation" pursued by Rome, and this gave results of the highest value while the vigour of the Roman people endured. Roman citizenship was granted to the provinces, but the real benefits of Roman citizenship could be enjoyed only at Rome itself; while we may notice that the Assembly of Rome, the Commitia, remained a primary assembly consisting of all the burghers, and thus, as the numbers grew, the assembly degenerated into a large mob, utterly unfit to transact any business. The Government of the Empire gradually destroyed the autonomy and spirit of self-reliance in the outlying provinces, while at the same time it became more and more centralized as the enemy pressed upon the frontiers, and simultaneously the central power was losing its vigour and becoming less and less able to supply the requisite force for repelling attack and holding the Empire together. Thus we see that this system failed owing to its inherent defects brought out by time and the stress of hostile attack. "Both these political failures were due to the absence of the principle of representation from the public life of Greece and Rome. The chief problem of civilization, from the political point of view, has always been how to secure concerted action among men on a great scale without sacrificing local independence. The ancient history of Europe shows that it is not possible to solve this problem without the aid of the principle of representation."[1]

The Gothic invaders gave renewed vigour to the provinces of the Roman Empire when they started them on their career as independent kingdoms with comparatively freer institutions.

England was not specially favoured in this respect, and, indeed, these representative institutions made

---

[1] Fiske, "American Political Ideas," p. 82.

more rapid advance to maturity in some of the countries of continental Europe than in England. Thus the Castilian cities were represented in the Cortes long before English towns sent representatives to the English parliament, and these members were fully equal in spirit, and had more power than the early members of the English parliament, but when the great struggle between them and the Crown in the reign of Charles V. in the 16th century came, they were overthrown, and the cause of representative liberty was lost in Spain. A similar fate befell the representative assemblies of other European countries. The series of wars carried on by France with England, with Flanders, with Castile, Navarre and Burgundy, led to the power of the States General being gradually destroyed.

So that while in England the war with France (which took place on French soil) and the wars of the Roses set back the advance of representative freedom, the peace which followed led to the advance in representative independence, which is to be seen in the character of the parliaments becoming more and more independent. As Mr. Bagehot says, "The Slavish parliament of Henry VIII. grew into the murmuring parliament of Queen Elizabeth, the mutinous parliament of James I., and the rebellious parliament of Charles I."[1] In France, during the same period, the wars with Italy, Spain, and Austria, and the subsequent internal wars, both religious and political, led to almost complete loss of representative

---

[1] "English Constitution," second edition, p. 281.

freedom. (Spencer, "Principles of Sociology," vol. ii. p. 623.)[1]

The cause of this loss of freedom and self-government was to be found in the necessity of a military organization in the distracted period of the Middle Ages, when no strong bond of control or union had been devised to correct the centrifugal tendencies exhibited by all neighbouring peoples in the absence of such a bond. The emperor had become a mere name, and exercised no controlling influence of this kind. The military type of society, as opposed to the industrial type, necessarily imposes a despotic rule upon the community, which is compelled to adopt it. The fighting power of the state must be at its maximum, and this can best be attained by the subordination of the individuals to one central head. "It is a very difficult thing for a free people to maintain its free constitution if it has to keep perpetually fighting for its life. The 'one man power,' less fit for carrying on the peaceful pursuits of life, is sure to be brought into the foreground in a state of endless warfare."[2]

We have only to observe the unquestioning obedience exacted from the soldier to his superior in

---

[1] For an example of the bad effects of war on internal freedom, see the reaction on England of the wars carried on with France at the end of the last century. No public meetings could be held without government leave—the penalty of death was imposed on those who remained together after being summoned to disperse. No public library or reading-room could be opened without government license. For other details see Buckle's "History of Civilization," chap. vii.

[2] Fiske, "American Political Ideas," p. 117.

grade to see that this type of society is necessarily opposed to anything like personal freedom of action. Fighting being the supreme interest of the state, it is only natural that all should be subordinated to this end. The headman who wields the military power naturally becomes the most powerful man in the nation, and as such becomes its ruler both in time ot war and peace, and his military or arbitrary methods are extended to the civil as well as military administrations of the country. We have seen in South Africa types of this kind of society in an early stage, in the military states ruled by Chaka, Dingaan, Cetywayo, Moselikatse, and Lobengula, who maintained all their able-bodied subjects as fighting regiments in a state of the most complete military organization, and, consequently, there was a total loss of any personal freedom, the individual being entirely at the mercy of the arbitrary will of the king. He might be executed at a moment's notice, without the slightest regard to his wishes or his merits; he was denied marriage until an advanced age, or until he had gained the right as a reward for military prowess. Thus we see that this type of society exhibits the same features whether it exist at the present day or in the past. As Herbert Spencer says, " Modern Dahomey and Russia, as well as ancient Peru, Egypt, and Sparta, exemplify that owning of the individual by the state in life, liberty, and goods, which is proper to a social system adapted for war. And that with changes further fitting a society for warlike activities, there spread throughout it an officialism, a dictation, and a superintendence akin to those under which soldiers live, we are shown by imperial Rome, by imperial Germany, and by England since its late aggressive activities." (Spencer, "Sociology," vol. ii. p. 602.)

The position of European states has been such that in all instances where they have been liable to invasion by their neighbours, military organization has been necessary, and this has entailed the destruction of those free institutions which were established in all the countries of Europe alike upon the break up of the Roman Empire.

"The political ideas of the Goths in Spain, of the Lombards in Italy, and of the Franks and Burgundians in Gaul, were as distinctly free as those of the Angles in Britain. But as the outcome of the long and uninterrupted turmoil of the Middle Ages, society throughout the continent of Europe remained predominantly military in type, and this fact greatly increased the tendency towards despotism which was bequeathed by Rome."[1]

There were, however, three countries of Europe where nature had offered a barrier more or less effective in providing against sudden attacks on the part of hostile forces. These three countries were Switzerland, Holland and England. Switzerland is the mountain crown of Europe. Its fastnesses were impenetrable to large military forces; the ways were known only to the local inhabitants, and indeed for a great part of the year the whole country was sealed with ice and snow; here were favourable conditions for preserving independence. The Austrian and

[1] Fiske, "American Political Ideas," p. 118.

Burgundian invader were alike repelled, and the brave people retained their democratic and free constitutions. So in contrast to the giant mountains, and yet related to them, were the low islands, separated by intricate and tortuous channels, formed by the Delta of the Rhine, and composed of the *débris* carried from the Alps of free Switzerland. Here a hardy people found a home secure from sudden invasion. Thus they too were left in comparative peace, and so were enabled to preserve and develop their early free institutions. It is interesting to observe in proof of the above how Venice rose to freedom by reason of a similar cause. When the invading Huns overran the mainland of Italy, the population near the coast fled to the low islands formed in the deltas of the great rivers which discharge into the Adriatic. Here they were comparatively safe, the tortuous ways in the lagunes being known only to themselves. These little island communities set up governments of their own which eventually combined for defence, while the contact with the sea and their commercial pursuits further developed this tendency to freedom. So also in Holland freedom was further expanded in the direction of liberty by a commercial and seafaring life.

And here we may remark that this influence of the sea in developing ideas of freedom in the people who devote themselves to carrying on their trade upon it has been most striking. Let us examine it for a moment. In the wreck of civilization on the destruction of the Roman Empire, and the dark night which then enveloped Europe, two little stars

of liberty appeared in the sixth century which grew
in brightness, and ran a brilliant career until about
the twelfth century. They were the little seafaring
and commercial republics of Amalfi and Naples, and
they were the first to kindle a spirit of freedom.
In the north of Italy we have seen that Venice in
like manner had its freedom developed by its contact
with the sea. So with Pisa and Genoa. So with
the maritime cities of Southern France—the towns
such as Avignon, Arles, Marseilles and others affected
to set up independent republics. So also Edward II.
and Edward III. entered into alliances with the
towns of Flanders to which neither their Court nor
the King of France were parties (Hallam, " Middle
Ages," i. p. 307). So also in Spain, the Catalan
headquarters of Barcelona emulated the Italian cities
in both branches of naval energy, war and commerce
(Hallam, iii. p. 390). And, finally, it is hardly
necessary to point out that England, the freest
country in the world, is also the most maritime.

To return, then, to Holland. When the time came,
she was ready to take her fair share, and indeed
more than her fair share, of the arduous work of
withstanding the brunt of the attack in the great
battle of freedom when she successfully coped with
the forces of Spain, the mightiest power of that day.
Venice, Holland, and Switzerland, being originally
composed of communities isolated by the tortuous
lagunes, by the arms of the Rhine, and by the
mountains of Switzerland respectively, all formed
federations in the first instance, and in the case of
Switzerland, the combination has lasted down to our

own day, while in Holland it endured throughout the most important period of its history.

And lastly, we see that England, strong in its insular position, and removed by the Channel from the great military system of continental Europe, has been enabled to develop its early free institutions, and to ripen them unhindered by any necessity for a military organization ready to repel sudden attack upon its frontiers.

Not only did political liberty continue to flourish in England, but the principles of local self-government were also firmly established. A vast weight and importance has been attached by eminent authorities to the contrast between the self-government of each local district in local matters as compared with a supreme central authority which sends its prefects, sub-prefects, and other officials to every department, providing by them for the control and direction of all local concerns. De Tocqueville, in his work on democracy in America, has devoted a chapter to emphasizing the distinction between a central government in imperial matters of general concern and a central government in matters of local interest, urging the importance of the former and calling attention to the bad effects of the latter. So also Professor Lieber, a German by birth, but an American citizen by choice, in his work on " Civil liberty and self-government," has urged the importance of this principle of local self-government; while the great historian, Niebuhr, in his work on "The internal administration of Great Britain," which was written with a view to inducing the Prussian Government to give more local liberty of control after the English model, says, "British liberty depends at least as much on the local self-appliances of local government as it does upon Parliament."

We realize this more fully when we consider that all the various local bodies, such as the parish vestry, the town council, and others of like character, train the people in the ideas and ways of parliamentary government. When Sir Philip Woodehouse attempted to destroy the divisional councils at the Cape, Mr. Molteno pointed out how valuable these local bodies were in preparing and fitting men to take their proper part in the Parliament, and he rightly declared in Parliament that Sir Philip Woodehouse's attempt in this direction was a part of his scheme for the destruction of representative institutions and of the local parliament itself.[1]

Sir Philip Woodehouse had on several occasions introduced Bills into Parliament for the abolition of the two chambers established by the Constitution ordinance in 1854—he proposed to substitute one chamber of eighteen members with a very large number of nominee members, with the view, as he openly said, of bringing the Legislature under the control of the nominee executive. He also made several attempts to withdraw the salaries of the officials from the control of Parliament. These measures bear an ominous resemblance to the measures which preceded the revolt of the American colonies. They were strenuously and successfully resisted by Mr. Solomon, Mr. Porter, and by Mr. Molteno, who saw that the results of such measures must inevitably be similar to their effect in America —the revolt of South Africa.

For the attempt of the British Government to withdraw salaries of officials from control of colonial legislatures in the case of America, see Lecky, "England in the Eighteenth

We see, then, the great value that is to be attached to these principles of representation and freedom which have been preserved and developed by England, and by her alone; and we have seen that in large measure this was due to the position which England occupies as an island, and in consequence being free from sudden invasion of its boundaries by its neighbours.

When in 1264 "the whole force of the country was summoned to London to resist the army which was coming from France under the Queen and her son Edmund, *the invading fleet was prevented by the weather from sailing until too late in the season.* . . . The papal legate, Guy Foulquois, who soon after became Clement IV., threatened the barons with excommunication, but the bull containing the sentence was taken by the men of Dover as soon as it arrived, and was thrown into the sea."[1] We all remember again how the invincible Armada was defeated and destroyed, and England's coasts remained free. So again in 1805, Napoleon collected his forces at Boulogne, but the silver streak imposed its veto on his attempt to invade England.

Century," vol. iv. p. 112. For modification of the Charter of Massachusetts making the upper chamber consist of nominees of the Crown, see Lecky, vol. iv. p. 166.

Compare with these the successful attempt of Lord Carnarvon, who, in 1875, through Sir Garnet Wolseley, destroyed the free legislative council of Natal and replaced it by a nominee council. Among the nominees were actually several members of Sir Garnet's military staff! The ways of despotism are ever similar!

[1] Stubbs's "Select Charters," p. 401, quoted by Fiske.

We have seen, then, by what means England formed and perfected its free imperial parliament and its local self-government, but England and the federations of Holland and Switzerland were small in area and population, and it was reserved for the nineteenth century to prove that Federal government had the power of holding together great bodies of men spread over vast territorial areas in orderly and peaceful relation with one another. The opportunity for the operation of this power was found in the settlement of America.

"The experiment of Federal union on a grand scale required as its conditions, first, a vast extent of unoccupied country which could be settled without much warfare by men of the same race and speech, and, secondly, on the part of the settlers, a rich inheritance of political training such as is afforded by long ages of self-government. The Atlantic coast of North America, easily accessible to Europe, yet remote enough to be freed from the political complications of the old world, furnished the first of these conditions; the history of the English people through fifty generations furnished the second. It was through English self-government that England alone, among the great nations of Europe, was able to found durable and self-supporting colonies. I have now to add that it was only England, among all the great nations of Europe, that could send forth colonists capable of dealing successfully with the difficult problem of forming such a political aggregate as the United States have become. For obviously the preservation of local self-government is essential to the very idea of a Federal union."[1]

Thus England handed on to America the principles of local self-government in full vigour, and in America, as in England, the ocean favoured the growth of liberty. We see these principles in operation when we find that on James II. sending out a royal order depriving the colony of the control of its militia, the sturdy men of Connecticut beat the drum to prevent the reading of the order. So, again, when England forgot her free principles and endeavoured to tax her colonies, they successfully resisted, and the ocean favoured their resistance. This series of events in the great progress of the operation of these free principles of self-government in securing freedom from outside control of communities who are able to govern themselves has been continued in South Africa too, where, as in the case of England and in the case of America, we have the ocean, which has favoured our liberties and will continue so to do. Let us consider this briefly. We have seen the Cape Colony united as one man in refusing to allow the landing of convicts sent to her shores, at the time of what is called the anti-convict agitation. A passive resistance, but of the most determined character, led to the abandonment by Earl Grey, the Secretary of State, of his intention, so obnoxious to a free and untainted community. Again, we have the great constitutional struggle for self-government carried on by the Parliament of the Cape with the autocratic governor, Sir P. Woodehouse, and its triumph, after ten years'

[1] Fiske, p. 91.

constant effort, in the acquisition of responsible government. Again, we have the noble struggle of the Boers of the Transvaal to regain their liberty basely taken from them. This, the latest event in this great struggle of ages, is also one of the noblest and most striking. As in America, so in Africa a constitutional struggle had been carried on by Solomon, Porter, and Molteno, and self-government had been won, but very soon its best fruits were torn away, and it was practically annulled and made useless by Lord Carnarvon, who, with a view to destroying self-government and forcing his views, sent out his proconsul, Sir Bartle Frere, a man who had recommended the destruction of the Parliament of New Zealand before he came to the Cape, a man who was versed in the harsh if necessary methods of treating subject peoples, a man utterly unfitted by his previous training to appreciate the working of constitutional government and of free assemblies. In Sir B. Frere's character we see exemplified the danger which besets a free country when it conquers and endeavours to rule a people in a lower stage of development;[1] free England conquered India and rules it despotically as a conquered country. As with the Roman Empire, which sent its proconsuls direct from Rome supported by great armies to rule the provinces,[2] in like manner did Lord Carnarvon

---

[1] Fiske, "American Political Ideas," p. 83.

[2] Sir Bartle Frere's apologist says, " In South Africa, as in India, it was essential to success, first, that the Resident should be known to have the whole power of the empire behind him."
—Life of Sir B. Frere, vol. ii. p. 353.

send Sir B. Frere, after governing in India, to impose his will on South Africa, and we see the modern proconsul ready to destroy those free institutions directly inherited from England, whether in New Zealand or the Cape. There was but little political life or knowledge at the Cape, and when its constitutional ministry was dismissed by Sir B. Frere, the Cape acquiesced. No Africander Bond or other association had yet been formed which would educate the isolated rural population to a sense of its constitutional rights and responsibilities, and which would quicken and give cohesion and force to such political views and desires as were common to a vast majority of the people. All that had been won by constitutional action at the Cape was now lost. America had had its war of independence, Africa was not to be spared, and its war of independence was fought single-handed by the men of Dutch extraction, true to the principles of liberty which we have already seen were preserved by Holland as well as England. This war finally compelled the attention of English statesmen to the fact that it was dangerous to go back upon what had been done when responsible government was granted, and to again directly interfere in the internal affairs of Africa in ignorance of the real conditions of the problem. It taught the Dutch to respect themselves, and the English to respect the Dutch. It will go far to give the young South African nation a pride in its past, and a confidence in its future. If British statesmen are wise, the lesson will be learned as it was learned in the case of the American war of independence with regard to America, and the days of active interference from afar in the internal affairs of South Africa will be over for ever.

We possess, as did America, the principles of self-government, and we must follow her further, for, as we have pointed out, the conditions of Africa are in many essential features similar to those of America, and the application of these principles of local self-government and federation will lead to a similar result in consolidating and preserving in peace and harmony the various states which are already established there, and those states which are destined to spring up in the common territory to the north.

We see these great principles of self-government practised by England and by the countries of English descent in the colonial world, giving power and energy and vigour in every part of the globe, and we see the great principle of Federal government following surely to bind them together into larger aggregates; witness the United States of America, the Federation of Canada, and the recent meetings of the Australian colonies for drafting a Federal Constitution.

For all these reasons the young South African nation must cherish its connection with England rather than with any other European power—all the other great European powers are under despotic rule owing to their supreme military organization, and could extend only despotic rule to any colonial dependencies—and this we see exemplified in the case of Germany's new dependencies. England is the freest country in the world, and one whose free institutions have proved themselves to be admirably fitted for transplantation to new lands, there to flourish anew as the institutions of no other European country have done or can do.

CHAPTER XIV.

CONNECTION OF SOUTH AFRICAN WITH UNIVERSAL HISTORY.

Gradual consolidation leads to widening peace area—War at first favours internal peace—Pax Romana—Civilizing result of Roman peace—Gradual removal of barbaric frontier from Europe—Similar work in Africa—Barbarism rolled back from Cape Peninsula—Country won for civilization and peace—Emigrant farmers put an end to murderous rule of Dingaan and Moselikatse—Terrible effects of Chaka's operations—800,000 natives destroyed—Boer settles between hostile clans—Saves remnant of mountain tribes—Boer colonization—Admirable system—Boer views of natives—No intermixture—Importance of this—Dutch and English native policy compared—Dr. Wallace's views—Boer taken his full share in costly work of civilization—As Rome moved frontier of barbarism eastward, so South African colonies and states are moving it northwards.

BEFORE we leave this great question of the Federation of South Africa, let us pause to consider what position this movement holds in the history of the world and the development of nations. There are no such things as isolated events in the history of any country; all have their roots in the past, and their unerring effects upon the future. We will briefly trace the connection of events in South Africa with the history of the world, and, further, we will examine whether there is any great goal, any noble ideal towards which this movement of Federation will carry us in common with other countries, and with the future of the whole world? The early history of all societies of men presents us with the common feature of constant warfare between the different tribes occupying a common territory, and originally springing from the same ancestors. We see the individuals composing these societies carrying on private war with their neighbours. The first step towards a more settled and more stable condition is to abolish private warfare and to substitute the more accurate and just methods of legal procedure and judicial regulations. And this change is at first favoured by a state of constant hostility, for, as Herbert Spencer points out, "joint aggressions upon men outside the society cannot prosper if there are many aggressions of man on man within the society. War implies co-operation; and co-operation is prevented by antagonism among those who are to co-operate. . . . The fact that success in war is endangered if his followers fight among themselves forces itself on the attention of the ruler." (Spencer, "Data of Ethics," p. 117.) Then we see the small groups combined into a larger political whole, thus extending the area over which internal peace prevails—we have seen this in operation with the small independent communities out of which Venice arose—and so enabling a certain advance to be made in the direction of the various arts and an accumulation of wealth, which must precede any advance in civilization. We see this process continued until we get larger and larger groups combined. We see, then, that "on the political side civilization means primarily the gradual substitution of a state of peace for a state of war. This change is a condition of all the other changes implied by the term civilization."[1] We may go deep down into the philosophy of things with Herbert Spencer, and learn how the progress of the world in every particular is on the one hand dependent on and advanced by a state of peace, and on the other retarded by a state of war, but the limits of this little work do not permit of this, and we must merely trace very rapidly the historical proof of this fact. As with the individuals and with the groups of small communities, so with the larger "a general diminution of warfare is rendered possible only by the union of small political groups into larger groups that are kept together by community of interests, and that can adjust their mutual relations by legal discussion without coming to blows."[2] Now, the Roman Empire rendered a service of this kind to the world. It established the Pax Romana over an immense area, and enabled civilization to become so rooted that it never again entirely died out. Rome took up the struggle against menacing barbarism; it gradually subdued and civilized the more local barbarous peoples of Spain and Gaul, and so civilized them that they were in a position to withstand and aid in defending Europe against the enormous hordes of

[1] Fiske, "American Political Ideas," p. 106.
[2] Fiske, Ibid.

yellow Mongolians, known as Huns, who poured down into Europe under Attila, and were destroyed at Chalons-sur-Marne. Cæsar had moved the frontier, to be defended against barbarians, to the Rhine; Charles the Great extended it to the Oder by the conquest and conversion of pagan Germany, and made the defence of Europe so much easier. In the thirteenth century it was further extended by the Teutonic knights, who, under the Emperor Frederick II., conquered the heathen Prussians and Lithuanians. In this same century Batu, the grandson of Jinghis Khan, came down into Europe, with a horde of more than a million Mongols, and tried to repeat the experiment of Attila. He penetrated as far as Silesia, and won a great battle at Liegnitz in 1241, but in spite of this he had to desist from the task of conquering Europe.

Finally, in the sixteenth century, the Russians, redeemed from their Mongolian oppressors, resumed the aggressive in this conflict of ages, began to do for Central Asia what the Romans did for Europe. The frontier against barbarism has been carried eastward to the Volga, and is now advancing to the Oxus.[1]

Now, in South Africa we have part of this same movement. We have seen the horde of barbarians gradually rolled back from the extremity of the Cape Peninsula, and a fine country won for civilization and peace. In this struggle the heat and burden of the day has been borne by the emigrant farmers from the Cape Colony, who met single-handed the forces of Dingaan, and, above all, who put an

[1] Fiske, "American Political Ideas," p. 113.

end for ever to the murderous raids of Moselikatse, and so rescued a country as large as France and Germany put together from the terrible sway of this chief, who, more than most African chiefs, delighted in slaughter and murder. This great service have they rendered to the cause of civilization. And let it not here be supposed that this has been accomplished by the perpetration of huge injustice upon the natives. This so-called rule of these chiefs merely signified the liberty on their part to overrun with fire and assagai the lands of their weaker neighbours, and in no sense was there any government of even the rudest character. The effects of this raiding were indeed terrible, and in order to give some idea of the evils inflicted upon these unfortunate peoples, and the nature of this *régime* of bloodshed and extermination to which the Boers have put an end, we may quote Theal's summary of the effects of the Zulu King Chaka's operations in the early decades of this century:—

"Vast numbers of people," says Theal, "of all ages died by the club and the assagai. In a short time the cattle were eaten up, and as the gardens ceased to be cultivated, a terrible famine arose. Thousands, tens of thousands, of people perished of starvation, other thousands fled from the wasted land, and many of those who remained behind became cannibals. It is impossible to form an estimate of the number of individuals of the mountain tribes who perished at the time. The losses of the Batlokua alone can be approximately computed. They were reduced from about one hundred and thirty thousand to fourteen or fifteen thousand, only a small proportion of the loss being from dispersion. If the destruction of what is now the Lesuto and in the north-east of the present Free State be estimated at three hundred thousand, that number must be greatly under the mark. And on the other side of the mountain (the Drakensburg) at least half a million had perished. Compared with this, the total loss of human life occasioned by all the wars in South Africa in which Europeans have engaged since first they set foot in the country sinks into insignificance."

South Africa was thus becoming over vast areas an absolute desert, and where the emigrant farmers interposed between the legions of Moselikatse and the remnant of the mountain tribes, they were heartily welcomed by the latter, and were the means of their salvation. Justice has not yet been done to this feature of Boer colonization. It has been hastily assumed that all the land in South Africa was fully occupied, and where Boer intruded native was necessarily cast out; but this is untrue. There was generally a great tract of land between two peoples unoccupied because of its liability to sudden incursion on the part of the stronger tribe, and these lands were willingly sold by the natives, who thus secured a protection from powerful and hostile neighbours such as had until then been unknown to them. And further, we can here only briefly notice the splendid system of colonization adopted by the Boers, which furnished them with an army at a moment's notice in case of sudden attack. The land was given out to any man who applied for it, in quantity sufficient for all his wants. He was no land speculator; he came to settle down with his family and his belongings, to make his home there and his children's home. He was immediately enrolled by the field cornet of his district, and made liable to military service. In this way a force was always available without cost to the state, and of such a character that it was not tempted to wanton aggression, as a standing army would be, for each man, being occupied with the operations of his farm, was not inclined to give service unless in case of dire need and unprovoked aggression on his country. In this way was the Boer admirably suited to be the pioneer in such a country and under conditions where he could not rely on any military force or the resources of a more populous and wealthy community. It would have been impossible for these early settlers to have supported the cost of a permanent military force.

Some have blamed them for the manner in which they look down upon the blacks, and in the early part of the century attempts were made on the part of the London Missionary Society to regard the black as a man and a brother, and act up to this by intermarrying with them. It cannot be open to doubt that it was a wise and healthy instinct which regarded such unions with indignation. Had there been any laxness in the manner in which this question had been regarded by the emigrant farmers, the most disastrous consequences would have ensued. There would have resulted a mongrel people, utterly wanting in moral force and vigour. Apart from all other considerations, such a people would quickly perish under the severe conditions of life which were the lot of these sturdy men. And that feeling with which the black races are regarded by South Africans can only be looked upon as one of those natural provisions which come into operation to preserve men and societies from forces which would otherwise disintegrate their character to an extent fatal to their existence. We must here guard ourselves against being misunderstood. We do not mean to imply that South Africans desire to see the destruction or extermination of the black races. They merely maintain that the blacks are at an inferior stage of development, and that this fact must be recognized in their treatment. The contrast between this view and that of Exeter Hall is roughly that between the relations of father and children and that between brother and brother. A father never quarrels with his children—he corrects them if wrong; while we often see brothers fall out. The English method leads to strife between the white and black brothers. We have such results as the Basuto war and the Zulu war, when vast numbers of natives are destroyed by the actual war, and also by subsequent anarchy and famine. It was no South African who in effect said, "All the natives of South Africa must be disarmed, and we must have our foot upon the neck of every native." This was reserved for the humane Sir Bartle Frere. So far from this was the South African view, that the burghers of the Cape Colony refused to carry out this policy in the case of the Basuto war. This question of the treatment of inferior races by superior white races has been carefully investigated and considered by the first of living naturalists—Dr. Alfred Russell Wallace, the co-discoverer with Darwin of the famous theories associated with that name—and he has unhesitatingly declared, from personal experience of the Dutch system in Java, in favour of the Dutch method of treatment of natives of inferior development. "If there is one thing," he says, "rather than another to which the grand law of continuity will apply, it is to human progress. There are certain stages through which society must pass in its onward march from barbarism to civilization. Now, one of these stages has always been some form or other of despotism, such as feudalism or servitude, or a despotic paternal government; and we have every reason to believe that it is not possible for humanity to leap over this transition epoch, and pass at once from pure savagery to free civilization. The Dutch system attempts to supply this missing link, and to bring the people on by gradual steps to that higher civilization which we (the English) try to force upon them at once. Our system has always failed. We demoralize and we extirpate, but we never really civilize. Whether the Dutch system can permanently succeed is but doubtful, since it may not be possible to compress the work of ten centuries into one; but, at all events, it takes nature as a guide, and is therefore more deserving of success and more likely to succeed than ours." ("The Malay Archipelago," p. 197.) [1]

Thus the Boer, going forth into the wilderness, and carrying with him his Bible and his ideas of order

---

[1] See Appendix for the complete passage.

and his principles of settled government, has unconsciously been taking his part, and indeed his full share of the arduous and costly work of redeeming the surface of the earth for the purposes of civilization, that is, of peace and good government from a political point of view.

As was done by Rome "in moving the civilized frontier northward and eastward against the disastrous encroachments of barbarous peoples," so the various colonies and states of South Africa are, in the great continent of Africa, doing the same work; some advancing and acting as pioneers, others coming after and consolidating and strengthening the position already won, and providing a base and renewed force for further advances on the part of those who are in the van. When we contemplate the constant hostilities in Africa, it must be borne in mind that "it is not easy for a turbulent community to live next to an orderly one without continually stirring up frontier disturbances which call for stern repression from the orderly community,"[1] and the ways of civilization cannot always be the ways of peace until a certain stage has been arrived at, not by one alone, but by all neighbouring peoples. And here let us see further the great ideal at which South Africa may aim, and which it will further by the Federation with which we are dealing in these pages.

[1] Fiske, "American Political Ideas," p. 110.

CHAPTER XV.

A NOBLE IDEAL.

Society at first militant type—*Contract* or industrial type replaces *Status* or military type—State now exists for members, not members for state—Coercion decreases and representation arises—Society no longer compelled to be self-contained—International commerce arises—Divisions between nations disappear—Consolidation now takes place by Federation—Advance in civilization dependent on cessation of war—Peaceful Federation is only further Consolidation—Cessation of war unwelcome to most—Action of High Commissioner—Character of rank and file—Hope of few—Historical development of peaceful Federation—Results achieved by United States—War of Secession—Fought to secure principle of decisions between states by judicial process, no longer by war—American system given peace to a vast area—Africa's ideal similar to give peace to area south of Zambesi and Cunene—Area as great as Europe omitting Russia—South Africa thus fitted to take its place among great federated groups of the world—Christian principles and ethical theory unite to confirm ideal—Words of Washington in conclusion.

As we have already seen, constant warfare among nations tends to the increase of despotism and the sacrifice of all other considerations to the supreme consideration of making the community a fighting machine. Those even who do not take part in the actual work of fighting are yet controlled in all their actions with a view to their contributing to the efficiency of those who are solely devoted to fighting, by growing food for them and otherwise providing the necessaries of life and the resources of war. The military leader becomes the head of the state both in times of peace and in times of war. Thus we have established the "militant type of society." This is the form of society characterized by *status*— a society the members of which stand one towards another in successive grades of subordination. From the despot down to the slave, all are masters of those below and subjects of those above.

"The relation of the child to the father, of the father to some superior, and so on up to the absolute head, is one in which the individual of lower status is at the mercy of one of higher status." (H. Spencer, "Principles of Sociology," vol. ii. p. 513.) Indeed, we may say that under the militant type of society the individual is owned by the state. But as the diminution of war takes place by reason of the consolidation of smaller groups into larger, a type of society differing from that of the previous military type is formed, and "with the formation of nations covering larger areas, the perpetual wars within each area have ceased, and though the wars which from time to time occur are on larger scales, they are less frequent, and are no longer the business of all freemen." (Spencer, loc. cit. p. 619.) Thus, the necessity for co-operation for defence grows less, and it becomes possible for the individuals who compose the state to enjoy greater freedom. The individuals no longer exist for the welfare of the state, but the state exists for the welfare of its members. We now find the condition of status so modified as to give place to a type in which each individual is free to follow his own inclinations and enjoy the fruit of his own labours, and his share of the results of his own efforts, in place of having an arbitrary share assigned to him by a superior authority. "Otherwise regarded, this system under which the efforts of each bring neither more nor less than their natural returns is the system of contract." (Spencer, loc. cit. p. 611.). . . . "We have seen that the *régime* of status is in all ways proper to the militant type . . . . but as with declining militancy and growing industrialism the power and range of authority decrease while uncontrolled action increases, the relation of contract becomes general, and in the fully developed industrial type it becomes universal. Under this universal relation of contract, when equitably administered, there arises that adjustment of benefit to effort which the arrangements of the industrial society have to achieve. If each as producer, distributor, manager, adviser, teacher, or aider of other kind, obtains from his fellows such payment for his service as its value, determined by the demand, warrants; then there results that correct apportioning of reward to merit which ensures the prosperity of the superior (individual)" (p. 611 of Spencer). Thus we come to a point where coercion no longer being necessary, the principle of representation can come in and take its proper place as a means for expressing the general views of the community. "Such control as is required under the industrial type can be exercised only by an appointed agency for ascertaining and executing the average will; and a representative agency is the one best fitted for doing this" (Spencer, loc. cit. p. 608). And we have a further most important effect produced by this development of the industrial type of society. The necessity for being self-supporting in all ways is imposed upon a society while it is at enmity with all its neighbours; but when confidence becomes extended it is ready to exchange the products which its soil or its position enables it to produce with the greatest facility and at the least cost for the different products which other countries in the same manner can produce at the least cost. Thus, a mutually advantageous intercourse results, and we find that "with the spread of industrialism, therefore, the tendency is towards the breaking down of the divisions between nationalities, and the running through them of a common organization; if not under a single government, then under a federation of governments" (Spencer, loc. lit. p. 615). But, far more than all this, the advance and progress of civilization inevitably depend upon a cessation of war and a continuance of mutual confidence between nations, resulting in peace over the largest areas.

And now we begin to perceive the connection of the foregoing rapid summary of the progress of civilization with our subject, for we see that the federation of Africa will be a step in the consolidation of the great free communities of the world and the ultimate federation of these into one great harmonious whole. Before we proceed to regard this fact from another point of view, let us summarize the observation and investigation of it from the ethical side in the words of Herbert Spencer. " The conclusion of profoundest moment to which all lines of argument converge, is that the possibility of a high social state, political as well as general, fundamentally depends upon the cessation of war. After all that has been said, it is needless to emphasize afresh the truth that persistent militancy, maintaining adapted institutions, must inevitably prevent, or else neutralize, changes in the direction of more equitable institutions and laws; while permanent peace will of necessity be followed by social amelioration of every kind.

" From war has been gained all that it had to give. The peopling of the earth by the more powerful and intelligent races is a benefit in great measure achieved; and what remains to be done calls for no other agency than the quiet pressure of a spreading industrial civilization on a barbarism which slowly dwindles. That integration of single groups into compound ones, and of these into doubly compound ones, which war has effected, until at length great nations have been produced, is a process already carried as far as seems either practicable or desirable. Empires formed of alien peoples habitually fall to pieces when the coercive power which holds them together fails, and even could they be held together, would not form harmoniously working wholes ; peaceful Federation is the only further consolidation to be looked for " (Spencer, loc. cit. p. 664). Thus we see that from the ethical and philosophical point of view the progress of this great idea of peaceful Federation gives us the great and only hope for a really higher phase of civilization. We have called this prospect a noble ideal to set before us, because it cannot yet become even palatable to a vast number of the most peaceful and highly civilized of the nations, much less an accomplished fact while in the words of Herbert Spencer, "As Attila, while conquering or destroying peoples and nations, regarded himself as the 'Scourge of God,' so we, as represented by a High Commissioner and a priest he quotes, think ourselves called on to chastise with rifles and cannon heathen who practise polygamy."[1]

If these be the acts of the highest products of humanity and present civilization as represented by the great pro-consuls who have been sent to govern us from England, still less is the hope of the early realization of the high ideal when we regard the average nature of the peoples of Europe. "If any one says that the men who form the land-grabbing nations of Europe cannot be ruled in their daily lives by an ethical sentiment, but must have it enforced by the fear of damnation, I am not prepared to contradict him. If a writer who, according to those who know, represents truly the natures of the gentlemen we send abroad, sympathetically describes one of them as saying to soldiers shooting tribes fighting for their independence, 'Give 'em hell, men,' I think those are possibly right who contend that such natures are to be kept in check only by fear of a God, Who will 'give 'em hell' if they misbehave."

[1] Spencer, "Data of Ethics," p. 240.

What hope is there then of any improvement? The same writer holds out the hope in these words, " But to the few, who, looking back on the changes which past thousands of years have witnessed, look forward to kindred changes which future thousands of years may be expected to bring, it will be a satisfaction to contemplate a humanity so adapted to harmonious social life that all needs are spontaneously and pleasurably fulfilled by each without injury to others" (H. Spencer, " Principles of Ethics," I. p. 474).

Having now shown deductively and from the philosophical side the benefits which Federation would confer upon the world, let us look at the question again from the inductive or practical point of view in the history of that great state which has already afforded us so many lessons and so many examples. Professor Fiske points out that " The United States to-day cling together with a coherency far greater than the coherency of any ordinary federation or league. Yet the primary aspect of the Federal Constitution was undoubtedly that of a permanent league, in which each state, while retaining its domestic sovereignty intact, renounced for ever its right to make war upon its neighbours, and relegated its international interests to the care of a central council, in which all the states were alike represented, and a central tribunal endowed with purely judicial functions of interpretation. It was the first attempt in the history of the world to apply on a grand scale to the relations between states the same legal methods of procedure which, as long applied in all civilized countries to the relations between individuals, have rendered private warfare obsolete. And it was so far successful that, during a period of seventy-two years, in which the United States increased fourfold in extent, tenfold in population, and more than tenfold in wealth and power, the Federal Union maintained a state of peace more profound than the *pax romana.*"

But here we may properly be asked to account for that terrible civil war which devastated the United States thirty years ago, and to explain the lesson which it has taught. Let us hear Fiske:—

"Twenty years ago this unexampled state of peace was suddenly interrupted by a tremendous war, which in its results, however, has served only to bring out with fresh emphasis the pacific implications of Federalism. With the eleven revolted states at first completely conquered and then reinstated with full rights and privileges in the Federal Union, with their people accepting in good faith the results of the contest, with their leaders not executed as traitors, but admitted again to seats in Congress and in the cabinet, and with all this accomplished without any violent constitutional changes,—I think we may fairly claim that the strength of the pacific implications of Federalism has been more strikingly demonstrated than if there had been no war at all. Certainly the world never beheld such a spectacle before." [1]

"Stated broadly, so as to acquire somewhat the force of a universal proposition, the principle of

---

[1] Fiske, "American Political Ideas," p. 29.

Federalism is just this: That the people of a state shall have full and entire control of their own domestic affairs, which directly concern them only, and which they will naturally manage with more intelligence and with more zeal than any distant governing body could possibly exercise; but that, as regards matters of common concern between a group of states, a decision shall in every case be reached, not by brutal warfare or by weary diplomacy, but by the systematic legislation of a central government which represents both states and people, and whose decisions can always be enforced, if necessary, by the combined physical power of all the states. This principle, in various practical applications, is so familiar to Americans to-day that we seldom pause to admire it, any more than we stop to admire the air which we breathe or the sun which gives us light and life. Yet I believe that if no other political result than this could to-day be pointed out as coming from the colonization of America by Englishmen, we should still be justified in regarding that event as one of the most important in the history of mankind. For obviously the principle of federalism, as thus broadly stated, contains within itself the seeds of permanent peace between nations; and to this glorious end I believe it will come in the fulness of time." [1]

"The object, therefore, for which the American government fought, was the perpetual maintenance of that peculiar state of things which the Federal Union had created,—a state of things in which,

---

[1] Fiske, "American Political Ideas," p. 134.

throughout the whole vast territory over which the Union holds sway, questions between states, like questions between individuals, must be settled by legal argument and judicial decisions, and not by wager of battle. Far better to demonstrate this point once for all, at whatever cost, than to be burdened hereafter, like the states of Europe, with frontier fortresses and standing armies and all the barbaric apparatus of mutual suspicion!"[1]

Thus we see that America has proved that the great principle of federalism has given peace and unity to an area of 3,603,000 square miles, an area as great as modern Europe and far larger than the Roman Empire. We see Canada federated, we see Australia about to follow its example and adopt the federal principle and lay the foundation of a mighty nation. Why should not South Africa follow these examples and found its federation? The area south of the Zambesi and Cunene rivers is roughly about 1,500,000 square miles, or about the area of the whole of Europe omitting Russia. It is a grand ideal to set before us, namely, that of consolidating and giving peace to this vast area, and so enabling South Africa to take its place as one of the vast federated groups of the world. In the words of Fiske: "Thus we may foresee in general outline how, through the gradual concentration of the preponderance of physical power into the hands of the most pacific communities, the wretched business of warfare must finally become obsolete all over the globe. The element of distance

[1] Fiske, "American Political Ideas," p. 135.

is now fast becoming eliminated from political problems, and the history of human progress politically will continue in the future to be what it has been in the past,—the history of the successive union of groups of men into larger and more complex aggregates. As this process goes on, it may after many more ages of political experience become apparent that there is really no reason, in the nature of things, why the whole of mankind should not constitute practically one huge federation,—each little group managing its local affairs in entire independence, but relegating all questions of international interest to the decision of one central tribunal, supported by the public opinion of the entire human race. I believe that the time will come when such a state of things will exist upon the earth, when it will be possible, with Tennyson, to celebrate 'the parliament of man and the federation of the world' Indeed, only when such a state of things has begun to be realized, can civilization, as sharply demarcated from barbarism, be said to have fairly begun. Only then can the world be said to have become truly Christian. Many ages of toil and doubt and perplexity will no doubt pass by before such a desideratum is reached. Meanwhile, it is pleasant to feel that the dispassionate contemplation of great masses of historical facts goes far towards confirming our faith in this ultimate triumph of good over evil." [1]

We have already seen that Herbert Spencer attaches supreme importance to the cessation of war.

[1] Fiske, "American Political Ideas," p. 157.

"For the diminution of this suffering, not only of the direct kind, but of the indirect kind, the one thing needful is the checking of international antagonisms and the diminution of those armaments which are at once the cause and consequence of them. With the depression of militant activities and decay of militant organizations, will come amelioration of political institutions as of all other institutions. Without them no such ameliorations are permanently possible. Liberty overtly gained in name and form will be unobtrusively taken away in fact" (Spencer, "Principles of Sociology," vol. ii. p. 665). We see, then, that both lines of investigation lead to the same result. The diminution of warfare is not only a noble ideal, but turns out to be the actual condition precedent to the development of the highest civilization. It appears, then, that in furthering the Federation of South Africa we are taking our part in the great work which the principles of Christianity enjoin upon us, "peace on earth, and goodwill towards men," and which the ethics based upon an elaborate, a powerful, and a cogent argument in accord with the principles of evolution as elaborated by Herbert Spencer, confirm in the fullest manner.

To those who have followed us thus far, and to those with whom it may rest to decide upon and to formulate the plan of Federal Government for South Africa, we will commend the immortal words of Washington, who, when the great Federal Convention had met, and many began to fear that the task of devising a constitution was beyond their powers, and palliative and half measures were suggested rather than any thorough-going reform, suddenly interposed and said in tones unwontedly solemn, with suppressed emotion: "It is too probable that no plan we propose will be adopted. Perhaps another dreadful conflict is to be sustained. If, to please the people, we offer what we ourselves disapprove, how can we afterwards defend our work? Let us raise the standard to which the wise and the honest can repair ; the event is in the hand of God."

APPENDIX I.

FIGURES from " Fiske's Civil Government in the United States," illustrating the acquisition of territory by the United States :—

	Sq. miles.
Area of United States in 1783 . . .	827,844
Austria-Hungary, German Empire, France and Spain	834,906
Louisiana Purchase, 1803, with the portion of Oregon territory retained in 1846 .	1,171,931
Austria-Hungary, German Empire, Sweden, Norway, Denmark, Belgium, France, Spain	1,171,154
Florida Purchase, 1819	59,268
England and Wales	58,320
Texan Annexation, 1845	375,239
Austria-Hungary, Italy, Switzerland .	370,472
Mexican Cessions, 1848-1853 . . .	591,318
German Empire, France and Spain . .	593,963
Alaska, 1867	577,390
Austria-Hungary, German Empire and Norway	575,314
United States since 1867	3,602,990
Europe	3,986,975

Area of the South African System.

	Sq. miles.
Cape Colony	225,338
Bechuanaland and Protectorate	300,000
Orange Free State	48,326
Transvaal	112,700
Zululand, Basutoland, Amatongaland	25,000
	711,354
British South Africa Company	750,000
German South-west Africa	322,000
Portuguese territory South of the Zambesi, say	100,000
	1,883,354
Europe	3,986,975
European Russia	2,080,961
Europe (without Russia)	1,906,014

APPENDIX II.

The following quotations taken from Dr. A. R. Wallace's work on "The Malay Archipelago," I have thought worthy of insertion here, as they raise a question which for South Africa has supreme importance.

The determination of the proper principles upon which the white races should treat the black in South Africa is of the highest moment to the welfare of both ; while the observations and opinions of a man of such high attainments as Dr. A. R. Wallace, especially when formed after a personal experience of the Dutch system extending over some years, must carry considerable weight. In speaking of the Celebes Islands he says :—

"Forty years ago the country was a wilderness, the people naked savages, garnishing their rude houses with human heads. Now it is a garden worthy of its sweet native name of 'Minahasa.' Good roads and paths traverse it in every direction; some of the finest coffee plantations in the world surround the villages, interspersed with extensive rice-fields more than sufficient for the support of the population.

"The people are now the most industrious, peaceable, and civilized in the whole Archipelago. They are the best clothed, the best housed, the best fed, and the best educated ; and they have made some progress towards a higher social state. I believe there is no example elsewhere of such striking results being produced in so short a time—results which are entirely due to the system of government now adopted by the Dutch in their Eastern possessions. The system is one which may be called a 'paternal despotism.' Now we Englishmen do not like despotism—we hate the name and the thing. and we would rather see people ignorant, lazy, and vicious, than use any but moral force to make them wise, industrious, and good. And we are right when we are dealing with men of our own race, and of similar ideas and equal capacities with ourselves. Example and precept, the force of public opinion, and the slow, but sure spread of education, will do everything in time; without engendering any of those bitter feelings, or producing any of that servility, hypocrisy, and independence, which are the sure results of a despotic government. But what should we think of a man who should advocate these principles of perfect freedom in a family or a school? We should say that he was applying a good general principle to a case in which the conditions rendered it inapplicable—the case in which the governed are in an admitted state of mental inferiority to those who governed them, and are unable to decide what is best for their permanent welfare. Children must be subjected to some degree of authority and guidance; and if properly managed they will cheerfully submit to it, because they know their own inferiority, and believe their elders are acting solely for their good. They learn many things the use of which they cannot comprehend, and which they would never learn without some moral and social if not physical pressure. Habits of order, of industry, of cleanliness, of respect and obedience, are inculcated by similar means. Children would never grow up into well-behaved and well-educated men, if the same absolute freedom of action that is allowed to men were allowed to them. Under the best aspect of education, children are subjected to a mild despotism for the good of ourselves and of society; and their confidence in the wisdom and goodness of those who ordain and apply this despotism, neutralizes the bad passions and degrading feelings, which under less favourable conditions are its general results.

"Now, there is not merely an analogy—there is in many respects an identity of relation between master and pupil or parent and child on the one hand, and an uncivilized race and its civilized rulers on the other. We know (or think we know) that the education and industry, and the common usages of civilized man, are superior to those of savage life; and, as he becomes acquainted with them, the savage himself admits this. He admires the superior acquirements of the civilized man, and it is with pride that he will adopt such usages as do not interfere too much with his sloth, his passions, or his prejudices. But as the wilful child or the idle schoolboy, who was never taught obedience, and never made to do anything which of his own free will he was not inclined to do, would in most cases obtain neither education nor manners; so it is much more unlikely that the savage, with all the confirmed habits of manhood and the traditional prejudices of race, should ever do more than copy a few of the least beneficial customs of civilization, without some stronger stimulus than precept very imperfectly backed by example.

"If we are satisfied that we are right in assuming the government over a savage race, and occupying their country ; and if we further consider it our duty to do what we can to improve our rude subjects and raise them up towards our own level, we must not be too much afraid of the cry of 'despotism' and 'slavery,' but must use the authority we possess to induce them to do work, which they may not altogether like, but which we know to be an indispensable step in their moral and physical advancement. The Dutch have shown much good policy in the means by which they have done this. They have in most cases upheld and strengthened the authority of the native chiefs, to whom the people have been accustomed to render a voluntary obedience ; and by acting on the intelligence and self-interest of these chiefs, have brought about changes in the manners and customs of the people, which would have excited ill-feeling and perhaps revolt had they been directly enforced by foreigners.

"In carrying out such a system much depends upon the character of the people ; and the system which succeeds admirably in one place could only be very partially worked out in another. In Minahasa the natural docility and intelligence of the race have made their progress rapid ; and how important this is, is well illustrated by the fact, that in the immediate vicinity of the town of Menado are a tribe called Banteks, of a much less tractable disposition, who have hitherto resisted all efforts of the Dutch Government to induce them to adopt any systematic cultivation. These remain in a ruder condition, but engage themselves willingly as occasional porters and labourers, for which their greater strength and activity well adapt them.

"No doubt the system here sketched seems open to serious objection. It is to a certain extent despotic, and interferes with free trade, free labour, and free communication. A native cannot leave his village without a pass, and cannot engage himself to any merchant or captain without a Government permit. The coffee has all to be sold to Government, at less than half the price that the local merchant would give for it, and he consequently cries out loudly against 'monopoly' and 'oppression.' He forgets, however, that the coffee plantations were established by the Government at great outlay of capital and skill ; that it gives free education to the people, and that the monopoly is in lieu of taxation. He forgets that the product he wants to purchase and make a profit by, is the creation of the Government, without whom the people would still be savages. He knows very well that free trade would, as its first result, lead to the importation of whole cargoes of arrack, which would be carried over the country and exchanged for coffee. That drunkenness and poverty would spread over the land; that the public coffee plantations would not be kept up; that the quality and quantity of the coffee would soon deteriorate; that traders and merchants would get rich, but that the people would relapse into poverty and barbarism. That such is invariably the result of free trade with any savage tribes who possess a valuable product, native or cultivated, is well known to those who have visited such people; but we might even anticipate from general principles that evil results would happen. If there is one thing rather than another to which the grand law of continuity or development will apply, it is to human progress. There are certain stages through which society must pass in its onward march from barbarism to civilization. Now one of these stages has always been some form or other of despotism, such as feudalism or servitude, or a despotic paternal government; and we have every reason to believe that it is not possible for humanity to leap over this transition epoch, and pass at once from pure savagery to free civilization. The Dutch system attempts to supply this missing link, and to bring the people on by gradual steps to the higher civilization, which we (the English) try to force upon them at once. Our system has always failed. We demoralize and we extirpate, but we never really civilize. Whether the Dutch system can permanently succeed is but doubtful, since it may not be possible to compress the work of ten centuries into one; but at all events it takes nature as a guide, and is therefore more deserving of success, and more likely to succeed, than ours."—" Malay Archipelago," pp. 194-197.

In the next extract we see the same conditions among peoples of a low state of development producing similar results. We know that in South Africa the preference by masters for the raw and unmissionized nations over the product of missionary efforts is universal.

In the concluding words of the extract below we find the true interpretation of these phenomena. The religions of Europe are far above the mental horizon of the native, and are therefore inoperative on his conduct.

"Captain Van der Beck was never tired of abusing the inhabitants of these Christian villages as thieves, liars. and drunkards, besides being incorrigibly lazy. In the city of Amboyna my friends, Doctors Mohnike and Doleschall, as well

as most of the European residents and traders, made exactly the same complaint, and would rather have Mohammedans for servants, even if convicts, than any of the native Christians. One great cause of this is the fact that with the Mohammedans temperance is a part of their religion, and has become so much a habit that practically the rule is never transgressed. One fertile source of want, and one great incentive to idleness and crime, is thus present with the one class, but absent in the other; but besides this the Christians look upon themselves as nearly the equals of the Europeans, who profess the same religion, and as far superior to the followers of Islam, and are therefore prone to despise work, and to endeavour to live by trade, or by cultivating their own land. It need hardly be said that with people in this low state of civilization religion is almost wholly ceremonial, and that neither are the doctrines of Christianity comprehended, nor its moral precepts obeyed."—
"Malay Archipelago," p. 270.

APPENDIX III.

THE CONSTITUTION OF THE UNITED STATES.

Preamble.

WE, the people of the United States, in order to form a more perfect union, establish justices, insure domestic tranquillity, provide for the common defence, promote the general welfare, and secure the blessings of liberty to ourselves and our posterity, do ordain and establish this Constitution for the United States of America.

Article I. Legislative Department.

Section I. Congress in General.

All legislative powers herein granted shall be vested in a Congress of the United States, which shall consist of a Senate and House of Representatives.

Section II. House of Representatives.

1. The House of Representatives shall be composed of members chosen every second year by the people of the several States, and the electors in each State shall have the qualifications requisite for electors of the most numerous branch of the State legislature.

2. No person shall be a Representative who shall not have attained the age of twenty-five years, and been seven years a citizen of the United States, and who shall not, when elected, be an inhabitant of that State in which he shall be chosen.

3. Representatives and direct taxes shall be apportioned among the several States which may be included within this Union, according to their respective numbers, which shall be determined by adding to the whole number of free persons, including those bound to service for a term of years, and excluding Indians not taxed, three-fifths of all other persons. The actual enumeration shall be made within three years after the first meeting of the Congress of the United States, and within every subsequent term of ten years, in such manner as they shall by law direct. The number of Representatives shall not exceed one for every thirty thousand, but each State shall have at least one Representative ; and until such enumeration shall be made, the State of *New Hampshire* shall be entitled to choose three, *Massachusetts* eight, *Rhode Island and Providence Plantations* one, *Connecticut* five, *New York* six, *New Jersey* four, *Pennsylvania* eight, *Delaware* one, *Maryland* six, *Virginia* ten, *North Carolina* five, *South Carolina* five, and *Georgia* three.

4. When vacancies happen in the representation from any State, the executive authority thereof shall issue writs of election to fill such vacancies.

5. The House of Representatives shall choose their speaker and other officers, and shall have the sole power of impeachment.

Section III. Senate.

1. The Senate of the United States shall be composed of two Senators from each State, chosen by the legislature thereof, for six years ; and each Senator shall have one vote.

2. Immediately after they shall be assembled in consequence of the first election, they shall be divided as equally as may be into three classes. The seats of the Senators of the first class shall be vacated at the expiration of the second year ; of the second class, at the expiration of the fourth year ; and of the third class, at the expiration of the sixth year, so that one-third may be chosen every second year ; and if vacancies happen by resignation or otherwise during the recess of the legislature of any State, the executive thereof may make

temporary appointments until the next meeting of the legislature, which shall then fill such vacancies.

3. No person shall be a Senator who shall not have attained to the age of thirty years, and been nine years a citizen of the United States, and who shall not, when elected, be an inhabitant of that State for which he shall be chosen.

4. The Vice-President of the United States shall be President of the Senate, but shall have no vote, unless they be equally divided.

5. The Senate shall choose their other officers, and also a President *pro tempore* in the absence of the Vice-President, or when he shall exercise the office of President of the United States.

6. The Senate shall have the sole power to try all impeachments. When sitting for that purpose, they shall be on oath or affirmation. When the President of the United States is tried, the Chief Justice shall preside : and no person shall be convicted without the concurrence of two-thirds of the members present.

7. Judgment in cases of impeachment shall not extend further than to removal from office, and disqualification to hold and enjoy any office of honour, trust, or profit under the United States ; but the party convicted shall, nevertheless, be liable and subject to indictment, trial, judgment, and punishment, according to law.

Section IV. Both Houses.

1. The times, places, and manner of holding elections for Senators and Representatives shall be prescribed in each State by the legislature thereof ; but the Congress may at any time by law make or alter such regulations, except as to the places of choosing Senators.

2. The Congress shall assemble at least once in every year, and such meeting shall be on the first Monday in December, unless they shall by law appoint a different day.

Section V. The Houses Separately.

1. Each house shall be the judge of the elections, returns, and qualifications of its own members, and a

majority of each shall constitute a quorum to do business; but a smaller number may adjourn from day to day, and may be authorized to compel the attendance of absent members, in such manner, and under such penalties, as each house may provide.

2. Each house may determine the rules of its proceedings, punish its members for disorderly behaviour, and with the concurrence of two-thirds, expel a member.

3. Each house shall keep a journal of its proceedings, and from time to time publish the same, excepting such parts as may in their judgment require secrecy, and the yeas and nays of the members of either house on any question shall, at the desire of one-fifth of those present, be entered on the journal.

4. Neither house, during the session of Congress, shall, without the consent of the other, adjourn for more than three days, nor to any other place than that in which the two houses shall be sitting.

Section VI. *Privileges and Disabilities of Members.*

1. The Senators and Representatives shall receive a compensation for their services, to be ascertained by law and paid out of the Treasury of the United States. They shall, in all cases except treason, felony, and breach of the peace, be privileged from arrest during their attendance at the session of their respective houses, and in going to and returning from the same; and for any speech or debate in either house they shall not be questioned in any other place.

2. No Senator or Representative shall, during the time for which he was elected, be appointed to any civil office under the authority of the United States, which shall have been created, or the emoluments whereof shall have been increased during such time; and no person holding any office under the United States shall be a member of either house during his continuance in office.

Section VII. *Mode of Passing Laws.*

1. All bills for raising revenue shall originate in the House of Representatives; but the Senate may propose or concur with amendments as on other bills.

2. Every bill which shall have passed the House of Representatives and the Senate shall, before it become a law, be presented to the President of the United States; if he approve he shall sign it, but if not he shall return it, with his objections, to that house in which it shall have originated, who shall enter the objections at large on their journal and proceed to reconsider it. If after such reconsideration two-thirds of that house shall agree to pass the bill, it shall be sent, together with the objections, to the other house, by which it shall likewise be reconsidered, and if approved by two-thirds of that house it shall become a law. But in all such cases the votes of both houses shall be determined by yeas and nays, and the names of the persons voting for and against the bill shall be entered on the journal of each house respectively. If any bill shall not be returned by the President within ten days (Sundays excepted) after it shall have been presented to him, the same shall be a law, in like manner as if he had signed it, unless the Congress by their adjournment prevent its return, in which case it shall not be a law.

3. Every order, resolution, or vote to which the concurrence of the Senate and the House of Representatives may be necessary (except on a question of adjournment) shall be presented to the President of the United States; and before the same shall take effect, shall be approved by him, or being disapproved by him, shall be repassed by two-thirds of the Senate and House of Representatives, according to the rules and limitations prescribed in the case of a bill.

Section VIII. Powers granted to Congress.

The Congress shall have power:

1. To lay and collect taxes, duties, imposts, and excises, to pay the debts and provide for the common defence and general welfare of the United States; but all duties, imposts, and excises shall be uniform throughout the United States;

2. To borrow money on the credit of the United States;

APPENDIX. 235

3. To regulate commerce with foreign nations and among the several States, and with the Indian tribes ;

4. To establish an uniform rule of naturalization, and uniform laws on the subject of bankruptcies throughout the United States ;

5. To coin money, regulate the value thereof, and of foreign coin, and fix the standard of weights and measures ;

6. To provide for the punishment of counterfeiting the securities and current coin of the United States;

7. To establish post-offices and post-roads ;

8. To promote the progress of science and useful arts by securing for limited times to authors and inventors the exclusive right to their respective writings and discoveries ;

9. To constitute tribunals inferior to the Supreme Court ;

10. To define and punish piracies and felonies committed on the high seas and offences against the law of nations ;

11. To declare war, grant letters of marque and reprisal, and make rules concerning captures on land and water ;

12. To raise and support armies, but no appropriation of money to that use shall be for a longer term than two years ;

13. To provide and maintain a navy ;

14. To make rules for the government and regulation of the land and naval forces.

15. To provide for calling forth the militia to execute the laws of the Union, suppress insurrections, and repel invasions ;

16. To provide for organizing, arming, and disciplining the militia, and for governing such part of them as may be employed in the service of the United States, reserving to the States respectively the appointment of the officers, and the authority of training the militia according to the discipline prescribed by Congress ;

17. To exercise exclusive legislation in all cases whatsoever over such district (not exceeding ten miles square) as may, by cession of particular States and the accept-

ance of Congress, become the seat of the Government of the United States, and to exercise like authority over all places purchased by the consent of the legislature of the State in which the same shall be, for the erection of forts, magazines, arsenals, dockyards, and other needful buildings; and

18. To make all laws which shall be necessary and proper for carrying into execution the foregoing powers, and all other powers vested by this Constitution in the Government of the United States, or in any department or office thereof.

Section IX. Powers denied to the United States.

1. The migration or importation of such persons as any of the States now existing shall think proper to admit shall not be prohibited by the Congress prior to the year one thousand eight hundred and eight, but a tax or duty may be imposed on such importation, not exceeding ten dollars for each person.

2. The privilege of the writ of habeas corpus shall not be suspended, unless when in cases of rebellion or invasion the public safety may require it.

3. No bill of attainder or ex post facto law shall be passed.

4. No capitation or other direct tax shall be laid, unless in proportion to the census or enumeration hereinbefore directed to be taken.

5. No tax or duty shall be laid on articles exported from any State.

6. No preference shall be given by any regulation of commerce or revenue to the ports of one State over those of another; nor shall vessels bound to or from one State be obliged to enter, clear, or pay duties in another.

7. No money shall be drawn from the Treasury but in consequence of appropriations made by law; and a regular statement and account of the receipts and expenditures of all public money shall be published from time to time.

8. No title of nobility shall be granted by the United States; and no person holding any office of profit or trust under them shall, without the consent of the

Congress, accept of any present, emolument, office, or title, of any kind whatever, from any king, prince, or foreign State.

Section X. *Powers denied to the States.*

1. No State shall enter into any treaty, alliance, or confederation ; grant letters of marque and reprisal ; coin money ; emit bills of credit ; make anything but gold and silver coin a tender in payment of debts ; pass any bill of attainder, ex post facto law, or law impairing the obligation of contracts, or grant any title of nobility.

2. No State shall, without the consent of Congress, lay any imposts or duties on imports or exports, except what may be absolutely necessary for executing its inspection laws ; and the net produce of all duties and imposts, laid by any State on imports or exports, shall be for the use of the Treasury of the United States ; and all such laws should be subject to the revision and control of the Congress.

3. No State shall, without the consent of Congress, lay any duty of tonnage, keep troops or ships of war in time of peace, enter into any agreement or compact with another State or with a foreign power, or engage in war, unless actually invaded or in such imminent danger as will not admit of delay.

ARTICLE II. EXECUTIVE DEPARTMENT.

Section I. *President and Vice-President.*

1. The executive power shall be vested in a President of the United States of America. He shall hold his office during the term of four years, and together with the Vice-President, chosen for the same term, be elected as follows :

2. Each State shall appoint, in such manner as the legislature thereof may direct, a number of electors, equal to the whole number of Senators and Representatives to which the State may be entitled in the Congress ; but no Senator or Representative, or person holding an office of trust or profit under the United States, shall be appointed an elector.

3. [The electors shall meet in their respective States and vote by ballot for two persons, of whom one at least shall not be an inhabitant of the same State with themselves. And they shall make a list of all the persons voted for, and of the number of votes for each; which list they shall sign and certify, and transmit sealed to the seat of government of the United States, directed to the President of the Senate. The President of the Senate shall, in the presence of the Senate and House of Representatives, open all the certificates, and the votes shall then be counted. The person having the greatest number of votes shall be the President, if such number be a majority of the whole number of electors appointed; and if there be more than one who have such majority, and have an equal number of votes, then the House of Representatives shall immediately choose by ballot one of them for President; and if no person have a majority, then from the five highest on the list the said House shall in like manner choose the President. But in choosing the President the votes shall be taken by States, the representation from each State having one vote; a quorum for this purpose shall consist of a member or members from two-thirds of the States, and a majority of all the States shall be necessary to a choice. In every case, after the choice of the President, the person having the greatest number of votes of the electors shall be the Vice-President. But if there should remain two or more who have equal votes, the Senate shall choose from them by ballot the Vice-President.] [1]

4. The Congress may determine the time of choosing the electors and the day on which they shall give their votes, which day shall be the same throughout the United States.

5. No person except a natural-born citizen, or a citizen of the United States at the time of the adoption of this Constitution, shall be eligible to the office of President; neither shall any person be eligible to that office who shall not have attained to the age of thirty-five years,

---

[1] This clause of the Constitution has been amended. See Amendments, Art. XII.

and been fourteen years a resident within the United States.

6. In case of the removal of the President from office, or of his death, resignation, or inability to discharge the powers and duties of the said office, the same shall devolve on the Vice-President, and the Congress may by law provide for the case of removal, death, resignation, or inability, both of the President and Vice-President, declaring what officer shall then act as President, and such officer shall act accordingly until the disability be removed or a President shall be elected.

7. The President shall, at stated times, receive for his services a compensation, which shall neither be increased nor diminished during the period for which he may have been elected, and he shall not receive within that period any other emolument from the United States or any of them.

8. Before he enter on the execution of his office he shall take the following oath or affirmation :

" I do solemnly swear (or affirm) that I will faithfully execute the office of President of the United States, and will to the best of my ability preserve, protect, and defend the Constitution of the United States."

Section II. Powers of the President.

1. The President shall be commander-in-chief of the Army and Navy of the United States, and of the militia of the several States when called into the actual service of the United States; he may require the opinion, in writing, of the principal officer in each of the executive departments, upon any subject relating to the duties of their respective offices, and he shall have power to grant reprieves and pardons for offences against the United States, except in cases of impeachment.

2. He shall have power, by and with the advice and consent of the Senate, to make treaties, provided two-thirds of the Senators present concur; and he shall nominate, and, by and with the advice and consent of the Senate, shall appoint ambassadors, other public ministers and consuls, judges of the Supreme Court, and all other officers of the United States, whose appoint-

ments are not herein otherwise provided for, and which shall be established by law ; but the Congress may by law vest the appointment of such inferior officers, as they think proper, in the President alone, in the courts of law, or in the heads of departments.

3. The President shall have power to fill up all vacancies that may happen during the recess of the Senate, by granting commissions which shall expire at the end of their next session.

Section III. *Duties of the President.*

He shall from time to time give to the Congress information of the state of the Union, and recommend to their consideration such measures as he shall judge necessary and expedient ; he may, on extraordinary occasions, convene both houses, or either of them, and in case of disagreement between them with respect to the time of adjournment, he may adjourn them to such time as he shall think proper ; he shall receive ambassadors and other public ministers ; he shall take care that the laws be faithfully executed, and shall commission all the officers of the United States.

Section IV. *Impeachment.*

The President, Vice-President, and all civil officers of the United States shall be removed from office on impeachment for and conviction of treason, bribery, or other high crimes and misdemeanours.

ARTICLE III. JUDICIAL DEPARTMENT.

Section I. *United States Courts.*

The judicial power of the United States shall be vested in one Supreme Court, and in such inferior courts as the Congress may from time to time ordain and establish. The judges, both of the supreme and inferior courts, shall hold their offices during good behaviour, and shall, at stated times, receive for their services a compensation which shall not be diminished during their continuance in office.

Section II. Jurisdiction of the United States Courts.

1. The judicial power shall extend to all cases, in law and equity, arising under this Constitution, the laws of the United States, and treaties made, or which shall be made, under their authority; to all cases affecting ambassadors, other public ministers, and consuls; to all cases of admiralty and maritime jurisdiction; to controversies to which the United States shall be a party; to controversies between two or more States; between a State and citizens of another State; between citizens of different States; between citizens of the same State claiming lands under grants of different States, and between a State, or the citizens thereof, and foreign States, citizens, or subjects.[1]

2. In all cases affecting ambassadors, other public ministers and consuls, and those in which a State shall be a party, the Supreme Court shall have original jurisdiction. In all the other cases before mentioned the Supreme Court shall have appellate jurisdiction, both as to law and fact, with such exceptions, and under such regulations as the Congress shall make.

3. The trial of all crimes, except in cases of impeachment, shall be by jury; and such trial shall be held in the State where the said crimes shall have been committed; but when not committed within any State, the trial shall be at such place or places as the Congress may by law have directed.

Section III. Treason.

1. Treason against the United States shall consist only in levying war against them, or in adhering to their enemies, giving them aid and comfort. No person shall be convicted of treason unless on the testimony of two witnesses to the same overt act, or on confession in open court.

2. The Congress shall have power to declare the punishment of treason, but no attainder of treason shall

---

[1] This clause has been amended. See Amendments, Art. XI.

work corruption of blood or forfeiture except during the life of the person attainted.

ARTICLE IV. THE STATES AND THE FEDERAL GOVERNMENT.

Section I. State Records.

Full faith and credit shall be given in each State to the public acts, records, and judicial proceedings of every other State. And the Congress may by general laws prescribe the manner in which such acts, records, and proceedings shall be proved, and the effect thereof.

Section II. Privileges of Citizens, etc.

1. The citizens of each State shall be entitled to all privileges and immunities of citizens in the several States.

2. A person charged in any State with treason, felony, or other crime, who shall flee from justice, and be found in another State, shall, on demand of the executive authority of the State from which he fled, be delivered up, to be removed to the State having jurisdiction of the crime.

3. No person held to service or labour in one State, under the laws thereof, escaping into another, shall, in consequence of any law or regulation therein, be discharged from such service or labour, but shall be delivered up on claim of the party to whom such service or labour may be due.[1]

Section III. New States and Territories.

1. New States may be admitted by the Congress into this Union ; but no new State shall be formed or erected within the jurisdiction of any other State ; nor any State be formed by the junction of two or more States or parts of States, without the consent of the legislatures of the States concerned as well as of the Congress.

2. The Congress shall have power to dispose of and

---

[1] This clause has been cancelled by Amendment XIII., which abolishes slavery.

make all needful rules and regulations respecting the territory or other property belonging to the United States ; and nothing in this Constitution shall be so construed as to prejudice any claims of the United States or of any particular State.

Section IV. Guarantee to the States.

The United States shall guarantee to every State in this Union a republican form of government, and shall protect each of them against invasion, and on application of the legislature, or of the executive (when the legislature eannot be convened), against domestic violence.

ARTICLE V. POWER OF AMENDMENT.

The Congress, whenever two-thirds of both houses shall deem it necessary, shall propose amendments to this Constitution, or, on the application of the legislatures of two-thirds of the several States, shall call a convention for proposing amendments, which in either case shall be valid to all intents and purposes as part of this Constitution, when ratified by the legislatures of three-fourths of the several States, or by conventions in three-fourths thereof, as the one or the other mode of ratification may be proposed by the Congress, provided that no amendments which may be made prior to the year one thousand eight hundred and eight shall in any manner affect the first and fourth clauses in the ninth section of the first article ; and that no State, without its consent, shall be deprived of its equal suffrage in the Senate.

ARTICLE VI. PUBLIC DEBT, SUPREMACY OF THE CONSTITUTION, OATH OF OFFICE, RELIGIOUS TEST.

1. All debts contracted and engagements entered into, before the adoption of this Constitution, shall be as valid against the United States under this Constitution as under the confederation.

2. This Constitution, and the laws of the United States which shall be made in pursuance thereof, and all treaties made, or which shall be made, under the authority of the United States, shall be the supreme law of the land ; and

the judges in every State shall be bound thereby, anything in the Constitution or laws of any State to the contrary notwithstanding.

3. The Senators and Representatives before mentioned, and the members of the several State legislatures, and all executive and judicial officers both of the United States and of the several States, shall be bound by oath or affirmation to support this Constitution ; but no religious test shall ever be required as a qualification to any office or public trust under the United States.

ARTICLE VII. RATIFICATION OF THE CONSTITUTION.

The ratification of the conventions of nine States shall be sufficient for the establishment of this Constitution between the States so ratifying the same.

> Done in convention by the unanimous consent of the States present,[1] the seventeenth day of September, in the year of our Lord one thousand seven hundred and eighty-seven, and of the Independence of the United States of America the twelfth. In witness whereof, we have hereunto subscribed our names :—

George Washington, President, and Deputy from VIRGINIA.
NEW HAMPSHIRE—John Langdon, Nicholas Gilman.
MASSACHUSETTS—Nathaniel Gorham, Rufus King.
CONNECTICUT—William Samuel Johnson, Roger Sherman.
NEW YORK—Alexander Hamilton.
NEW JERSEY—William Livingston, David Brearly, William Patterson, Jonathan Dayton.
PENNSYLVANIA—Benjamin Franklin, Thomas Mifflin, Robert Morris, George Clymer, Thomas Fitzsimons, Jared Ingersoll, James Wilson, Gouverneur Morris.
DELAWARE—George Read, Gunning Bedford, Jr., John Dickinson, Richard Bassett, Jacob Broom.
MARYLAND—James McHenry, Daniel of St. Thomas Jenifer, Daniel Carrol.
VIRGINIA—John Blair, James Madison, Jr.
NORTH CAROLINA—William Blount, Richard Dobbs Spaight, Hugh Williamson.

[1] Rhode Island sent no delegates to the Federal Convention.

SOUTH CAROLINA—John Rutledge, Charles Cotesworth Pinckney, Charles Pinckney, Pierce Butler.
GEORGIA—William Few, Abraham Baldwin.
    Attest: William Jackson, *Secretary*.

AMENDMENTS.[1]

ARTICLE I.

Congress shall make no law respecting an establishment of religion, or prohibiting the free exercise thereof; or abridging the freedom of speech or of the press; or the right of the people peaceably to assemble, and to petition the government for a redress of grievances.

ARTICLE II.

A well-regulated militia being necessary to the security of a free State, the right of the people to keep and bear arms shall not be infringed.

ARTICLE III.

No soldier shall, in time of peace, be quartered in any house without the consent of the owner, nor in time of war, but in a manner to be prescribed by law.

ARTICLE IV.

The right of the people to be secure in their persons, houses, papers, and effects, against unreasonable searches and seizures, shall not be violated, and no warrants shall issue but upon probable cause, supported by oath or affirmation, and particularly describing the place to be searched, and the person or things to be seized.

ARTICLE V.

No person shall be held to answer for a capital or otherwise infamous crime, unless as a presentment or

---

[1] Amendments I. to X. were proposed by Congress, Sept. 25th, 1789, and declared in force Dec. 15th, 1791.

indictment of a grand jury, except in cases arising in the land or naval forces, or in the militia, when in actual service in time of war or public danger; nor shall any person be subject for the same offence to be twice put in jeopardy of life and limb; nor shall be compelled in any criminal case to be a witness against himself, nor be deprived of life, liberty, or property, without due process of law; nor shall private property be taken for public use without just compensation.

Article VI.

In all criminal prosecutions the accused shall enjoy the right to a speedy and public trial, by an impartial jury of the State and district wherein the crime shall have been committed, which district shall have been previously ascertained by law, and to be informed of the nature and cause of the accusation; to be confronted with the witness against him; to have compulsory process for obtaining witnesses in his favour, and to have the assistance of counsel for his defence.

Article VII.

In suits at common law, where the value in controversy shall exceed twenty dollars, the right of trial by jury shall be preserved, and no fact tried by a jury shall be otherwise re-examined in any court of the United States, than according to the rules of the common law.

Article VIII.

Excessive bail shall not be required, nor excessive fines imposed, nor cruel and unusual punishments inflicted.

Article IX.

The enumeration in the Constitution of certain rights shall not be construed to deny or disparage others retained by the people.

APPENDIX.

ARTICLE X.

The powers not delegated to the United States by the Constitution, nor prohibited by it to the States, are reserved to the States respectively or to the people.

ARTICLE XI.[1]

The judicial power of the United States shall not be construed to extend to any suit in law or equity, commenced or prosecuted against one of the United States by citizens of another State, or by citizens or subjects of any foreign State.

ARTICLE XII.[2]

1. The electors shall meet in their respective States and vote by ballot for President and Vice-President, one of whom, at least, shall not be an inhabitant of the same State with themselves ; they shall name in their ballots the person voted for as President, and in distinct ballots the person voted for as Vice-President, and they shall make distinct lists of all persons voted for as President and of all persons voted for as Vice-President, and of the number of votes for each ; which lists they shall sign and certify, and transmit sealed to the seat of the government of the United States, directed to the President of the Senate. The President of the Senate shall, in the presence of the Senate and House of Representatives, open all the certificates, and the votes shall then be counted. The person having the greatest number of votes for President shall be the President, if such number be a majority of the whole number of electors appointed ; and if no person have such majority, then from the persons having the highest numbers not exceeding three on the list of those voted for as President, the House of Representatives shall choose immediately, by ballot, the

---

[1] Proposed by Congress March 5th, 1794, and declared in force Jan. 8th, 1798.
[2] Proposed by Congress Dec. 12th, 1803, and declared in force Sept. 25th, 1804.

President. But in choosing the President the votes shall be taken by States, the representation from each State having one vote; a quorum for this purpose shall consist of a member or members from two-thirds of the States, and a majority of all the States shall be necessary to a choice. And if the House of Representatives shall not choose a President whenever the right of choice shall devolve upon them, before the fourth day of March next following, then the Vice-President shall act as President, as in the case of the death or other constitutional disability of the President.

2. The person having the greatest number of votes as Vice-President shall be the Vice-President, if such number be a majority of the whole number of electors appointed; and if no person have a majority, then from the two highest numbers on the list the Senate shall choose the Vice-President; a quorum for the purpose shall consist of two-thirds of the whole number of Senators, and a majority of the whole number shall be necessary to a choice.

3. But no person constitutionally ineligible to the office of President shall be eligible to that of Vice-President of the United States.

Article XIII.[1]

1. Neither slavery nor involuntary servitude, except as a punishment for crime whereof the party shall have been duly convicted, shall exist within the United States or any place subject to their jurisdiction.

2. Congress shall have power to enforce this article by appropriate legislation.

Article XIV.[2]

1. All persons born or naturalized in the United States, and subject to the jurisdiction thereof, are citizens of the

---

[1] Proposed by Congress Feb. 1st, 1865, and declared in force Dec. 18th, 1865.

[2] Proposed by Congress June 16th, 1866, and declared in force July 28th, 1868.

United States and of the State wherein they reside. No State shall make or enforce any law which shall abridge the privileges or immunities of citizens of the United States ; nor shall any State deprive any person of life, liberty, or property, without due process of law ; nor deny to any person within its jurisdiction the equal protection of the laws.

2. Representatives shall be apportioned among the several States according to their respective numbers, counting the whole number of persons in each State, excluding Indians not taxed. But when the right to vote at any election for the choice of electors for President and Vice-President of the United States, Representatives in Congress, the executive and judicial officers of a State, or the members of the legislature thereof, is denied to any of the male inhabitants of such State, being twenty-one years of age, and citizens of the United States, or in any way abridged, except for participation in rebellion, or other crime, the basis of representation therein shall be reduced in the proportion which the number of such male citizens shall bear to the whole number of male citizens twenty-one years of age in such State.

3. No person shall be a Senator or Representative in Congress, or elector of President and Vice-President, or hold any office, civil or military, under the United States or under any State, who, having previously taken an oath as a member of Congress, or as an officer of the United States, or as a member of any State legislature, or as an executive or judicial officer of any State, to support the Constitution of the United States, shall have engaged in insurrection or rebellion against the same, or given aid or comfort to the enemies thereof. But Congress may, by a vote of two-thirds of each house, remove such disability.

4. The validity of the public debt of the United States, authorized by law, including debts incurred for payment of pensions and bounties for services in suppressing insurrection or rebellion, shall not be questioned. But neither the United States nor any State shall assume or pay any debt or obligation incurred in aid of insurrection or rebellion against the United States, or any

claim for the loss or emancipation of any slave ; but all such debts, obligations, and claims shall be held illegal and void.

5. The Congress shall have power to enforce, by appropriate legislation, the provisions of this article.

Article XV.[1]

1. The right of citizens of the United States to vote shall not be denied or abridged by the United States or by any State on account of race, colour, or previous condition of servitude.

2. The Congress shall have power to enforce this article by appropriate legislation.

[1] Proposed by Congress Feb. 26th, 1869, and declared in force March 30th, 1870.

INDEX.

A.

ACHÆAN League, 109, 183.
Act of Settlement, 144.
Adriatic, 189.
Ætolian League, 183.
Africa, 196.
Africa, East Coast and West, 78, 87.
Africander Bond, 197.
African Lakes, Central, 77.
Aigion, 99.
Alps, 189.
Amalfi, Republic of, 190.
Amatongaland area, 224.
Amboyna, 228.
America: Question as to future government of, in 1787, 1; Critical period of history, 1, 9, 15.
America, Union of, p. 2 [*See* "United States"].
Angles, 188.
Anglo-Saxon, 181, 182.
Angra Pequena, 82.
Arles, 190.
Armada, Spanish, 193.
Asia, Central, 203.
Attila, 203, 215.
Australia, 88; Federation of, 198, 219.
Austria, 167, 168, 185.
Autonomy: Practical, in case of South African colonies and states, 7; Dangers of condition without central controlling power, 7, 8; of American colonies, 13; not lost by Union, 71; Danger of, 73.
Avignon, 190.

B.

BAGEHOT, 185.
Balfour, Blanche, "1200 miles in an ox-waggon," 79.
Bancroft, 158.
Banteks, 227.
Barbarism: Rome takes up struggle against, 202; South African states and colonies move frontier northward as Rome did eastward, 209.
Barcelona, 190.
Barkly, Sir Henry, has leave to summon meeting of colonies and states, 5.
Basutoland area, 224.
Basuto War, 4, 46, 207.
Batlokua, 204.
Batu, 203.
Bavaria, 160.
Bechuanaland, Area of, 224.
Bechuanaland absorbed by Cape, 66.
Belgium, 130.
Berlin Conference recognizes paper protectorates of European Powers, 47; Scramble for Africa after, 47.
Berne, 99, 168.
Bill of Rights, 122, 143.
Bismarck plan for securing Africa, 76, 77, 85.
Boers: Struggle for liberty, 196; Put an end to murderous native régime, 204; System of colonization, 205; Furnishes army at small cost, 205-206; Has taken his share of costly work of civilization, 208.

Britain, xi., 74, 87, 95; Benefit conferred on, by Federation of colonies and states, 164, 191.
British Kaffraria, x.
Bryce, xii., 10, 122, 129, 133, 135, 138, 142, 146, 147, 148, 158, 161-165, 172.
Buckle, 186.
Bulwer Lytton, Sir E., refuses to allow Federation, and recalls Sir George Grey, 4.
Burghers of Cape Colony refuse to disarm Basutos, 207.
Burgundian, 168, 185, 188, 189.

C.

CABINET: none in America, 128, 129; Principles of Government by, 130.
Cæsar, 203.
Cairo, 76.
California, 132.
Cameroons, 79.
Canada, 88.
Canada: Objects reserved for Dominion legislature, 118; Constitution of, 119, 124; French régime in, 176, 177, 179; Federation of, 198, 219.
Cape Colony: Responsible Government in, 4; Free State and Transvaal President's views on adoption of Responsible Government, 4; calls in British Government, 21; Transvaal populated from, 25; Customs union with Free State, 37; Railway arrangement with South African Republic, 37; South Africa populated from, 39; and Chartered Company, 47; and Transvaal, 55; deprived of its emigrants, 94; Sir George Grey desires to Federate, 163; Sir P. Woodehouse attempts to destroy Free Parliament, 192; Area of, 224.
Cape Parliament, 83.
Cape Peninsula, 203.
Cape Town, 170.
Carnarvon, Lord: Troubles due to his attempt to force policy on South Africa, viii.; Unwise attempt to force Federation, 5; objects to annexation of Walwich Bay, 83-85; Troubles due to his policy, 85; destroys Free Legislative Council in Natal, 193; destroys self-government, 196.
Castile, Cities of, 185.
Catalan, 190.
Catholic, 168, 175.
Celebes, 225.
Cetywayo, 187.
Chaka, 187, 204.
Chalons-sur-Marne, Huns destroyed at, 203.
Charles I., 185.
Charles V., 185.
Charles the Great, 203.
Chartered Company, 12; forces oppose Transvaal people in Limpopo, 29; Customs union with Cape, 37; Alternative occupation of Foreign Power, 47; secures northern territories for South Africa, 47, 48; Mission temporary, 52; Area of territory, 224.
Clement IV., 93.
Clinton, General George, 80.
Colonies [See "Cape" and "Natal"].
Commitia Assembly at Rome remains primary assembly, 184.
Confederation despatch, Lord Carnarvon's, 83.
Congress, Constitution over-rides, 120; differs from English Parliament, 121, 125, 128; Nature of, 131-140; Defined, 230; Powers of, 234, 238, 242, 243, 250.
Congress of States before Union formed makes use of implied war powers, 14; Driven out of Philadelphia by drunken soldiery, 14; Sole bond between revolted colonies, 17; powerless to repress disorders in states, 32, 104, 108.
Connecticut: Elects its own Governor, 10; Feeling between, and New York, 11; and Massachu-

INDEX. 253

setts, 11; True Republic, 13;
opposes commercial policy of
neighbours, imposes duties on
Massachusetts, 19; Quarrel with
Pennsylvania, 27; Land claims,
50, 51; resists Royal order, 195,
231.
Constantine, 130.
Constitution: Establishment of, by
reflection and choice, 2; of confederated states before U.S.A.
formed, 18; Origin of Convention
to draft, 36, 107, 112, 114, 115,
117; Description of American,
119-123; Danger of change in
English, 120; American, defines
powers of states and Federal
Government, 121; Paramount
character of, 143-149; General
provisions of American, 150-158;
Success of American, 165, 166;
Text of American, 230-250.
Contract not to be impaired, 237.
Contract succeeds status as peace
advances, 211, 212.
Convention, Constitutional, meets
in Independence Hall, 36, 107;
met at critical moment, 171.
Cortes, Cities represented in, 185.
Crown Colony, 175.
Cunene River, 39, 82, 84, 219.

D.

DAHOMEY, 187.
Dalton, J. N., "Federal States of
the World," 119.
Damaraland, 85.
Danes, 181.
Dar es Salaam, 79.
Delagoa Bay, German plan to
secure, 77, 80, 82, 86.
Derby, Lord, 85.
De Tocqueville, 191.
Diamond Fields, Annexation of, 6.
Dicey, 122-124, 151, 152, 158.
Dingaan, 90, 187, 203.
Doleschall, 228.
Downing Street, 91.
Drakensberg, 205.

Duruy, 181.
Dutch, 197; system in Java, 208,
225-228.
Dutch Republics never formed a
union, viii.

E.

EDWARD II., 190.
Edward III., 190.
Egypt, 187.
Emigrant farmers from Cape
Colony bear brunt of attacks of
Dingaan and Moselikatse, 203.
Emperor Frederic II., 203.
Emperor of Germany, 77.
England: Liberty, 79, 81; hands
back Transvaal, 90; Parliament
supreme in, 120, 121, 130, 133,
141, 143, 171; will protect South
African seaboard, 172; Why,
to be preferred as paramount
power in South Africa, 175, 198;
Colonial rivalry with France, 175-
177; Vitality of English colonies
due to self-government, 178;
How freedom secured in, 180;
History of, struggle for, 184-186;
Despotic recent tendency, 188;
freest, also most maritime, 190;
Strength of insular position, 191-
194; hands on local self-
government to America, 195.
English Government: Unwise policy
of, 3; Interference of, 80; treatment of Walwich Bay question,
84-86.
English statesmen, Duty of, viii.,
ix.
Europe, 81; South African connection with, 174-199; Area, 224.
Evolution, 221.
Exeter Hall, 80, 207.

F.

FEDERALIST, xii.
Federal Court, Description of, 138-
149, 240, 241.
Federal Government: Advantages

of, 159-173; Advances universal peace, 213; Essential principles of, 218.
Federal Union would enable England to withdraw from internal affairs in South Africa, xi.; Form of, 93-116; Before U.S.A. formed, 100; Objects and machinery of, 117-137.
Federation looked on as result of responsible government, 5; Prospects ruined by Lord Carnarvon's action, 5.
Federation, only further consolidation to be looked for, 214.
Federation of South Africa, place in universal history, 200-209.
Fiske, xii., 11, 13, 15, 16, 18-20, 23, 28-33, 36, 50-53, 108, 158, 165, 166, 178, 179, 180, 182, 183, 184, 186, 203, 209, 216, 217, 218, 219, 222.
Flanders, 185, 190.
Florida, 81, 82.
France insults U.S.A., 34; Hostility of, 49; System of patrols, 56, 81, 82, 99, 122, 130, 133, 141, 167, 175, 176; Colonial system of, 175-177, 180, 185, 193.
Franklin, Benjamin, leading member of Convention, 17, 172.
Franks, 188.
Frederic II., Emperor, 203.
Freeman, xii., 97, 100; Success of American Constitution, 166, 167.
Frere, Sir Bartle, magnifies danger of Gaika and Galeka war, 62, 84; introduces despotism at the Cape, 196, 197; desires to disarm and suppress all natives, 207.
Froude, J. A., Unconstitutional agitation at Cape, 83.

G.

GAUL, 188, 202.
Geneva, 99, 168.
Genoa, 190.

Germany, viii.; appealed to by Transvaal, 75; Policy in South Africa, 76-79; Harshness of native treatment, 79, 85, 86, 87; Bad colonial system of, 178, 179; Despotism of, 188; Despotic rule in colonies caused by despotic rule at home, 198; Pagan, 203.
German East Africa, 79.
German Empire, 133, 134, 160.
Germans, Primitive, 181.
Gladstone prevents annexation of St. Lucia Bay by Germany, 78; Confession of failure, 87; As to ignorance of feeling in Transvaal, 89; hands back Transvaal, 90.
Goths, 181, 184, 188.
Government, Form of, in American colonies, 10, 13.
Governor of Cape, ix., x.
Greece, 129, 180, 183, 184.
Grey, Earl, Secretary of State for Colonies, attempts to force convicts on Cape, 195.
Grey, Lord, 88.
Grey, Sir George, *Dedication* and xii.; Endeavours to federate, dismissed by the Colonial Secretary, 4; Cofidence in, 25; Condition of country on arrival in South Africa, 61; His policy, 62; Opinion in favour of Federation, 163, 164.
Griqualand, West, absorption by Cape, 66.
Grondwet, 123.

H.

HALLAM, 190.
Hamilton, leading member of Convention, 17; in *Federalist*, 43, 44, 46, 69, 71, 135, 136, 172.
Hebrews, 79.
Hellas, 167.
Henry III., 182.
Henry VIII., 185.
High Commissioner, ix., x.; Arbitrary action of, 4; Action in diamond-fields annexation, 5, 46, 86.

INDEX. 255

87 ; compared with Attila in Zulu War, 215.
History, South African, 200-209; Universal, 200-209.
Holland and U.S.A, 34, ; supports Protestantism, 175 ; remains free, 180, 188, 189, 190, 191, 194.
House of Commons, 86, 87, 182.
House of Representatives, Description of, 136-137, 230-231, 233-234.
Huguenots forbidden French Canada, 177.
Huns, 189, 203.

I.

IDEAL for South Africa, 210-222.
Illinois, 99.
Imperial Secretary, ix.
India, 88, 170 ; Danger of reaction of despotic rule in, on England and Colonies, 196.
Inyack Island, 86.
Ireland, 144.
Italy, 130, 133, 180, 185, 188, 190.

J.

JAMES I., 185.
James II. sends out royal order depriving Connecticut of control of militia, 195.
Java, Dutch sy tem of native treatment in, 218.
Jay, in *Federalist*, 1.
Jinghis Khan, 203.
Justinian, 130.

K.

KENT, 158.
Kimberley, 83.
Kimberley, Lord, gives authority to Sir H. Barkly to summon meeting of colonies and states, 5, 86.
King John, 182.

Kruger, President : Action in case of "drifts," Difficulties of, 24.

L.

LANGUAGES, Similar distribution of Dutch and English, 40.
Lanyon, Sir Owen, 89.
Lecky, "History of England in eighteenth century," 192, 193.
Lesuto, Destruction in, by Chaka, 205.
Lieber, Professor, 191.
Liegnitz, 203.
Limpopo River, 77.
Lithuanians, 203.
Lobengula, 187.
Lombard, 168, 188.
London, 193.
London Missionary Society, 206.
Louis XIV.: Bureaucratic ideas enforced in Canada, 176.
Louisiana, 81, 82, 132.
Lycian league, 109.

M.

MADISON: Leading member of Convention, 17 ; proposes discussion by all states of commercial questions, 36, 172.
Magna Charta, 122, 143.
Maine, 132.
Maine, Sir Henry, 12 , 125, 129, 142, 152, 169.
Malay Archipelago, 225, 228, 229.
Maps, xxii., 1, 81.
Maryland : Constitution limited monarchy, 13 ; acts with Virginia over Potomac, 35 ; suggests uniform system of duties, 36 ; refuses to ratify Convention unless land surrendered, 51, 231.
Marseilles, 190.
Massachusetts : Feeling between, and Carolina and Connecticut, 11, 12 ; Land claims, 50, 51, 107; Modification of its Charter making nominee upper chamber, 193.

Megalopolis, 98, 99.
Menado, 227.
Middle Ages, 186.
Military militant type of society, 211.
Mill, J. S., 107, 108, 147.
Minahasa, 225, 227.
Ministry, Cape, 84, 85.
Mississippi, 87, 101.
Mohammedans, 229.
Mohinke, 228.
Molteno, Sir John, x.; First Premier of Cape, 4; Confidence in, 26; No racial feeling, 41; enters into Sir G. Grey's plans, 62; constructs railways and telegraphs, 62; refuses aid of Imperial troops, 63; His plan of annexation, 66; desires to annex Walwich Bay, 82-84; Warning of, 89. on Foreign interference, 91-92; Points out importance of local self-government, 192; carries on constitutional struggle, 196.
Mongolians, 203.
Monroe, 41.
Montreal, 177.
Moselikatse, 90, 187, 204, 205.
Munster, Count, 85.

N.

NAMAQUALAND, Great, 85.
Naples, Republic of, 190.
Napoleon, 82, 193.
Natal: Seizure of, 3; erected into separate government in 1845, 3; receives responsible government, 7; Jealous of Chartered Company, 29; regrets loss of area occupied by Chartered Company, 47; and Transvaal, 55, 97; Sir George Grey suggests federation of, 163; The Legislative Council destroyed by Lord Carnarvon and Sir G. Wolseley, 193.
Natives: Treatment of, favoured by Union, 61, 63; Possible rising of, in Natal, 66; Gradual extension of Cape authority over, 66; Management of a federal object, '119; Dr. Wallace's views of treatment of, 208, 225-229.
Naturalization, 248.
Navarre, 185.
New England, 177.
New Hampshire: Quarrel with New York over Green Mountains, 28, 29; Troubles in, 32, 231.
New York: Feeling between, and Connecticut, 11, 12; Selfish conduct of, 19; George Clinton's bad influence, 20; Hostile action to New Jersey, 21; Quarrel with New Hampshire, 28; Land claims, 50; cedes land to Union, 51, 80, 98, 99, 132, 177, 231.
New Zealand, 88; Sir B. Frere advises destruction of Parliament of, 196, 197.
Niebuhr, 191.
Nobility, Title of, 151, 153, 154, 236.
Normans, 182.
North America, 194.

O.

ODER, 203.
Orange Free State: Formed on abandonment of Orange River sovereignty in 1854, 3; Volksraad resolution favours Union, 4; now free from foreign control, 7; regrets absorption of vacant South Africa by Chartered Company, 29; Issue of paper money, 33; Customs union with Cape, 37; Railway arrangements with Cape, 37; Strained feeling over diamond fields, 266; and Chartered Company, 47; Plan of Germany to secure, 76, 97, 124, 125; Sir George Grey desires to Federate, 163; Chaka's raids, 205; Area of, 224.

INDEX.

Orange River, 82, 85.
Oxus, 203.

P.

PACIFIC, 161.
Palgrave, Francis, Commissioner to examine Walwich Bay territory, 84.
Parliament, x. xi. ; Supreme in England, 120, 124, 125, 144; Cape, Sir P. Woodehouse attempts to destroy, 192.
Patriotism of American statesmen, 17, 33 ; of South African statesmen, 34.
Pax Romana, 202.
Peel, Sir R., 88.
Pennyslvania : Form of Government limited monarchy, 13; Council does not assist Congress, 14; puts import duty against Delaware and New Jersey, 19 ; Quarrel with Connecticut, 27 ; Cruel conduct of, 28, 125, 231.
Peru, 187.
Petition of Right, 122.
Piedmont, 168.
Pisa, 190.
Pondoland absorbed by Cape, 66.
Pope supports despotism, 175.
Porter, William, Attorney-General of Cape, vii., viii. ; trusted by Boers, 26, 192; carries on Constitutional struggle at Cape, 196.
Portugal, 87 ; Bad colonial system, 178.
Portuguese, 81, 84.
Portuguese territory, south of Zambesi, Area of, 224.
Pottinger, Sir Henry, Governor of Cape, first uses title of High Commissioner, ix.
President, American Constitution, 119, 125 ; Duties of, and election, 126-129, 140, 158.
President of United States, 232, 234, 237-240, 247, 248.
Protestant, 168, 175.
Providence, 231.
Prussia, 133, 141, 191, 203.

Q.

QUEBEC, 177.
Queen Elizabeth, 185.

R.

RANDOLPH, leading member of Convention, 17, 107.
Reichstag, 85.
Religion inoperative on Native conduct, Ceremonial, 228, 229.
Representation : How arises, 212 ; Value of principle of, 180; developed by England, 180 ; Teutonic origin of, 180.
Representative, 230, 233, 244, 249.
Responsible Government, 4 ; favours union, 5 ; Solution of South African difficulties, 6; Acquisition of, at Cape, 196.
Revolution, French, 171.
Rhaetia, 168.
Rhine, 169, 189, 190, 203.
Rhode Island : Elects its own Governor, 10 ; True Republic, 13 ; Serious troubles owing to paper money, 30 ; not represented in Constitutional Convention, 36 ; Circumscribed area of, 50, 132, 231.
Rhodes, Cecil, secures Northern Territory for South Africa, 48.
Rhodesia : New population of, 35, 68 ; Rapid development of, 170.
Robinson, Sir H. : Elimination of Imperial factor, 43.
Romans, Conquest by, 75.
Rome, 144, 180, 181, 183, 184, 188, 189, 196, 202, 209.
Roses, War of, set back internal freedom, 185.
Russia, 168, 187, 203, 224.

S.

ST. LUCIA BAY, 78.
Salisbury, Lord, 86.
Scandinavia, 181.

S

Scotland, 144.
Secretary of State for Colonies, 83, 85, 86, 87, 163.
Seeley, Sir John, viii.; "Success of American system of settlement of new territory," 161; "Self-Government in America," 175.
Self-Government, Importance of, 191, 192.
Senate, Description of, 131-136, 230, 231, 233-235.
Senator, 232, 233, 244, 249.
Sheppard, x.
Sherman, Roger, 172.
Sidgwick, H., "Elements of Politics," 107.
Silesia, 203.
Smith, W. H., Leader of House of Commons, 86.
Solomon, Saul, x.; Discusses Union, 4, 192; carries on Constitutional struggle at Cape, 196.
South Africa: Dangers of disunion, vii.; Difficulties not racial, vii.; English non-interference in, vii., 2, 3, 5; Change in position of colonies and states since responsible government introduced, 6; Importance of Uitlander question to, 24; Rural population, backbone of, 26; Complementary natures of English and Dutch, 26; Territorial troubles, 29; Railway conferences and customs union, 37; Circumstances favouring closer union, 38; Geographical definition, 39; Monroe doctrine for, 41: Elimination of Imperial factor, 43; Territorial disputes, 46; Northern territory compared with Westward territory in America, 4, 8; Plan of dealing with common land, 54; ports of, 55; Revenue must be from Customs' duties, 56; Saving in cost of collection, 57; Benefit of free interchange of products, 58, 59; Native policy, 61; Saving in cost of government effected by union, 63; Form of government guaranteed, 65; Danger to, from Uitlander position, 67; from Autonomy of states, 73; Exclusion of Foreign interference, 73-92; Complications of politics, 88, 116; Area of, 224; Maps of, 1, 81; Must be ready to acquire land of S. African system now in Foreign hands, 172, 173; Connection with Europe, 174, 199.
South African history, connection with Universal history, 200-209.
South African Republic, x.; Independence recognized by Sand River Convention 1852, 3; has recourse to arms, 6; Traffic to, 12; Isolation of, compared with New York, 20; Action on "Drifts" question, 21-24; Duties imposed on Cape produce, 23; Uitlander population, 24; Regrets absorption of vacant South Africa by Chartered Company, 29; Issue of paper money, 33; Railway arrangements with Cape, 37; Refuses Franchise to Cape Colonists, 46; and Chartered Company, 47; Chafes under commercial dependence on Colonies, 55; Desires its own port, 55, 66, 67; Danger from Uitlander condition, 67; Appeal to Germany, 75; Plan of Germany to secure, 76; Allies herself with Portuguese, 80; Mr. Gladstone's ignorance of feeling in, 89; Military exaction of taxes, 89, 97, 124; Balance of population being upset, 170; Area of, 224.
South America, 169.
South-West Africa: Acquisition of, by Germany, 76-79: Bad system in, 178; Area of, 224.
Spain: Insults U.S.A., 34; Hostility of, 49; Disunion of, 74, 81, 82, 90, 99, 101, 175, 180, 185, 188, 190, 202.
Sparta, 187.
Spencer, Herbert, 154, 186, 187, 188, 201, 202, 211, 212, 213, 214, 215, 216, 220, 221.
States, African [See "Orange Free

State" and "South African Republic"].
States-General of France, 185.
Status, 211.
Story, 158.
Stubbs' Select Charters, 193.
Swiss Confederation, 148; Character of, 167; Value of precedent to South Africa, 168, 180, 188, 189, 190.
Switzerland, 99, 106, 108.

T.

TABLE BAY, 92.
Tacitus, 181.
Tennyson, 220.
Teutonic knights, 203.
Teutons, 180, 181.
Theal, Description of havoc made by Chaka, 204.
Ticino, 168.
Ting, 181.
Title of nobility not to be granted, 151, 153, 154, 236.
Transkei absorbed by Cape Colony, 66.
Transvaal [See "South African Republic"].
Treason defined, 241.
Turkey, 168.

U.

UITLANDERS: Danger of present condition, 67, 170.
United States, 2; Danger of disunion, 3; European opinion of, 16, 34; Constitutional Convention, 17, 36; League of Friendship constitutes no central representative of states, 18; No power to levy taxes, 18; Commercial war of States, 19; Territorial troubles, 27; Financial troubles, 30; Commercial questions made basis of negotiations for union, 35; Westward territory compared with Northern territory at Cape, 48, 81;
Attachment to State governments, 97, 105, 106; Area of, 223; Map of, 81.
Universal History, connection with South African history, 200-209.
Uri, 168.

V.

VAN DER BECK, 228.
Vaud, 168.
Venice, 189, 190, 201.
Vice-President of United States, 232, 237-240.
Virginia: Population of, when revolt took place, 10; Tobacco does duty for money, 30; Acts as to navigation of Potomac with Maryland, 35; Kentucky refuses to be separated from, 48; Takes possession of land east of Mississippi, 49, 50, 51; and Kentucky, 53, 177, 231.
Volga, 203.
Volksraad of Orange Free State in favour of Union, 4, 164.
Vote, Right to, 250.

W.

WALLACE, Doctor Alfred Russell; Views of English and Dutch native systems, 208; Extract from his Malay Archipelago, 225.
Walwich Bay, 82, 83, 84, 85, 86.
War: Cessation of, essential for peace, 213; has given all it is capable of, 214, 221.
Washington, George: Letter to American people as to formation of Union, 15; President of Constitutional convention, 17, 36; Asked to be king, 19; Peacemaker in Territorial disputes, 29; His remedy for Disunion, 29; Suggests common system of duties, 36; Patriotic foresight of, 172; Exhortation of, 221.
Weber, Ernest von, Scheme for

securing Africa for Germany, 76-79.
William the Conqueror, 182.
Witenagemote, 181.
Wolfe, 179.
Wolseley, Sir Garnet, destroys free Legislative Council in Natal, 193.
Woodehouse, Sir Philip, xi. ; Arbitrary action of, 4; Attempts to destroy self-government at Cape, 192; Endeavours to abolish free Parliament at Cape, 192 ; Struggle with Parliament of Cape, 195.
Wurtemberg, 160.

Z.

ZAMBESI, 39, 85, 219.
Zulu War, 207.
Zululand, Area, 224.
Zululand, War in, 85.
Zurich, 99, 168.

THE END.

St. Dunstan's House, Fetter Lane,
London, E.C. *August*, 1895.

Select List of Books in all Departments of Literature

PUBLISHED BY

Sampson Low, Marston & Company, Ld.

AARON, Dr. E. M., *The Butterfly Hunters in the Caribbees*, 7s. 6d.
ABBEY, C. J., *Religious Thought in Old English Verse*, 5s.
—— and PARSONS, *Quiet Life*, from drawings; motive by Austin Dobson, 31s. 6d.
ABERDEEN, Earl of. See Prime Ministers.
ABNEY, Capt., *Colour Vision*, 12s. 6d.
—— *Instruction in Photography*, 3s. 6d.
—— *Instantaneous Photography*, 1s.
—— *Negative Making*, 1s.
—— *Photography with Emulsions*, 3s.
—— *Platinotype Printing*, 2s. 6d.
—— *Thebes*, 63s.
—— and H. P. ROBINSON, *Art of Silver Printing*, 2s. 6d.
—— and CUNNINGHAM, *Pioneers of the Alps*, new ed. 21s.
About Some Fellows, by "an Eton boy," 2s. 6d.; now edit. 1s.
ADAM, G. M., *An Algonquin Maiden*, 5s.
—— *Sir J. A. Macdonald's Life*, 16s.
ADAMS, Charles K., *Historical Literature*, 12s. 6d.

AINSLIE, P., *Priceless Orchid*, new ed., 3s. 6d. and 2s. 6d.
AITKEN, R. *Memorials of Burns*, 5s.
ALBERT, Prince. See Bay. S.
ALCOTT, L. M., *Jo's Boys*, 5s.
—— *Comic Tragedies*, 5s.
—— *Life, Letters and Journals*, by Ednah D. Cheney, 6s.; 3s. 6d.
See also " Low's Standard Series for Girls" and Rose Library.
ALDEN, W. L. See Low's Standard Series of Girls' Books.
ALFORD, Lady Marian, *Needlework as Art*, 21s.; l. p. 84s.
ALGER, J. G., *Englishmen in the French Revolution*, 7s. 6d.
—— *Glimpses of the French Revolution*, 6s.
Amateur Angler in Dove Dale, by E. M., 1s. 6d., 1s.
American Catalogue of Books, 1886-94, each 15s. and 18s.
AMICIS, E. de, *Heart*, 3s. 6d.
AMPHLETT, F. H., *Lower and Mid Thames*, 1s.
ANDERSEN, H. C., *Fairy Tales*, illust. by Scandinavian artists, 6s.
ANDERSON, W., *Pictorial Arts of Japan*, 4 parts, 168s.
Angler's strange Experiences, by Cotswold Isys, new edit., 3s. 6d.

ANNESLEY, C., *Standard Opera Glass*, 8th edit., 3s.
Antipodean Notes; a nine months' tour, by Wanderer, 7s. 6d.
APPLETON, *European Guide*, new edit., 2 parts, 10s. each.
ARCHER, F., *How to write a Good Play*, buckram, 6s.
ARDEN, J., *Triumph of Theresa*, 21s.
ARLOT'S *Coach Painting*, from the French by A. A. Fesquet, 6s.
ARMSTRONG, *South Pacific Fern Album*, actual fronds, 63s. net.
—— ISABEL J., *Two Roving Englishwomen in Greece*, 6s.
ARMYTAGE, HON. MRS., *Wars of Queen Victoria's Reign*, 5s.
ARNOLD, *On the Indian Hills, Coffee Planting, &c.*, new ed., 7s. 6d.
—— REV. F., *Cheerful Thoughts*, 2 vols. 21s.
—— R., *Ammonia and Ammonium Compounds*, illust. 5s.
Art of the World, 252s. nett.
ARTHUR, T. C., *Reminiscences*, 16s.
—— J. K., *Kangaroo and Kauri*, 7s. 6d.
Artistic Japan, vols. I.-VI.. 15s. each.
Artists at Home, photos, 42s.
ASHE, R. P., *Two Kings of Uganda*, 3s. 6d.
—— *Uganda, England's latest Charge*, stiff cover, 1s.
ATCHISON, C. C., *Winter Cruise in Summer Seas*, 7s. 6d.
ATKINSON, J. B. *Overbeck*. See Great Artists.
ATTWELL, *Italian Masters, in the National Gallery*, 3s. 6d.
AUDSLEY, G. A., *Chromolithography*, 63s.
—— *Ornamental Arts of Japan*, 2 vols. morocco, 23l. 2s.; four parts, 15l. 15s.

AUDSLEY, W. and G. A., *Outlines of Ornament in all Styles*, 31s. 6d.
AUERBACH, B., *Brigitta* (B. Tauchnitz), 2s.; sewed, 1s. 6d.
—— *On the Heights* (B. Tauchnitz), 3 vols. 6s.; sewed, 4s. 6d.
—— *Spinoza* (B. Tauchnitz), a novel, 2 vols. 4s.
AUSTEN, F. V., *Elfie's Visit to Cloudland*, 3s. 6d.
BACON. See Eng. Philosophers.
—— DELIA, *Biography*, 10s. 6d.
BADDELEY, W. ST. CLAIR, *Love's Vintage;* sonnets &c., 5s.
—— *Tchay and Chianti*, 5s.
—— *Travel-tide*, 7s. 6d.
BAKER, JAMES, *John Westacott*, new edit. 3s. 6d.
—— *Foreign Competitors*, 1s.
See also Low's Standard Novels.
—— R. HINDLE, *Organist and Choirmaster's Diary*, 2s. 6d.
BALDWIN, JAMES, *Story of Siegfried*, illust. 6s.
—— *Story of Roland*, illust. 6s.
—— *Story of the Golden Age*, illust. 6s.
BALL, J. D., *Things Chinese*, new edit., 10s. 6d.
BALLIN, A. S., *Science of Dress*, 6s.
BAMFORD, A. J., *Turbans and Tails*, 7s. 6d.
BANCROFT, G., *History of America*, new ed. 6 vols. 73s. 6d.
Barbizon Painters. See Great Artists.
BARLOW, ALFRED, *Weaving by Hand and Power*, new ed. 25s.
—— P. W., *Kaipara, New Z.*, 6s.
—— W., *Matter and Force*, 12s.
BARR, AMELIA E., *Preacher's Daughter*, 5s.
—— *Flower of Gala Water*, 5s.

In all Departments of Literature. 3

BARROW, J., *Mountain Ascents (in England)*, new edit. 5s.
BARRY, J. W., *Corsican Studies*, 12s.; new edit. 6s.
BASSETT, *Legends of the Sea and Sailors*, 7s. 6d.
BATHGATE, A., *Waitaruna, a Story of New Zealand*, 5s.
Bayard Series, edited by the late J. Hain Friswell; flexible cloth extra, 2s. 6d. each.
Chevalier Bayard, by Berville.
St. Louis, by De Joinville.
Essays of Cowley.
Abdallah, by Laboullaye.
Table-Talk of Napoleon.
Vathek, by Beckford.
Cavalier and Puritan Songs.
Words of Wellington.
Johnson's Rasselas.
Hazlitt's Round Table.
Browne's Religio Medici.
Ballad Stories of the Affections, by Robert Buchanan.
Coleridge's Christabel, &c.
Chesterfield's Letters.
Essays in Mosaic, by Ballantyne.
My Uncle Toby.
Rochefoucauld, Reflections.
Socrates, Memoirs from Xenophon.
Prince Albert's Golden Precepts.

BEACONSFIELD, See Prime Ministers.
BEALE, A. A., *Feeding in Infancy*, 6d. and 1s.
BEATTIE, T, *Pambaniso*, 6s.
BEAUGRAND, *Young Naturalists*, new edit. 5s.
BECKER, A.L., *First German Book*, 1s.; *Exercises*, 1s.; *Key* to both, 2s. 6d.; *Idioms*, 1s. 6d.
BECKFORD. See Bayard Series.
BEECHER, H. W., *Biography*, new edit. 10s. 6d.
BEETHOVEN. See Great Musicians.
BEHNKE, E., *Child's Voice*, 3s. 6d.

BELL, Mrs. A., *History of Art*, 10s. 6d.
—— Hon. H. J., *Obeah, Witchcraft in the West Indies*, 3s. 6d.
—— *Witch's Legacy*, 2s. 6d.
—— *Gold Coast Geography*.
—— L., *Little Sister to the Wilderness*, 3s. 6d.
—— *Love Affairs of an Old Maid*, 3s. 6d.
BENTHALL, J., *Hebrew Poets*, 10s. 6d.
Berlioz, Life of, 10s. 6d.
BERRY, C. A. See Preachers.
BIART, *Lucien*. See Low's Standard Books and Rose Library.
BICKERDYKE, *Irish Midsummer Night's Dream*, 1s.
BICKERSTETH, ASHLEY, B.A., *Harmony of History*, 2s. 6d.
Outlines of Roman History, 2s. 6d.
—— E. and F., *Doing and Suffering*, new ed., 2s. 6d.
—— E. H., Bishop of Exeter, *Clergyman in his Home*, 1s.
—— *From year to year*, original poetical pieces, morocco or calf, 10s. 6d.; padded roan, 5s.; cloth, 3s. 6d.
—— *Hymnal Companion to the Common Prayer*, full lists post free.
—— *Master's Home Call*, new edit. 1s.
—— *Octave of Hymns*, sewn, 3d., with music, 1s.
—— *The Reef, Parables*, illust.,
—— *Shadow of the Rock*, 2s. 6d.
—— *Shadowed Home*, n. ed. 5s.
—— Miss M., *Japan as we saw it*, illust. from photos., 21s.
BIGELOW, JOHN, *France and the Confederate Navy*, 7s. 6d.
BILLROTH, *Care of the Sick*, 6s.
BIRD, F. J., *Dyer's Companion*, 42s.
—— H.E., *Chess Practice*, n.e., 1s.

BLACK, WILLIAM. See Low's Standard Novels.
—— R., *Death no Bane*, 5s.
—— *History of Horse Racing in France*, 14s.
BLACKBURN, C. F., *Catalogue Titles, Index Entries, &c.* 14s.
——*Rambles in Books*, cr. 8vo. 5s.; edit. de luxe, 15s.
—— H., *Art in the Mountains*, new edit. 5s.
—— *Artistic Travel*, 7s. 6d.
—— *Breton Folk*, n. e., 10s. 6d.
BLACKMORE, R. D., *Georgics of Virgil*, 4s. 6d.; cheap edit. 1s. See also Low's Standard Novels.
BLAIKIE, *How to get Strong*, new edit. 5s.
—— *Sound Bodies for our Boys and Girls*, 2s. 6d.
Boas, Textbook of Zoology. 2 vols.
Bobby, a Story, by Vesper, 1s.
BOCK, *Temples & Elephants*, 21s.
Bonaparte, Decline and fall of, by Wolseley, 3s. 6d.
BONWICK, JAMES, *Colonial Days*, 2s. 6d.
—— *Colonies*, 1s. each; 1 vol. 5s.
—— *Daily Life of the Tasmanians*, 12s. 6d.
—— *First Twenty Years of Australia*, 5s.
—— *Irish Druids*, 6s.
—— *Last of the Tasmanians*, 16s.
—— *Port Philip*, 21s.
—— *Romance of Wool Trade*, 6s.
—— *Lost Tasmanian Race*, 4s.
BOSANQUET, C., *Jehoshaphat*, 1.
——*Lenten Meditations*, Ser. I. 1s. 6d.; II. 2s.
—— *Tender Grass for Lambs*, 2s. 6d.

BOULTON, N. W. *Rebellions, Canadian life*, 9s.
BOURKE, *On the Border with Crook*, illust., roy. 8vo, 21s.
—— *Snake Dance of Arizona*, with coloured plates, 21s.
BOUSSENARD. See Low's Standard Books.
BOWEN, F., *Modern Philosophy*, new ed. 16s.
BOWER, G. S., and WEBB, *Law of Electric Lighting*, 12s. 6d.
BOWNE, B. P., *Metaphysics*, 12s. 6d.
BOYESEN, H. H., *Against Heavy Odds*, 5s.; also 3s. 6d.
—— *History of Norway*, 7s. 6d.
—— *Modern Vikings*, 3s. 6d.
Boys, vols. I., II., 7s. 6d. each.
BRACE, C. L., *Life*, 8s. 6d.
BRADSHAW, *New Zealand as it is*, 12s. 6d.
—— *New Zealand of To-day*, 14s.
BRANNT, *Fats and Oils*, 42s.
—— *Scourer and Dyer*, 10s. 6d.
—— *Soap and Candles*, 35s.
—— *Vinegar, Acetates*, 25s.
—— *Distillation of Alcohol*, 12s. 6d.
—— *Metal Worker's Receipts*, 12s. 6d.
—— *Metallic Alloys*, 12s. 6d.
—— *Petroleum*, 35s.
—— and WAHL, *Techno-Chemical Receipt Book*, 10s. 6d.
BRETON, JULES, *Life of an Artist*, an autobiography, 7s. 6d.
BRETT, EDWIN J., *Ancient Arms and Armour*, 105s. nett.
BRIGHT, JOHN, *Letters of*, 5s.
BRINE, ADMIRAL L., *Travels*, 21s.
BRISSE, *Menus and Recipes*, French & English, new ed. 3s. 6d.
Britons in Brittany, 2s. 6d.

BROOKS, G., *Industry and Property*, 3s. 6d.
—— NOAH, *Boy Settlers*, 6s.; new ed., 3s. 6d.
—— *Statesmen*, 8s. 6d.
BROWN, A. J., *Rejected of Men*, and other poems, 3s. 6d.
—— A. S. *Madeira and Canary Islands for Invalids*, n. ed. 2s. 6d.
—— *South Africa*, 2s. 6d.
—— ROBERT. See Low's Standard Novels.
BROWNE, LENNOX, and BEHNKE, *Voice, Song, & Speech*, 15s.; new edit. 5s.
—— *The Child's Voice*, 3s. 6d.
—— *Voice Use*, 3s. 6d.
BRYCE, G., *Manitoba*, 7s. 6d.
—— *Short History of the Canadian People*, 7s. 6d.
BULKELEY, OWEN T., *Lesser Antilles*, 2s. 6d.
BUNYAN. See Low's Standard Series.
BURDETT-COUTTS, *Brookfield Stud*, 5s.
—— BARONESS, *Woman's Mission*, Congress papers, 10s. 6d.
BURNABY, EVELYN, *Ride from Land's End to John o' Groats*, 3s. 6d.
—— MRS., *High Alps in Winter*, 14s. See also Main.
BURNLEY, JAMES, *History of Wool and Wool-combing*, 21s.
BURTON, W. K., *Works on Japan*. List on application.
BUTLER, COL. SIR W. F., *Campaign of the Cataracts*, 18s.
—— See also Low's Standard Books.
BUXTON, ETHEL M. WILMOT, *Wee Folk*, 5s.
BYNNER. See Low's Standard Novels.
CABLE, G. W., See Low's Standard Novels.

CADOGAN, LADY ADELAIDE, *Drawing-room Comedies*, illust. 10s. 6d., acting edit. 6d.
—— *Illustrated Games of Patience*, col. diagrams, 12s. 6d.
—— *New Games of Patience*, with coloured diagrams, 12s. 6d.
CAHUN. See Low's Standard Books.
CALDECOTT, RANDOLPH, *Memoir*, by Henry Blackburn, 5s.
—— *Sketches*, pict. bds. 2s. 6d.
CALL, ANNIE PAYSON, *Power through Repose*, 3s. 6d.
—— *As a Matter of Course*, 3s. 6d.
CALLAN, H., M.A., *Wanderings on Wheel*, 1s. 6d.
CALVERT, EDWARD (*artist*), *Memoir*, imp. 4to, 63s. nett.
Cambridge Trifles, 2s. 6d.
Cambridge Staircase, 2s. 6d.
CAMPBELL, LADY COLIN, *Book of the Running Brook*, 5s.
CAMPELLO, COUNT, *Life*, 5s.
CANTERBURY, ARCHBISHOP. See Preachers.
Capitals of the World, plates and text, 2 vols., 4to, 63s. nett.
CARBUTT, MRS., *Five Months Fine Weather; Canada, &c.*, 5s.
CARLETON, WILL, *City Ballads*, illust. 12s. 6d.
—— *City Legends*, ill. 12s. 6d.
—— *Farm Festivals*, ill. 12s. 6d.
—— *City Ballads*, 1s. } 1 vol.,
—— *City Legends*, 1s. } 2s. 6d.
—— *City Festivals*, 1s.
—— *Farm Ballads*, 1s. }
—— *Farm Festivals*, 1s. } 1 vol., 3s. 6d.
—— *Farm Legends*, 1s. }
—— *Poems*, 6 vols. in case, 8s.
—— See also Rose Library.
CARLYLE, T., *Conversations with*, 6s.

CARMICHAEL, H. See Low's Standard Novels.
CARNEGIE, ANDREW, *American Four-in-hand in Britain*, 10s. 6d.; also 1s.
—— *Triumphant Democracy*, 6s.; new edit. 1s. 6d.; paper, 1s.
CAROVÉ, *Story without an End*, illust. by E. V. B., 7s. 6d.
CARPENTER. See Preachers.
CARSON, H. L., *Supreme Court of U.S.* 84s.
CAVE, *Picturesque Ceylon*, 2 vols., 21s. and 28s. nett.
Celebrated Racehorses, fac-sim. portraits, 4 vols., 126s.
CÉLIÈRE. See Low's Standard Books.
Changed Cross, &c., poems, 2s. 6d.
Chant-book Companion to the Common Prayer, 2s.; organ ed. 4s.
CHAPIN, *Mountaineering in Colorado*, 10s. 6d.
CHAPLIN, J. G., *Bookkeeping*, 2s. 6d.
CHARLES, J. F. See Playtime Library.
CHARLEY, SIR W., *Crusade against the Constitution*, 7s. 6d.
CHATTOCK, *Notes on Etching*, new edit. 10s. 6d.
CHENEY, A. N., *Fishing with the Fly*, 12s. 6d.
CHERUBINI. See Great Musicians.
Choice Editions of choice books, illustrated by Cope, Creswick, Birket Foster, Horsley, Harrison Weir, &c., 2s. 6d.; re-issue, 1s. each.
Bloomfield's Farmer's Boy.
Campbell's Pleasures of Hope.
Coleridge's Ancient Mariner.
Elizabethan Songs and Sonnets.
Goldsmith's Deserted Village.
Goldsmith's Vicar of Wakefield.
Gray's Elegy in a Churchyard.
Keats' Eve of St. Agnes.

Choice Editions—continued.
Milton's Allegro.
Poetry of Nature, by H. Weir.
Rogers' Pleasures of Memory.
Shakespeare's Songs and Sonnets.
Tennyson's May Queen.
Wordsworth's Pastoral Poems.
Chopin, Life of, 10s. 6d.
CHRISTIAN, S., *Lydia*, 2s. 6d.
—— *Sarah*, 2s. 6d.
—— *Two Mistakes*, 3s. 6d.
CHURCH, W. C., *Life of Ericsson*, new ed., 16s.
CHURCHILL, LORD RANDOLPH, *Men, Mines and Animals in South Africa*, 6s.; 2s. 6d.
CLARK, A., *Woe to the Conquered*, 21s.
—— *Dark Place of the Earth*, 6s.
—— Mrs. K. M., *Southern Cross Fairy Tale*, 5s.
—— *Persephone, Poems*, 5s.
CLARKE, PERCY, *Three Diggers*, 6s.
—— *Valley Council*; 6s.
Claude le Lorrain. See Great Artists.
CLIVE BAYLY, *Vignettes from Finland*.
COCHRAN, W., *Pen and Pencil in Asia Minor*, 21s.
COLLINGWOOD, H. See Low's Standard Books.
COLLYER, ROBERT, *Things Old and New, Sermons*, 5s.
CONDER, J., *Flowers of Japan and Decoration*, coloured Plates, 42s. nett.
—— *Landscape Gardening in Japan*, 52s. 6d. nett.; supplement. 36s. nett.
CONYBEARE, E., *School Chronology*, 1s.
CORDINGLEY, W. G., *Guide to the Stock Exchange*, 5s.
CORREGGIO. See Great Artists.

COWEN, JOSEPH, M.P., Life and Speeches, 14s.
COWPER, F., Hunting of the Auk, 5s.
COX, DAVID. See Great Artists.
—— J. CHARLES, Gardens of Scripture; Meditations, 5s.
COZZENS, F., American Yachts, pfs. 21l.; art. pfs. 31l. 10s.
—— S. W. See Low's Standard Books.
CRADDOCK. See Low's Standard Novels.
CRAIG, W. H., Dr. Johnson and the Fair Sex.
CRAIK, D., Millwright and Miller, 21s.
CROCKER, Education of the Horse, 8s. 6d. nett.
CROKER, MRS. B. M. See Low's Standard Novels.
CROSLAND, MRS. NEWTON, Landmarks of a Literary Life, 7s. 6d.
CROUCH, A. P., Glimpses of Feverland (West Africa), 6s.
—— On a Surf-bound Coast, 7s. 6d.; new edit. 5s.
CRUIKSHANK, G. See Great Artists.
CUDWORTH, W., Abraham Sharp, Mathematician, 26s.
CUMBERLAND, STUART. See Low's Standard Novels.
CUNDALL, J., Shakespeare, 3s. 6d., and 2s.
—— History of Wood Engraving, 2s.
CURTIS, C. B., Velazquez and Murillo, with etchings, 31s. 6d.; large paper, 63s.
CUNNINGHAM & ABNEY, Pioneers of the Alps, 21s.
—— Almer's Fuhrerbuch, 30s.
CUSHING, W., Anonyms, 2 vols. 52s. 6d.

CUSHING, W., Initials and Pseudonyms, 25s.; ser. II., 21s.
CUTCLIFFE, H. C., Trout Fishing, new edit. 3s. 6d.
CUTHELL, E. E., Baireuth Pilgrimage, 12s.
DALY, MRS. DOMINIC, Digging, Squatting in N. S. Australia, 12s.
D'ANVERS, N., Architecture and Sculpture, new edit 5s.
—— Elementary Art, Architecture, Sculpture, Painting, new edit. 12s. and 10s. 6d.
—— Painting, new ed. by F. Cundall, 6s.
DAUDET, ALPHONSE, Port Tarascon, by H. James, 7s. 6d.; also 5s. and 3s. 6d.
DAVIES, C., Modern Whist, 4s.
—— REV. D., Talks with Men, 6s.
DAVIS, C. T., Manufacture of Leather, 52s. 6d.
—— Manufacture of Paper, 28s.
—— Manufacture of Bricks, 25s.
—— Steam Boiler Incrustation, 8s. 6d.
—— G. B., International Law, 10s. 6d.
—— R. H., Our English Cousins, 6s.
DAWIDOWSKY, Glue, Gelatine, Veneers, Cements, 12s. 6d.
Day of my Life, by an Eton boy, new edit. 2s. 6d.; also 1s.
Days in Clover, by the "Amateur Angler," 1s.; illust., 2s. 6d.
DELLA ROBBIA. See Great Artists.
DEMAGE, G., Plunge into Sahara, 5s.
DERRY (B. of). See Preachers.
DE WINT. See Great Artists.
DIGGLE, J. W., Bishop Fraser's Lancashire Life, new edit. 12s. 6d.; popular ed. 3s. 6d.
—— Sermons for Daily Life, 5s.

DIRUF, O., *Kissingen*, 5s. and 3s. 6d.
DOBSON, AUSTIN, *Hogarth*, illust. 24s.; l. paper 52s. 6d.; new ed. 12s. 6d.
DOD, *Peerage, Baronetage, and Knightage, for 1895*, 10s. 6d.
DODGE, MRS., *Hans Brinker*. See Low's Standard Books.
Doing and Suffering; memorials of E. and F. Bickersteth, 2s. 6d.
DONKIN, J. G., *Trooper and Redskin*; Canada police, 8s. 6d.
DONNELLY, IGNATIUS, *Atlantis, the Antediluvian World*, 12s. 6d.
—— *Cæsar's Column*, authorised edition, 3s. 6d.
—— *Doctor Huguet*, 3s. 6d.
—— *Great Cryptogram*, Bacon's Cipher in the so-called Shakspere Plays, 2 vols., 30s.
—— *Ragnarok: the Age of Fire and Gravel*, 12s. 6d.
DORE, GUSTAVE, *Life and Reminiscences*, by Blanche Roosevelt, fully illust. 24s.
DOUGALL, J. D., *Shooting Appliances, Practice*, n. ed. 7s. 6d.
DOUGLAS, JAMES, *Bombay and Western India*, 2 vols., 42s.
DU CHAILLU, PAUL. See Low's Standard Books.
DUFFY, SIR C. G., *Conversations with Carlyle*, 6s.
DUMAS, A., *Company of Jehu*, 7s.
—— *First Republic*, 7s.
—— *Last Vendée*, 7s.
DUNCKLEY ("Verax.") See Prime Ministers.
DUNDERDALE, GEORGE, *Prairie and Bush*, 6s.
Dürer. See Great Artists.
DYER, T. F., *Strange Pages*, 3s. 6d.
DYKES, J. Osw. See Preachers.

EBERS, G., *Per Aspera*, 2 vols., 21s.; new ed., 2 vols., 4s.
—— *Cleopatra*, 2 vols., 6s.
—— *In the Fire of the Forge*, 2 vols., 6s.
EDMONDS, C., *Poetry of the Anti-Jacobin*, new edit. 7s. 6d.
EDWARDS, *American Steam Engineer*, 12s. 6d.
—— *Modern Locomotive Engines*, 12s. 6d.
—— *Steam Engineer's Guide*, 12s. 6d.
—— M. B., *Dream of Millions, &c.*, 1s.
—— See also Low's Standard Novels.
EDWORDS. *Camp Fires of a Naturalist, N. Am. Mammals*, 6s.
EGGLESTON, G. CARY, *Juggernaut*, 6s.
Egypt. By S. L. POOLE, 3s. 6d.
ELIAS, N., *Tarikh i Rishidi*, 30s. nett.
Elizabethan Songs. See Choice Editions.
ELVEY, SIR GEORGE, *Life*, 8s. 6d.
EMERSON, DR. P. H., *English Idylls*, new ed., 2s.
—— *Pictures of East Anglian Life*, 105s.; large paper, 147s.
—— *Son of the Fens*, 6s.
—— See also Low's 1s. Novels.
—— and GOODALL, *Life on the Norfolk Broads*, plates, 126s.; large paper, 210s.
—— and GOODALL, *Wild Life on a Tidal Water*, copper plates, 25s.; *édit. de luxe*, 63s.
—— RALPH WALDO, *in Concord*, a memoir by E. W. Emerson, 7s. 6d.
EMERY, G. F., *Guide to Parish Councils Act*, 1d. each.
—— *Parish Councils*, 2s.

In all Departments of Literature.

EMERY, G. F., *Parish Meetings*, 2s.
English Catalogue, 1872-80, 42s.; 1881-9, 52s. 6d.; 1890-94, 5s. each.
English Catalogue, Index vol. 1856-76, 42s.; 1874-80, 18s.; 1881-89, 31s. 6d.
English Philosophers, edited by E. B. Ivan Müller, 3s. 6d. each.
Bacon, by Fowler.
Hamilton, by Monck.
Hartley and James Mill, by Bower.
Shaftesbury & Hutcheson; Fowler.
Adam Smith, by J. A. Farrer.
ERCKMANN-CHATRIAN. See Low's Standard Books.
ESLER, E. RENTOUL, *The Way they Loved at Grimpat*, 3s. 6d.
—— *Maid of the Manse*, 3s. 6d.
—— *Mid Green Pastures*, 3s. 6d.
—— *Way of Transgressors*.
ESMARCH, F., *Handbook of Surgery*, with 647 new illust. 24s.
EVANS, G. E., *Repentance of Magdalene Despar, &c.*, poems, 5s.
—— S. & F., *Upper Ten*, a story, 1s.
—— W. E., *Songs of the Birds, Analogies of Spiritual Life*, 6s.
EVELYN. See Low's Stand. Books.
—— JOHN, *Life of Mrs. Godolphin*, 7s. 6d.
EVES, C. W., *West Indies*, n. ed. 7s. 6d.
Explorers of Africa, 2 vols., 25s.
EYRE-TODD, *Anne of Argyle*, 6s.
FAGAN, L., *History of Engraving in England*, illust. from rare prints, £25 nett.
FAIRBAIRN. See Preachers.
Faith and Criticism; Essays by Congregationalists, 6s.

Familiar Words. See Gentle Life Series.
FARINI, G. A., *Through the Kalahari Desert*, 21s.
Farragut, Admiral, by Capt. Mahan, 6s.
FAWCETT, *Heir to Millions*, 6s.
—— *American Push*, 6s.
—— See also Rose Library.
FAY, T., *Three Germanys*, 2 vols. 35s.
FEILDEN, H. ST. J., *Some Public Schools*, 2s. 6d.
—— Mrs., *My African Home*, 7s. 6d.
FENN, G. MANVILLE. *Black Bar*, illust. 5s., 3s. 6d. and 2s. 6d.
—— *Fire Island*, 6s.
—— See also Low's Stand. Bks
FFORDE, B., *Subaltern, Policeman, and the Little Girl*, 1s.
—— *Trotter, a Poona Mystery*, 1s.
FIELDS, JAMES T., *Memoirs*, 12s. 6d.
—— *Yesterdays with Authors*, 10s. 6d.
FINCK, HENRY T., *Pacific Coast Scenic Tour*, fine pl. 10s. 6d.
FISHER, G. P., *Colonial Era in America*, 7s. 6d.
FITZGERALD, PERCY, *Book Fancier*, 5.; large paper, 12s. 6d.
FITZPATRICK, T., *Autumn Cruise in the Ægean*, 10s. 6d.
—— *Transatlantic Holiday*, 10s. 6d.
FLEMING, S., *England and Canada*, 6s.
FLETCHER, *Public Libaries in America*, 3s. 6d.
Fly Fisher's Register of Date, Place, Time Occupied, &c., 4s.
FOLKARD, R., *Plant Lore, Legends and Lyrics*, n. ed., 10s. 6d.

FOREMAN, J., *Philippine Islands*, 21s.
FOSTER, B., *Some Places of Note*, 63s.
—— F. P., *Medical Dictionary*, 180s. nett.
FRANC, MAUD JEANNE, *Beatrice Melton*, 4s.
—— *Emily's Choice*, n. ed. 5s.
—— *Golden Gifts*, 4s.
—— *Hall's Vineyard*, 4s.
—— *Into the Light*, 4s.
—— *John's Wife*, 4s.
—— *Little Mercy;* 4s.
—— *Marian, a Tale*, n. ed. 5s.
—— *Master of Ralston*, 4s.
—— *Minnie's Mission*, 4s.
—— *No longer a Child*, 4s.
—— *Silken Cords*, a Tale, 4s.
—— *Two Sides to Every Question*, 4s.
—— *Vermont Vale*, 5s.
A plainer edition is issued at 2s. 6d.
Frank's Ranche; or, My Holiday in the Rockies, n. ed. 5s.
FRASER, Sir W. A., *Hic et ubique*, 3s. 6d. ; large paper, 21s.
FREEMAN, J., *Melbourne Life, lights and shadows*, 6s.
French and English Birthday Book, by Kate D. Clark, 7s. 6d.
French Readers. See LOW.
Fresh Woods and Pastures New, by the Amateur Angler, 1s. 6d.
FRIEZE, Duprè, *Florentine Sculptor*, 7s. 6d.
FRISWELL. See Gentle Life.
Froissart for Boys. See Lanier.
FROUDE, J. A. See Prime Ministers.
FRY, H., *History of North Atlantic Navigation*, 7s. 6d.
Gainsborough and Constable. See Great Artists.

GARLAND, HAMLIN, *Prairie Folks*, 6s.
GASPARIN, *Sunny Fields and Shady Woods*, 6s.
GEFFCKEN, *British Empire*, translated, 7s. 6d.
Gentle Life Series, edited by J. Hain Friswell, 16mo, 2s. 6d. each.
Gentle Life.
About in the World.
Like unto Christ.
Familiar Words, 6s.; also 3s. 6d.
Montaigne's Essays.
Gentle Life, second series.
Silent hour; essays.
Half-length Portraits.
Essays on English Writers.
Other People's Windows, 6s. & 2s. 6d.
A Man's Thoughts.
GESSI, ROMOLO PASHA, *Seven Years in the Soudan*, 18s.
GHIBERTI & DONATELLO. See Great Artists.
GIBBS, W. A., *Idylls of the Queen*, 1s., 5s., & 3s.; Prelude, 1s.
GIBSON, W. H., *Happy Hunting Grounds*, 31s. 6d.
GILES, E., *Australia Twice Traversed, 1872-76*, 2 vols. 30s.
GILL, J. See Low's Readers.
GILLIAT. See Low's Stand. Novels.
Giotto, by Harry Quilter, illust. 15s. See also Great Artists.
GLADSTONE, W. E. See Prime Ministers.
GLAVE, E. J., *Congoland, Six Years' Adventure*, 7s. 6d.
Goethe's Faustus, in the original rhyme, by Alfred H. Huth, 5s.
—— *Prosa*, by C. A. Buchheim (Low's German Series), 3s. 6d.
GOLDSMITH, O., *She Stoops to Conquer*, by Austin Dobson, illust. by E. A. Abbey, 84s.
—— See also Choice Editions.

In all Departments of Literature.

GOOCH, FANNY C., *Face to Face with the Mexicans*, 16s.
GOODMAN, E. J., *The Best Tour in Norway*, new edit., 7s. 6d.
GOODYEAR, W. H., *Grammar of the Lotus, Ornament and Sun Worship*, 63s. nett.
GORDON, E. A., *Clear Round, Story from other Countries*, 7s. 6d.
—— J. E. H., *Physical Treatise on Electricity and Magnetism*, 3rd ed. 2 vols. 42s.
—— *School Electricity*, 5s.
—— Mrs. J. E. H., *Decorative Electricity*, illust. 12s.; n. ed. 6s.
—— *Eunice Anscombe*, 7s. 6d.
GOUFFÉ, *Cookery Book*, 10s. 6d.
GOUGH, E. J. See Preachers.
Gounod, Life and Works, 10s. 6d.
GOWER, LORD RONALD. See Great Artists.
GRAESSI, *Italian Dictionary*, 3s. 6d.; roan, 5s.
Grant, General, Memoirs, 6s.
Great Artists, Illustrated Biographies, 2s. 6d. per vol. except where the price is given.
Barbizon School, 2 vols.
Claude le Lorrain.
Correggio, 2s.
Cox and De Wint.
George Cruikshank.
Della Robbia and Cellini, 2s.
Albrecht Dürer.
Figure Painters of Holland. By Lord Ronald Gower.
Fra Angelico, Masaccio, &c.
Fra Bartolommeo; Leader Scott.
Gainsborough and Constable.
Ghiberti and Donatello, by Leader Scott, 2s. 6d.
Giotto, by H. Quilter; 4to, 15s.
Hogarth, by Austin Dobson.
Hans Holbein.
Landscape Painters of Holland.
Landseer, by F. G. Stephens.
Leonardo da Vinci, by J P. Richter.

Great Artists—continued.
Little Masters of Germany, by W. B. Scott; éd. de luxe, 10s. 6d.
Mantegna and Francia.
Meissonier, 2s.
Michelangelo.
Mulready.
Murillo, by Ellen E. Minor, 2s.
Overbeck, by J. B. Atkinson.
Raphael, by N. D'Anvers.
Rembrandt, by J. W. Mollett.
Reynolds, by F. S. Pulling.
Romney and Lawrence, 2s.
Rubens, by Kett.
Tintoretto, by Osler.
Titian, by Heath.
Turner, by Monkhouse.
Vandyck and Hals, by P. R. Head.
Velasquez, by Edwin Stowe.
Vernet & Delaroche.
Watteau, by Mollett, 2s.
Wilkie, by Mollett.

Great Musicians, biographies, edited by F. Hueffer, 3s. each:—
Bach.
Beethoven.
Cherubini.
English Church Composers.
Handel.
Haydn.
Mendelssohn.
Mozart.
Purcell.
Rossini.
Schubert.
Schumann.
Richard Wagner.
Weber.

GRIEB, *German Dictionary*, n. ed. 2 vols., fine paper, cloth, 21s.
"GRINGO," *Land of the Aztecs*. 6s.
GROHMANN, *Camps in the Rockies*, 12s. 6d.
GROVES. See Low's Std. Bks.
GUILLÉ. *Instruction and Amusements of the Blind*, ill., 5s.
GUIZOT, *History of England*, illust. 3 vols. re-issue, 10s. 6d. ea.
—— *History of France*, illust. re-issue, 8 vols. 10s. 6d. each.
—— Abridged by G. Masson, 5s.
GUNN, E. S., *Romance of Paradise*, 3s. 6d.

GUYON, Madame, *Life*, 6s.
HADLEY, J., *Roman Law*, 7s. 6d.
HALE, *How to Tie Salmon-Flies*, 12s. 6d.
HALFORD, F. M., *Dry Fly-fishing*, n. ed. 25s. nett.
—— *Floating Flies*, 15s.
HALL, *How to Live Long*, 2s.
HALSEY, F. A., *Slide Valve Gears*, 8s. 6d.
HAMILTON. See English Philosophers.
—— E. *Fly-fishing for Salmon*, 6s.; large paper, 10s. 6d.
—— *Riverside Naturalist*, 14s.
—— J. A., *Mountain Path*, 3s. 6d.
HANCOCK, H., *Mechanics*, 5s.
HANDEL. See G. Musicians.
HANDS, T., *Numerical Exercises in Chemistry*, 2s. 6d.
Handy Guide to Dry-fly Fishing, by Cotswold Isys, new ed., 1s.
Handy Guide Book to Japanese Islands, 6s. 6d.
HARKUT. See Low's Stand. Novels.
HARRIS, J., *Evening Tales*, 6s.
—— W. B., *Land of an African Sultan*, 10s. 6d., 5s., and 2s. 6d.
HARRISON, Mary, *Modern Cookery*, 6s. and 3s. 6d.
—— *Skilful Cook*, n. ed. 3s. 6d.
—— W., *London Houses*, Illust. n. edit., 2s. 6d.
—— *Memor. Paris Houses*, 6s.
HATTON. See Low's Standard Novels.
HAWEIS, H.R., *Broad Church*, 6s.
—— *Poets in the Pulpit*, new edit. 6s.; also 3s. 6d.
—— Mrs., *Housekeeping*, 2s. 6d.
—— *Beautiful Houses*, n. ed. 1s.

HAYDN. See Great Musicians.
HAZLITT. See Bayard Ser.
HEAD, Percy R. See Illus. Text Books and Great Artists.
HEARN, L., *Youma*, 5s.
HEATH, Gertrude, *Tell us Why*, 2s. 6d.
HEGINBOTHAM, *Stockport*, I., II., III., IV., V., 10s. 6d. each.
HELDMANN, B. See Low's Standard Books for Boys.
HENTY, G. A. See Low's Standard Books for Boys.
—— Richmond, *Australiana*, 5s.
HERNDON, W. H, *Life of A. Lincoln*, 2 vols. 12s.
HERRICK, R., *Poetry Edited by Austin Dobson*, illust. by E. A. Abbey, 42s.
HERVEY, Gen., *Records of Crime, Thuggee, &c.*, 2 vols., 30s.
HICKS, C. S., *Our Boys, and what to do with Them; Merchant Service*, 5s.
—— *Yachts, Boats, and Canoes, Design and Construction*, 10s. 6d.
HILL, G. B., *Footsteps of Johnson*, 63s.; édition de luxe, 147s.
—— Katharine St., *Grammar of Palmistry*, new ed., 1s.
HINMAN, R., *Eclectic Physical Geography*, 5s.
Hints on proving Wills without Professional Assistance, n. ed. 1s.
Historic Bindings in the Bodleian Library, many plates, 94s. 6d., 84s., 52s. 6d. and 42s.
HODDER, E., *History of South Australia*, 2 vols., 24s.
HOEY, Mrs. Cashel. See Low's Standard Novels.
HOFFER, *Caoutchouc & Gutta Percha*, by W. T. Brannt, 12s. 6d.
HOFFMAN, C., *Paper Making*, 100s.

HOGARTH. See Gr. Artists, and Dobson, Austin.
HOLBEIN. See Great Artists.
HOLDER, CHARLES F., *Ivory King*, 8s. 6d.; new ed. 3s. 6d.
—— *Living Lights*, n. ed. 3s. 6d.
HOLLINGSHEAD, J., *My Life Time*, 2 vols., 21s.
HOLMAN, T., *Life in the Royal Navy*, 1s.
—— *Salt Yarns*, new ed., 1s.
HOLMES, O. WENDELL, *Before the Curfew*, 5s.
—— *Guardian Angel*, 2s. and 2s. 6d.
—— *Over the Tea Cups*, 6s.
—— *Iron Gate, &c., Poems*, 6s.
—— *Last Leaf*, holiday vol., 42s.
—— *Mechanism in Thought and Morals*, 1s. 6d.
—— *Mortal Antipathy*, 8s. 6d., 2s. and 1s.
—— *Our Hundred Days in Europe*, new edit. 6s., 3s. 6d., and 2s. 6d., large paper, 15s.
—— *Poetical Works*, new edit., 2 vols. 10s. 6d.
—— *Works*, prose, 10 vols.; poetry, 3 vols.; 13 vols. 84s.
—— See also Low's Standard Novels and Rose Library.
Homer, *Iliad*, translated by A. Way, vol. I., 9s.; II., 9s.; Odyssey, in English verse, 7s. 6d.
Horace in Latin, with Smart's literal translation, 2s. 6d.; translation only, 1s. 6d.
HOSMER, J., *German Literature*, a short history, 7s. 6d.
How and where to Fish in Ireland, by Hi-Regan, 3s. 6d.
HOWARD, BLANCHE W., *Tony the Maid*, 3s. 6d.
—— See also Low's Standard Novels.

HOWELLS, W. D. *Undiscovered Country*, 3s. 6d. and 1s.
HOWORTH, SIR H. H., *Glacial Nightmare & the Flood*, 2 vols., 30s.
—— *Mammoth and the Flood*, 18s.
HUEFFER. F. See Great Musicians.
HUGHES, HUGH PRICE. See Preachers.
—— W., *Dark Africa*, 2s.
HUGO'S *Notre Dame*, 10s. 6d.
HUME, FERGUS, *Creature of the Night*, 1s. See also Low's Standard Novels and 1s. Novels.
HUMFREY, MARIAN, *Obstetric Nursing*, 2 vols., 3s. 6d. each.
Humorous Art at the Naval Exhibition, 1s.
HUMPHREYS, JENNET, *Some Little Britons in Brittany*, 2s. 6d.
HUNTINGDON, *The Squire's Nieces*, 2s. 6d. (Playtime Library.)
HYDE, *A Hundred Years by Post*, Jubilee Retrospect, 1s.
HYNE, G. J., *Sandy Carmichael*, 5s., 3s. 6d., and 2s. 6d.
Hymnal Companion to the Book of Common Prayer, separate lists gratis.
Illustrated Text-Books of Art-Education, edit. by E. J. Poynter, R.A., 5s. each.
Architecture, Classic and Early Christian, by Smith and Slater.
Architecture, Gothic and Renaissance, by T. Roger Smith.
German, Flemish, and Dutch Painting.
Painting, Classic and Italian, by Head, &c.
Painting, English and American.
Sculpture, modern; Leader Scott.
Sculpture, by G. Redford.
Spanish and French artists; Smith.
Water Colour Painting, by Redgrave.

INDERWICK, F. A., *Interregnum*, 10s. 6d.
—— *Prisoner of War*, 5s.
—— *King Edward and New Winchelsea*, 10s. 6d.
—— *Sidelights on the Stuarts*, new edit. 7s. 6d.
INGELOW, JEAN. See Low's Standard Novels.
INGLIS, HON. JAMES, *Our New Zealand Cousins*, 6s.
—— *Sport and Work on the Nepaul Frontier*, 21s.
—— *Tent Life in Tiger Land*, with coloured plates, 18s.
IRVING, W., *Little Britain*, 10s. 6d. and 6s.
JACKSON, John, *Compendium*, 1s.
—— *New Style Vertical Writing Copy-Books*, 1—15, 2d. each.
—— *New Code Copy-Books*, 25 Nos. 2d. each.
—— *Shorthand of Arithmetic*, Companion to Arithmetics, 1s. 6d.
—— *Theory and Practice of Handwriting*, with diagrams, 5s.
JALKSON, LOWIS, *Ten Centuries of European Progress*, 3s. 6d.
JAMES, CROAKE, *Law and Lawyers*, new edit. 7s. 6d.
JAMES and MOLE'S *French Dictionary*, 3s. 6d. cloth; roan, 5s.
JAMES, *German Dictionary*, 3s. 6d. cloth; roan, 5s.
JANVIER, *Aztec Treasure House*. See also Low's Standard Books.
Japanese Books, untearable.
1. Rat's Plaint, by Little, 5s.
2. Smith, Children's Japan, 3s. 6d.
3. Bramhall, Niponese Rhymes, 5s.
4. Princess Splendor, fairy tale. 2s.
JEFFERIES, RICHARD, *Amaryllis at the Fair*, 7s. 6d.
—— See also Low's Stan. Books.

JEFFERSON, R. L., *A Wheel to Moscow*, 2s. 6d.
JEPHSON, A. J. M., *Emin Pasha relief expedition*, 21s.
—— *Stories told in an African Forest*, 8s. 6d.
JOHNSTON, H. H., *The Congo, from its Mouth to Bóló bó*, 21s. and 2s. 6d.
JOHNSTON-LAVIS, H. J., *South Italian Volcanoes*, 15s.
JOHNSTONE, D. L., *Land of the Mountain Kingdom*, 2s. 6d.
JOINVILLE. See Bayard Ser.
JONES, REV. J. M. See Preachers.
JULIEN, F., *Conversational French Reader*, 2s. 6d.
—— *English Student's French Examiner*, 2s.
—— *First Lessons in Conversational French Grammar*, n. ed. 1s.
—— *French at Home and at School*, Book I. accidence, 2s.; key, 3s.
—— *Petites Leçons de Conversation et de Grammaire*, n. ed. 3s.
—— *Petites Leçons*, with phrases, 3s. 6d.
—— *Phrases of Daily Use*, separately, 6d.
KARR, H. W. SETON, *Shores and Alps of Alaska*, 16s.
Keene (C.), *Life*, by Layard, 24s.; l.p., 63s. nett; n. ed., 12s. 6d.
KENNEDY, E. B., *Blacks and Bushrangers*, 5s., 3s. 6d., and 2s. 6d.
—— *Out of the Groove*, 6s.
KERSHAW, S. W., *Protestants from France in their English Home*, 6s.
KILNER, E. A., *Four Welsh Counties*, 5s.
KINGSLEY, R. G., *Children of Westminster Abbey*, 5s.

In all Departments of Literature. 15

KINGSTON, W. H. G. See Low's Standard Books.
KIRKALDY, W. G., *David Kirkaldy's Mechanical Testing*, 84s.
KNIGHT, E. F., *Cruise of the Falcon*, 7s. 6d.; new edit. 2s. 6d.
KNOX, T. W., *Boy Travellers with H. M. Stanley*, new edit. 5s.
—— *John Boyd's Adventures*, 6s.
KRUMMACHER, *Dictionary Everyday German*, 5s.
KUNHARDT, C. P., *Small Yachts*, new edit. 50s.
—— *Steam Yachts*, 16s.
KWONG, *English Phrases*, 21s.
LABILLIERE, *Federal Britain*, 6s.
Lafayette, General, Life, 12s.
LALANNE, *Etching*, 12s. 6d.
LAMB, CHAS., *Essays of Elia*, with designs by C. O. Murray, 6s.
Landscape Painters of Holland. See Great Artists.
LANDSEER. See Great Artists.
LANGE, P., *Pictures of Norway*, 52s. 6d.
LANIER, S., *Boy's Froissart,* 7s. 6d.; *King Arthur*, 7s. 6d.; *Percy*, 7s. 6d.
LANSDELL, HENRY, *Through Siberia*, 2 vols., 30s.
—— *Russian Central Asia*, 2 vols. 42s.
—— *Through Central Asia*, 12s.
—— *Chinese Central Asia*, 2 vols., fully illustrated, 36s.
LARDEN, W., *School Course on Heat*, 5th ed., entirely revised, 5s.
LARNED, W. C., *Churches and Castles*, 10s. 6d.
LAURENCE, SERGEANT, *Autobiography*, 6s.
LAURIE, A. See Low's Stand. Books.
LAWRENCE. See Romney in Great Artists.

LAYARD, MRS., *West Indies*, 2s. 6d.
—— G.S., *His Golf Madness*, 1s.
—— See also Keene.
LEA, H. C., *Inquisition in the Middle Ages*, 3 vols., 42s.
LEANING, J., *Specifications*, 4s.
LEARED, A., *Morocco*, n. ed. 16s.
LEECH, H. J., *John Bright's Letters*, 5s.
LEFFINGWELL, W. B., *Shooting*, 18s.
—— *Wild Fowl Shooting*, 10s. 6d.
LEFROY, W., DEAN OF NORWICH. See Preachers of the Age.
LEIBBRAND, DR., *This Age Ours*, 6s.
Leo XIII. Life, 18s.
Leonardo da Vinci. See Great Artists.
—— *Literary Works*, by J. P. Richter, 2 vols. 252s.
LEVETT YEATS, S. See Low's Standard Novels.
LIEBER, *Telegraphic Cipher*, 42s. nett.
Like unto Christ. See Gentle Life Series.
Lincoln, Abraham, true story of a great life, 2 vols., 12s.
LITTLE, ARCH. J., *Yang-tse Gorges*, n. ed., 10s. 6d.
—— See also Japanese Books.
LITTLE, W. J. KNOX-. See Preachers of the Age.
Little Masters of Germany. See Great Artists.
LODGE, *Life of George Washington*, 12s.
LOFTIE, W. J., *Orient Line Guide*, 3s. 6d.
LONG, JAMES, *Farmer's Handbook*, 4s. 6d.

LONGFELLOW, *Maidenhood*, with coloured plates, 2s. 6d.
—— *Nuremberg*, photogravure illustrations, 31s. 6d.
—— *Song of Hiawatha*, 21s.
LOOMIS, E., *Astronomy*, 8s. 6d.
LORD, Mrs. FREWEN, *Tales from Westminster Abbey*, 2s. 6d.; new edition, 1s.
—— *Tales from St. Paul's*, 1s.
LORNE, MARQUIS OF, *Canada and Scotland*, 7s. 6d.
—— See also Prime Ministers.
Louis, St. See Bayard Series.
Low's Chemical Lecture Charts, 31s. 6d.
—— *French Readers*, ed. by C. F. Clifton, I. 3d., II. 3d., III. 6d.
—— *German Series*. See Goethe, Meissner, Sandars, and Schiller.
—— *London Charities*, annually, 1s. 6d.; sewed, 1s.
——*Illustrated Germ. Primer*, 1s.
—— *Infant Primers*, I. illus. 3d.; II. illus. 6d.
—— *Pocket Encyclopædia*, with plates, 3s. 6d.; roan, 4s. 6d.
—— *Readers*, Edited by John Gill, I., 9d.; II., 10d.; III., 1s.; IV., 1s. 3d.; V., 1s. 4d; VI., 1s. 6d.

Low's Stand. Library of Travel and Adventure. 2s. 6d. per vol.
Ashe (R. P.), Two Kings of Uganda; also 3s. 6d.
Butler (Sir W. F.) The Great Lone Land: A Record of Travel and Adventure in North and West America.
Churchill (Lord R.), Men, Mines, and Animals in South Africa.
Harris (W. B.), The Land of an African Sultan: Travels in Morocco.
Holmes (Dr. O. W.), Our Hundred Days in Europe.

Low's Stand. Library of Travel—continued.
Johnston (H. H.), The River Congo, from its Mouth to Bólóbó.
Knight (E. F.), Cruise of the *Falcon*: A Voyage to South America in a Thirty-Ton Yacht; also 3s. 6d.
Spry (W. J. J.), The Cruise of the *Challenger*; also 7s. 6d.
Stanley (H. M.) How I Found Livingstone; also 3s. 6d.
Wingate (Major F. R.), Ten Years' Captivity in the Mahdi's Camp, 1882-1892; also 6s.
Other Volumes in preparation.

Low's Standard Novels, Library Edition (except where price is stated), cr. 8vo., 6s.; also popular edition (marked with *), small post 8vo, 2s. 6d.
Baker, John Westacott, 3s. 6d.
—— Mark Tillotson.
*Black (William) Adventures in Thule.
*—— The Beautiful Wretch.
*—— Daughter of Heth.
*—— Donald Ross of Heimra.
*—— Green Pastures & Piccadilly.
—— The Handsome Humes.
—— Highland Cousins.
*—— In Far Lochaber.
*—— In Silk Attire.
*—— Judith Shakespeare.
*—— Kilmeny.
*——Lady Silverdale's Sweetheart.
*—— Macleod of Dare.
*—— Madcap Violet.
—— The Magic Ink.
*—— Maid of Killeena.
*—— New Prince Fortunatus.
*—— The Penance of John Logan.
*—— Princess of Thule.
*—— Sabina Zembra.
*—— Shandon Bells.
*—— Stand Fast, Craig Royston!
*—— Strange Adventures of a House Boat.
*—— Strange Adventures of a Phaeton.
*—— Sunrise.
*—— Three Feathers.

Low's Stand. Novels—continued.
*Black (William) White Heather.
* —— White Wings.
* —— Wise Women of Inverness.
—— Wolfenberg.
* —— Yolande.
*Blackmore (R. D.) Alice Lorraine.
* —— Christowell.
* —— Clara Vaughan.
* —— Cradock Nowell.
* —— Cripps the Carrier.
* —— Erema, or My Father's Sin.
* —— Kit and Kitty.
* —— Lorna Doone.
* —— Mary Anerley.
—— Perlycross.
* —— Springhaven.
* —— Tommy Upmore.
Bremont, Gentleman Digger.
*Brown (Robert) Jack Abbott's Log.
Byrner, Agnes Surriage.
—— Begum's Daughter.
Cable (G. W.) Bonaventure, 5s.
—— John March, Southerner.
Carmichael (H.), Rooted in Dishonour.
Catherwood (M. H.), Lady of Fort St. John.
Coleridge (C. R.) English Squire.
Craddock, Despot of Broomsedge.
*Croker (Mrs. B. M.) Some One Else.
*Cumberland (Stuart) Vasty Deep.
DeLeon, Under the Stars & Crescent.
*Edwards (Miss Betham) Half-way.
Eggleston, Juggernaut.
Emerson (P. H.), Son of the Fens.
Eyre-Todd, Anne of Argyle.
French Heiress in her own Chateau.
Gilliat, Story of the Dragonnades.
Harkut, The Conspirator.
*Hatton, Old House at Sandwich.
* —— Three Recruits.
Hicks (J.), Man from Oshkosh.
*Hoey (Mrs. Cashel) Golden Sorrow.
—— Out of Court.
—— Stern Chase.
*Holmes (O. W.), Guardian Angel.
* —— Over the Teacups.
Howard (Blanche W.) Open Door.
Hume (Fergus), Fever of Life.
—— Gates of Dawn.

Low's Stand. Novels—continued.
Ingelow (Jean) Don John.
—— John Jerome, 5s.
—— Sarah de Berenger.
Lathrop, Newport, 5s.
Macalpine, A Man's Conscience.
*MacDonald (Geo.) Adela Cathcart.
* —— Guild Court.
* —— Mary Marston.
* —— A Dish of Orts.
* —— Stephen Archer, &c.
* —— The Vicar's Daughter.
* —— Weighed and Wanting.
Macmaster, Our Pleasant Vices.
Martin, Even Mine Own Familiar Friend.
Musgrave (Mrs.) Miriam.
*Oliphant, Innocent.
Osborn, Spell of Ashtaroth, 5s.
Penderel (R.) Wilfred Waide.
Pendleton, Sons of Ham, 5s.
Prince Maskiloff.
Raife (R.), Sheik's White Slave.
*Riddell (Mrs.) Alaric Spenceley.
* —— Daisies and Buttercups.
* —— Senior Partner.
—— Struggle for Fame.
*Russell (W. Clark) Betwixt the Forelands.
—— The Emigrant Ship.
* —— Frozen Pirate.
* —— Jack's Courtship.
* —— John Holdsworth.
* —— Little Loo.
* —— The Lady Maud.
* —— Mrs. Dines' Jewels.
* —— My Watch Below.
* —— An Ocean Free Lance.
* —— A Sailor's Sweetheart.
* —— The Sea Queen.
* —— A Strange Voyage.
* —— Wreck of the *Grosvenor*.
Ryce, Rector of Amesty.
Steuart, In the Day of Battle.
—— Kilgroom.
Stockton (F. R.) Ardis Claverden.
—— Bee-man of Orn, 5s.
* —— Dusantes and Mrs. Leeks and Mrs. Aleshine, 1 vol., 2s. 6d. and 2s. only.
—— Hundredth Man.
—— The late Mrs. Null.

Low's Stand. Novels—continued.

Stoker (Bram) Snake's Pass.
Stowe (Mrs.) Poganuc People.
Thanet (O.), Stories of a Western Town.
Thomas, House on the Scar.
Thomson (Joseph) Ulu.
Tourgee, Murvale Eastman.
Tytler (S.) Duchess Frances.
*Vane, From the Dead.
—— Polish Conspiracy.
*Walford (Mrs.), Her Great Idea.
Warner, Little Journey in the World.
Wilcox, Senora Villena.
Woolson (Constance F.) Anne.
—— East Angels.
—— For the Major, 5s
—— Jupiter Lights.
Yeats (S. L.), Honour of Savelli.

Low's Shilling Novels.

Edwards, Dream of Millions.
Emerson, East Coast Yarns.
—— Signor Lippo.
Evans, Upper Ten.
Forde, Subaltern, &c.
—— Trotter: a Poona Mystery.
Hewitt, Oriel Penhaligon.
Holman, Life in the Royal Navy.
—— Salt Yarns.
Hume (F.), Creature of the Night.
—— Chinese Jar.
Ignotus; Visitors' Book.
Layard, His Golf Madness.
Married by Proxy.
Rux, Roughing it after Gold.
—— Through the Mill.
Vane, Lynn's Court Mystery.
Vesper, Bobby, a Story.

Low's Standard Books for Boys,
with numerous illustrations, 2s. 6d. each; gilt edges, 3s. 6d.

Ainslie, Priceless Orchid.
Biart (Lucien) Young Naturalist.
—— My Rambles in the New World.
Boussenard, Crusoes of Guiana.
—— Gold Seekers, a sequel.
Butler (Col. Sir Wm.) Red Cloud.
Cahun (Leon) Captain Mago.
—— Blue Banner.
Célière, Exploits of the Doctor.

Low's Stand. Books for Boys—continued.

Collingwood, Under the Meteor Flag
—— Voyage of the *Aurora*.
Cozzens (S. W.) Marvellous Country.
Dodge (Mrs.) Hans Brinker.
Du Chaillu (Paul) Gorilla Country.
—— Wild Life on the Equator.
Erckmann-Chatrian, Bros. Rantzau.
Evelyn, Inca Queen.
Fenn (G. Manville) Off to the Wilds.
—— Silver Cañon.
—— The Black Bar.
Groves (Percy) Charmouth Grange.
Heldmann (B.) *Leander* Mutiny.
Henty (G. A.) Cornet of Horse.
—— Jack Archer.
—— Winning his Spurs.
Hyne, Sandy Carmichael.
Janvier, Aztec Treasure House.
Jefferies (Richard) Bevis, Story of a Boy.
Johnstone, Mountain Kingdom.
Kennedy, Blacks and Bushrangers.
Kingston (W. H. G.) Ben Burton.
—— Captain Mugford.
—— Dick Cheveley.
—— Heir of Kilfinnan.
—— Snowshoes and Canoes.
—— Two Supercargoes.
—— With Axe and Rifle.
Laurie (A.) Axel Eberson.
—— Conquest of the Moon.
—— New York to Brest.
—— Secret of the Magian.
MacGregor (John) *Rob Roy* Canoe.
—— *Rob Roy* in the Baltic.
—— Yawl *Rob Roy*.
Maclean, Maid of the *Golden Age*.
Mael, P., Under the Sea to the Pole.
Malan (A. N.) Cobbler of Cornikeranium.
Meunier, Great Hunting Grounds.
Muller, Noble Words and Deeds.
Norway (G.) How Martin Drake found his Father.
Perelaer, The Three Deserters.
Reed (Talbot Baines) Roger Ingleton, Minor.
—— Sir Ludar.
Reid (Mayne) Strange Adventures.

Low's Stand. Books for Boys— continued.
Rousselet (Louis) Drummer-boy.
—— King of the Tigers.
—— Serpent Charmer.
—— Son of the Constable.
Russell (W. Clark) Frozen Pirate.
Stanley, My Kalulu.
Tregance, Louis, in New Guinea.
Van Hare, Life of a Showman.
Verne, Adrift in the Pacific.
—— Cæsar Cascabel.
—— Family without a Name.
—— Purchase of the North Pole.
Winder (F. H.) Lost in Africa.

Low's Standard Series of Girls' Books by popular writers, cloth gilt, 2s.; gilt edges, 2s. 6d. each.
Alcott (L. M.) A Rose in Bloom.
—— An Old-Fashioned Girl.
—— Aunt Jo's Scrap Bag.
—— Eight Cousins, illust.
—— Jack and Jill.
—— Jimmy's Cruise.
—— Little Men.
—— Little Women & L.Wo.Wedded
—— Lulu's Library, illust.
—— Recollections of Childhood.
—— Shawl Straps.
—— Silver Pitchers.
—— Spinning-Wheel Stories.
—— Under the Lilacs, illust.
—— Work and Beginning Again, ill.
Alden (W. L.) Jimmy Brown, illust.
—— Trying to Find Europe.
Bunyan, Pilgrim's Progress, 2s.
De Witt (Madame) An Only Sister.
Franc (Maud J.), Stories, 2s. 6d. edition, see page 9.
Holm (Saxe) Draxy Miller's Dowry.
Robinson (Phil) Indian Garden.
—— Under the Punkah.
Roe (E. P.) Nature's Serial Story.
Saintine, Picciola.
Samuels, Forecastle to Cabin, illust.
Sandeau (Jules) Seagull Rock.
Stowe (Mrs.) Dred.
—— Ghost in the Mill, &c.
—— Minister's Wooing.
—— My Wife and I.
—— We and our Neighbours.

Low's Standard Series of Books for Girls—continued.
Tooley (Mrs.) Harriet B. Stowe.
Warner, In the Wilderness.
—— My Summer in a Garden.
Whitney (Mrs.) Leslie Goldthwaite.
—— Faith Gartney's Girlhood.
—— The Gayworthys.
—— Hitherto.
—— Real Folks.
—— Wo Girls.
—— The Other Girls: a Sequel.
*** *A new illustrated list of books for boys and girls, with portraits, sent post free on application.*

LOWELL, J. R., *Among my Books*, I. and II., 7s. 6d. each.
—— *Vision of Sir Launfal*, illus. 63s.
LUMMIS, C. F., *Tramp, Ohio to California*, 6s.
—— *Land of Poco Tiempo* (New Mexico), 10s. 6d., illust.
MACDONALD, D.,*Oceania*,6s.
—— *Sweet Scented Flowers*, 5s.
—— GEORGE. See Low's Stand. Novels.
—— SIR JOHN A., *Life*, 16s.
MACGOUN, *Commercial Correspondence*, 5s.
MACGREGOR, J., *Rob Roy in the Baltic*, n. ed. 3s. 6d. and 2s. 6d.
—— *Rob Roy Canoe*, new edit., 3s. 6d. and 2s. 6d.
—— *Yawl Rob Roy*, new edit., 3s. 6d. and 2s. 6d.
MACKENNA, *Brave Men in Action*, 10s. 6d.
MACKENZIE, SIR MORELL, *Fatal Illness of Frederick the Noble*, 2s. 6d.
—— *Essays*, 7s. 6d.
MACKINNON and SHADBOLT, *S. African Campaign*, 50s.
MACLAREN,A. See Preachers.
MACLEAN, H. E. See Low's Standard Books.

MACMASTER. See Low's Standard Novels.
MACMULLEN, J. M., *History of Canada*, 3rd ed., 2 vols., 25s.
MACMURDO, E., *History of Portugal*, 3 vols., 21s. each.
MAEL, PIERRE, *Under the Sea to the North Pole*, 5s. and 2s. 6d.
MAHAN, CAPT. A. T., *Admiral Farragut*, 6s.
—— *Influence of Sea Power on the French Revolution*, 2 vols. (British naval history), 30s.
—— *Sea Power in History*, 18s.
MAIN, MRS., *My Home in the Alps*, 3s. 6d.
—— *Hints on Snow Photography*, 1s. 6d.
—— See also Burnaby, Mrs.
MALAN. See Low's Stand. Books
—— C. F. DE M., *Eric and Connie's Cruise*, 5s.
Manchester Library, Reprints of Classics, per vol., 6d.; sewed, 3d. List on application.
MANLEY, *Notes on Fish and Fishing*, 6s.
MANTEGNA and FRANCIA. See Great Artists.
MARBURY, *Favourite Flies*, with coloured plates, &c., 24s. nett.
MARCH, F. A., *Comparative Anglo-Saxon Grammar*, 12s.
—— *Anglo-Saxon Reader*, 7s. 6d.
MARKHAM, ADM., *Naval Career during the old war*, 14s.
—— CLEMENTS R., *War Between Peru and Chili*, 10s. 6d.
MARSH, A. E. W., *Holiday in Madeira*, 5s.
—— G. P., *Lectures on the English Language*, 18s.
—— *Origin and History of the English Language*, 18s.
MARSHALL, W. G., *Through America*, new edit. 7s. 6d.
MARSTON, E, *How Stanley wrote "In Darkest Africa,"* 1s.
—— See also Amateur Angler, Frank's Ranche, and Fresh Woods.
—— R. B., *Walton and Some Earlier Angling Writers*, 4s. 6d.
—— See also Walton's "Compleat Angler."
—— WESTLAND, *Eminent Recent Actors*, n. ed., 6s.
MARTIN, J. W., *Float Fishing and Spinning*, new edit. 2s.
MATHESON, ANNIE, *Love's Music, and other lyrics*, 3s. 6d.
MATTHEWS, J. W., *Incwadi Yami*, 20 Years in S. Africa, 14s.
MAUCHLINE, ROBERT, *Mine Foreman's Handbook*, 21s.
MAURY, M. F., *Life*, 12s. 6d.
MAURY, M. F., *Physical Geography and Meteorology of the Sea*, new ed. 6s.
MAURY, GENL. H., *Recollections*, 7s. 6d.
MEISSNER, A. L., *Children's Own German Book* (Low's Series), 1s. 6d.
—— *First German Reader* (Low's Series), 1s. 6d.
—— *Second German Reader* (Low's Series), 1s. 6d.
MEISSONIER. See Great Artists.
MELBOURNE, LORD. See Prime Ministers.
MELIO, G. L., *Swedish Drill*, entirely new edition, 2s. 6d.
Member for Wrottenborough, by ARTHUR A'BECKETT, 3s. 6d.
Men of Achievement, 8s. 6d. each.
Noah Brooks, *Statesmen*.
Gen. A. W. Greeley, *Explorers*.
Philip G. Hubert, *Inventors*.
W. O. Stoddard, *Men of Business*.

MENDELSSOHN. *Family*, 1729-1847, Letters and Journals, new edit., 2 vols., 30s.
—— See also Great Musicians.
MERIWETHER, LEE, *Mediterranean*, new ed., 6s.
MERRYLEES, J., *Carlsbad*, new edition, 3s. 6d.
MERRIFIELD, J., *Nautical Astronomy*, 7s. 6d.
MESNEY, W., *Tungking*, 3s. 6d.
Metal Workers' Recipes and Processes, by W. T. Brannt, 12s.6d.
MEUNIER, V. See Low's Standard Books.
Michelangelo. See Great Artists.
MIJATOVICH, C., *Constantine*, 7s. 6d.
MILL, JAMES. See English Philosophers.
MILLS, J., *Alternative Chemistry*, answers to the ordinary course, 1s.
—— *Alternative Elementary Chemistry*, 1s. 6d.; answers, 1s.
—— J., *Chemistry for students*, 3s. 6d.
MILNE, J., AND BURTON, *Volcanoes of Japan*, collotypes by Ogawa, part i., 21s. nett.
MITCHELL, D.G.(Ik. Marvel) *English Lands, Letters and Kings*, 2 vols. 6s. each.
—— *Writings*, new edit. per vol. 5s.
MITFORD, J., *Letters*, 3s. 6d.
—— MISS, *Our Village*, illus. 5s.
MODY, MRS., *German Literature*, outlines, 1s.
MOFFATT, W., *Land and Work*, 5s.
MOINET. See Preachers.
MOLLETT. See Great Artists.
MOLONEY, J. A., *With Captain Stairs to Katanga*, 8s. 6d.
MONKHOUSE. See G. Artists.

Montaigne's Essays, revised by J. Hain Friswell, 2s. 6d.
MONTBARD (G.), *Among the Moors*, 16s. ; ed. de Luxe, 63s.
MOORE, J.M., *New Zealand for Emigrant, Invalid, and Tourist*, 5s.
MORLEY, HENRY, *English Literature in the Reign of Victoria*, 2s. 6d.
MORSE, E. S., *Japanese Homes*, new edit. 10s. 6d.
MORTEN, H., *Hospital Life*, 1s.
—— *Illnesses & Accidents*, 2s. 6d.
—— & GETHEN, *Tales of the Children's Ward*, 3s. 6d.
MORTIMER, J., *Chess Player's Pocket-Book*, new edit. 1s.
MOSS, F. J., *Great South Sea, Atolls and Islands*, 8s. 6d.
MOTTI, PIETRO, *Elementary Russian Grammar*, 2s. 6d.
—— *Russian Conversation Grammar*, 5s.; Key, 2s.
MOULE, H.C.G. See Preachers.
MOUTON, E., *Adventures of a Breton Boy*, 5s.
MOXLY, *West India Sanatorium; Barbados*, 3s. 6d.
MOZART. See Gr. Musicians.
MULERTT, H., *Gold Fish Culture*, 5s.
MULLER, E. See Low's Standard Books.
MULLIN, J.P., *Moulding and Pattern Making*, 12s. 6d.
MULREADY. See Gt. Artists.
MURDOCH, *Ayame San*, a Japanese Romance, 30s. nett.
MURILLO. See Great Artists.
MURPHY, *Beyond the Ice*, from Farleigh's Diary, 3s. 6d.
MUSGRAVE, MRS. See Low's Standard Novels.
My Comforter, &c., Religious Poems, 2s. 6d.
Napoleon I. See Bayard Series.

Napoleon I., *Decline and Fall of.*
See Wolseley.
NELSON, WOLFRED, *Panama, the Canal,* &c., 6s.
Nelson's Words and Deeds, 3s. 6d.
NETHERCOTE, *Pytchley Hunt,* 8s. 6d.
New Zealand, chromos, by Barraud, text by Travers, 168s.
NICHOLS, W. L., *Quantocks,* 5s.; large paper, 10s. 6d.
NICOLS, A., *Salmonidæ,* 5s.
Nineteenth Century, a Monthly Review, 2s. 6d. per No.
NISBET, HUME, *Life and Nature Studies,* illustrated, 6s.
NIVEN, R., *Angler's Lexicon,* 6s.
NORMAN, C. B., *Corsairs of France,* 18s.
NORMAN, J. H., *Monetary Systems of the World,* 10s. 6d.
—— *Ready Reckoner of Foreign and Colonial Exchanges,* 2s. 6d.
NORWAY, 50 photogravures by Paul Lange, text by E. J. Goodman, 52s. 6d. nett.
—— S., *How Martin Drake,* 5s. and 2s. 6d.
NOTTAGE, C. G., *In Search of a Climate,* illust. 25s.
Nugent's French Dictionary, 3s.
O'BRIEN, *Fifty Years of Concession to Ireland,* 2 vols. 32s.
OGAWA, *Open-Air Life in Japan,* 15s. nett; *Out of doors Life in Japan,* 12s. nett.
OGDEN, J., *Fly-tying,* 2s. 6d.
Ohrwalder's Ten Years' Captivity; Mahdi's Camp, 6s. & 2s. 6d.
Orient Line Guide, fourth edit. by W. J. Loftie, 3s. 6d.
ORTOLI, *Evening Tales,* done into English by J. C. Harris, 6s.
ORVIS, C. F., *Fly Fishing,* with coloured plates, 12s. 6d.

OSBORN, H. S., *Prospector's Guide,* 8s. 6d.
OTTO, E., *French and German Grammars, &c.* List on application.
Our Little Ones in Heaven, 5s.
Out of Doors Life in Japan, Burton's photos. See Ogawa.
Out of School at Eton, 2s. 6d.
OVERBECK. See Great Artists.
OWEN, *Marine Insurance,* 15s.
PAGE, T. N., *Marse Chan,* illust. 6s.
—— *Meh Lady,* a Story of Old Virginian Life, illus. 6s.
PALAZ, A., *Industrial Photometry,* 12s. 6d.
PALGRAVE, R. F. D. *Chairman's Handbook,* 12th edit. 2s.
—— *Oliver Cromwell,* 10s. 6d.
PALLISER, MRS. BURY, *China Collector's Companion,* 5s.
—— *History of Lace,* n. ed. 21s.
PANTON, *Homes of Taste,* 2s. 6d
PARKE, T. H., *Emin Pasha Relief Expedition,* 21s.
—— *Health in Africa,* 5s.
PARKER, E. H., *Chinese Account of the Opium War,* 1s. 6d.
—— J., *Thermo Dynamics,* 10s. 6d.
PARKS, LEIGHTON, *Winning of the Soul, &c.,* sermons, 3s. 6d.
Parliamentary Pictures and Personalities (from the *Graphic*), illust., 5s.; ed. de luxe, 21s. nett.
PATTERSON, CAPT., *Navigator's Pocket Book,* 5s.
PEACH, *Annals of Swainswick,* near Bath, 10s. 6d.
Peel. See Prime Ministers.
PELLESCHI, G., *Gran Chaco of the Argentine Republic,* 8s. 6d.
PEMBERTON, C., *Tyrol,* 1s. 4d.

PENDLETON, L. See Low's Standard Novels.
PENNELL, *Fishing Tackle*, 2s.
—— *Sporting Fish*, 15s. & 30s.
Penny Postage Jubilee, 1s.
Pensions for all at Sixty, 6d.
PERL, H., *Venice*, 28s.
PHELPS, E. S., *Struggle for Immortality*, 5s.
—— SAMUEL, *Life*, by W. M. Phelps & Forbes-Robertson, 12s.
PHILBRICK, F. A., AND WESTOBY, *Post and Telegraph Stamps*, 10s. 6d.
PHILLIMORE, C. M., *Italian Literature*, new. edit. 3s. 6d.
——See also Gt. Artists, *Fra An.*
PHILLIPS, L. P., *Dictionary of Biographical Reference*, n.o. 25s.
—— E., *How to Become a Journalist*, 2s. 6d.
—— W., *Law of Insurance*, 2 vols. 73s. 6d.
PHILPOT, H. J., *Diabetes*, 5s.
—— *Diet Tables*, 1s. each.
PICKARD, S. F., *Whittier's Life*, 2 vols., 18s.
PIERCE, *Memoir of C. Sumner*, 2 vols., 36s.
Playtime Library, 2s. 6d. each.
Charles, Where is Fairy Land?
Humphreys, Little Britons.
Huntingdon, Squire's Nieces.
PLUNKETT (solid geometry) *Orthographic Projection*, 2s. 6d.
POE, E. A., *Raven*, ill. by G. Doré, 63s.
Poems of the Inner Life, 5s.
Poetry of the Anti-Jacobin, 7s. 6d.
POPE, W. H., *Fly Fisher's Register*, 4s.
—— F. L., *Electric Telegraph*, 12s. 6d.
PORCHER, A., *Juvenile French Plays*, with Notes, 1s.

PORTER, NOAH, *Memoir*, 8s. 6d.
Portraits of Racehorses, 4 vols. 126s.
POSSELT, *Structure of Fibres, Yarns and Fabrics*, 63s.
—— *Textile Design*, illust. 28s.
POTTER, F. S., *Walter Gaydon*, 5s.
POYNTER. See Illustrated Text Books.

Preachers of the Age, 3s. 6d. ea.
Living Theology, by His Grace the Archbishop of Canterbury.
The Conquering Christ, by Rev. A. Maclaren.
Verbum Crucis, by the Bishop of Derry.
Ethical Christianity, by Hugh P Hughes.
Knowledge of God, by the Bishop of Wakefield.
Light and Peace, by H. R. Reynolds.
Journey of Life, by W. J. Knox-Little.
Messages to the Multitude, by C. H. Spurgeon.
Christ is All, by H. C. G. Moule, M.A.
Plain Words on Great Themes, by J. O. Dykes.
Children of God, by E. A. Stuart.
Christ in the Centuries, by A. M. Fairbairn.
Agoniæ Christi, by Dr. Lefroy.
The Transfigured Sackcloth, by W. L. Watkinson.
The Gospel of Work, by the Bishop of Winchester.
Vision and Duty, by C. A. Berry.
The Burning Bush; Sermons, by the Bishop of Ripon.
Good Cheer of Jesus Christ, by C. Moinet, M.A.
A Cup of Cold Water, by J. Morlais Jones.
The Religion of the Son of Man, by E. J. Gough, M.A.

PRICE, *Arctic Ocean to Yellow Sea*, illust., new ed., 7s. 6d.

Prime Ministers, a series of political biographies, edited by Stuart J. Reid, 3s. 6d. each.
Earl of Beaconsfield, by J. Anthony Froude.
Viscount Melbourne, by Henry Dunckley ("*Verax*").
Sir Robert Peel, by Justin McCarthy.
Viscount Palmerston, by the Marquis of Lorne.
Lord John Russell, by Stuart J. Reid.
Right Hon. W. E. Gladstone, by G. W. E. Russell.
Earl of Aberdeen, by Baron Stanmore.
Marquis of Salisbury, by H. D. Traill.
Earl of Derby, by G. Saintsbury.

⁂ An edition, limited to 250 copies, medium 8vo, half vellum, cloth sides, gilt top, 9 vols. 4l. 4s. nett.

Prince Maskiloff. See Low's Standard Novels.
Prince of Nursery Playmates, new edit. 2s. 6d.
PRITT, T. N., *North Country Flies,* coloured plates, 10s. 6d.
Publisher's Circular, weekly, 1½d.
Purcell. See Great Musicians.
PYLE, HOWARD, *Robin Hood,* 10s. 6d.
QUILTER, HARRY, *Giotto, Life, &c.* 15s. See also Great Artists.
RAFTER & BAKER, *Sewage Disposal,* 24s.
RAIFE, R., *Sheik's White Slave,* 6s.
RAPHAEL. See Great Artists.
REDFORD, *Sculpture.* See Illustrated Text-books.
REDGRAVE, *Century of English Painters,* new ed., 7s. 6d.
REED, T. B. See Low's St. Bks.
REID, MAYNE, CAPTAIN. See Low's Standard Books.

REID, STUART J. See Prime Min.
Remarkable Bindings in British Museum; 73s. 6d. and 63s.
REMBRANDT. See Gr. Artists.
REYNOLDS. See Gr. Artists.
REMUSAT, MADAME DE, *Memoirs,* 7s. 6d.
—— HENRY R. See Preachers.
RICHARDS, J. W., *Aluminium,* new edit. 21s.
RICHTER, *Italian Art in the National Gallery,* 42s.
—— See also Great Artists.
RIDDELL, MRS. J. H. See Low's Standard Novels.
RIPON, BP. OF. See Preachers.
RIVIÈRE, J., *Recollections,* 3s. 6d.
ROBERTS, LORD, *Rise of Wellington,* 3s. 6d.
—— W., *English Bookselling,* earlier history, 3s. 6d.
ROBERTSON, DR. AL., *Fra Paolo Sarpi,* 6s.
—— *Count Campello,* 5s.
ROBIDA, A., *Toilette,* coloured plates, 7s. 6d.; new ed. 3s. 6d.
ROBINSON, H. P., *Works on Photography.* List on application.
ROBINSON, PHIL., *Noah's Ark,* n. od. 3s. 6d.
—— *Sinners & Saints,* 10s. 6d.; new ed. 3s. 6d.
—— See also Low's Stan. Ser.
—— SERJ., *Wealth and its Sources,* 5s.
—— J. R., *Princely Chandos,* illust., 12s. 6d.
—— *Last Earls of Barrymore,* 12s. 6d.
—— "*Old Q.*" 7s. 6d. and 21s.
—— "*Romeo*" Coates, 7s. 6d.
ROCKSTRO, *History of Music,* now ed. 14s.
RODRIGUES, *Panama Can.,* 5s.

ROE, E. P. See Low's St. Ser.
ROLFE, *Pompeii*, n. ed., 7s. 6d., with Photos, 14s.
ROMNEY. See Great Artists.
ROOPER, G., *Thames and Tweed*, 2s. 6d.
ROSE, J., *Mechanical Drawing Self-Taught*, 16s.
—— *Key to Engines*, 8s. 6d.
—— *Practical Machinist*, new ed. 12s. 6d.
—— *Steam Engines*, 31s. 6d.
—— *Steam Boilers*, 12s. 6d.

Rose Library. Per vol. 1s., unless the price is given.
Alcott (L. M.) Eight Cousins, 2s.
—— Jack and Jill, 2s.
—— Jimmy's cruise in the *Pinafore*, 2s.; cloth, 3s. 6d.
—— Little Women.
—— Little Women Wedded; Nos. 4 and 5 in 1 vol. cloth, 3s. 6d.
—— Little Men, 2s.; cl. gt., 3s. 6d.
—— Old-fashioned Girls, 2s.; cloth, 3s. 6d.
—— Rose in Bloom, 2s.; cl. 3s. 6d.
—— Silver Pitchers.
—— Under the Lilacs, 2s.; cl.3s.6d.
—— Work, 2 vols. in 1, cloth, 3s.6d.
Stowe (Mrs.) Pearl of Orr's Island.
—— Minister's Wooing.
—— We and Our Neighbours, 2s.
—— My Wife and I, 2s.
—— Dred, 2s.; cl. gt., 3s. 6d.
Dodge (Mrs.) Hans Brinker, 1s.; cloth, 5s.; 3s. 6d.; 2s. 6d.
Holmes, Guardian Angel, cloth, 2s.
Carleton (W.) City Ballads, 2 vols. in 1, cloth gilt, 2s. 6d.
—— Legends, 2 vols. in 1, cloth gilt, 2s. 6d.
—— Farm Ballads, 6d. and 9d.; 3 vols. in 1, cloth gilt, 3s. 6d.
—— Farm Festivals, 3 vols. in 1, cloth gilt, 3s. 6d.
—— Farm Legends, 3 vols. in 1, cloth gilt, 3s. 6d.
Biart, Bernagius' Clients, 2 vols.
Howells, Undiscovered Country.

Rose Library—Continued.
Clay (C. M.) Baby Rue.
—— Story of Helen Troy.
Whitney, Hitherto, 2 vols. 3s. 6d.
Fawcett (E.) Gentleman of Leisure.
Butler, Nothing to Wear.
ROSSETTI. See Wood.
ROSSINI, &c. See Great Mus.
Rothschilds, by J. Reeves, 7s. 6d.
Roughing it after Gold, by Rux, new edit. 1s.
ROUSSELET. See Low's Standard Books.
Royal Naval Exhibition, illus.1s.
RUBENS. See Great Artists.
RUSSELL, G.W. E., *Gladstone*. See Prime Ministers.
—— H., *Ruin of Soudan*, 21s.
—— W. CLARK, Mrs. *Dines' Jewels*, cloth, 2s. 6d., boards, 2s.
—— *Nelson's Words and Deeds*, 3s. 6d.
—— *Sailor's Language*, 3s. 6d.
—— See also Low's Standard Novels.
—— W. HOWARD, *Prince of Wales' Tour*, ill. 52s. 6d.
Russia's March towards India, by an Indian Officer, 2 vols., 16s.
Russian Art, 105s.
St. *Dunstan's Library*, 3s. 6d. each.
1. A Little Sister to the Wilderness, by L. Bell.
2. Corona of the Nantahalas, by L. Pendleton.
3. Two Mistakes, by Sydney Christian.
4. Love Affairs of an Old Maid, by L. Bell.
Saints and their Symbols, 3s. 6d.
SAINTSBURY, G., *Earl of Derby*. See Prime Ministers.
SALISBURY, LORD. See Prime Ministers.
SAMUELS. See Low's Standard Series.

SAMUELSON, JAMES, *Greece, her Condition and Progress*, 5s.
SANBORN, KATE, *A Truthful Woman in S. California*, 3s. 6d.
SANDARS, *German Primer*, 1s.
SANDLANDS, *How to Develop Vocal Power*, 1s.
SAUER, *European Commerce*, 5s.
—— *Italian Grammar* (Key, 2s.), 5s.
—— *Spanish Dialogues*, 2s. 6d.
—— *Spanish Grammar* (Key, 2s.), 5s.
—— *Spanish Reader*, 3s. 6d.
SCHAACK, *Anarchy*, 16s.
SCHERER, *Essays in English Literature*, by G. Saintsbury, 6s.
SCHILLER'S *Prosa*, 2s. 6d.
SCHUBERT. See Great Mus.
SCHUMANN. See Great Mus.
SCHWAB, *Age of the Horse ascertained by the teeth*, 2s. 6d.
SCHWEINFURTH, *Heart of Africa*, 2 vols., 3s. 6d. each.
Scientific Education of Dogs, 6s.
SCOTT, LEADER, *Renaissance of Art in Italy*, 31s. 6d.
—— See also Great Artists and Illust. Text Books.
—— SIR GILBERT, *Autobiography*, 18s.
Scribner's Magazine, monthly, 1s.; half-yearly volumes, 8s. 6d.
Sea Stories. See Russell in Low's Standard Novels.
SENIOR, W., *Near and Far*, 2s.
—— *Waterside Sketches*, 1s.
SEVERN, JOSEPH, *Life, Letters, and Friendships*, by Sharp, 21s.
Shadow of the Rock, 2s. 6d.
SHAFTESBURY. See English Philosophers.
SHAKESPEARE, ed. by R. G. White, 3 vols. 36s.; l. paper, 63s.
—— *Annals; Life & Work*, 2s.

SHAKESPEARE, *Hamlet*. 1603, 7s. 6d.
—— *Heroines*, by living painters, 10s.
—— *Home and Haunts of*, 31s.
—— *Macbeth*, with etchings, 10s. and 52s. 6d.
—— *Songs and Sonnets.* See Choice Editions.
SHALER, N. S., *The U.S. of America*, 36s.
SHEPHERD, *British School of Painting*, 2nd edit. 5s. and 1s.
SHERMAN, GENL., *Letters*, 16s.
SHUMWAY, *Tuberculosis*, 3s. 6d. nett.
SIDNEY, SIR PHILIP, *Arcadia*, new ed., 6s.
SIMSON, *Ecuador and the Putumayor River*, 8s. 6d.
SKOTTOWE, *Hanoverian Kings*, new edit. 3s. 6d.
SLOANE, T. O., *Home Experiments in Science*, 6s.
SLOANE, W. M., *French War and the Revolution*, 7s. 6d.
SMITH, CHARLES W., *Theories and Remedies for Depression in Trade, &c.*, 2s.
—— *Commercial Gambling the Cause of Depression*, 3s. 6d.
—— G., *Assyria*, 18s.
—— *Chaldean Account of Genesis*, new edit. by Sayce, 18s.
—— SYDNEY, *Life*, 21s.
—— T. ASSHETON, *Reminiscences* by Sir J. E. Wilmot, 2s. 6d. and 2s.
—— T. ROGER. See Illustrated Text Books.
—— W. A., *Shepherd Smith, the Universalist*, 8s. 6d.
—— HAMILTON, and LEGROS' *French Dictionary*, 2 vols. 16s., 21s., and 22s.
SMITT, PROF., *Scandinavian Fishes*, 2 Parts, 252s. nett.

SNOWDEN (J. K.), *Tales of the Yorkshire Wolds*, 3s. 6d.

SOMERSET, *Our Village Life*, with coloured plates, 5s.

SPIERS, *French Dictionary*, new ed., 2 vols. 18s., half bound, 21s.

SPRY. See Low's Standard Library of Travel.

SPURGEON, C. H. See Preachers.

STANLEY, H. M., *Congo*, new ed., 2 vols., 21s.

——— *Coomassie&Magdala*,3s.6d.

——— *Early Travels*, 2 vols., 12s. 6d.

——— *Emin's Rescue*, 1s.

——— *In Darkest Africa*, 2 vols., 42s.; new edit. 1 vol. 10s. 6d.

———*My Dark Companions and their Strange Stories*, illus. 7s. 6d.

——— See also Low's Standard Library and Low's Stand. Books.

START, *Exercises in Mensuration*, 8d.

STEPHENS. See Great Artists.

STERNE. See Bayard Series.

STERRY, J. ASHBY, *Cucumber Chronicles*, 5s.

STEUART, J. A., *Letters to Living Authors*, new edit. 2s. 6d.; édit. de luxe, 10s. 6d.

——— See also Low's Standard Novels.

STEVENI (W. B.). *Through Famine-Stricken Russia*, 3s. 6d.

STEVENS, J. W., *Leather Manufacture*, illust. 18s.

STEWART, DUGALD, *Outlines of Moral Philosophy*, 3s. 6d.

STOCKTON, F. R., *Ardis Claverden*, 6s.

——— *Clocks of Rondaine*, 7s. 6d.

——— *Mrs. Lecks*, 1s.

——— *The Dusantes*, a sequel to *Mrs. Lecks*, 1s.

STOCKTON, F. R., *Personally Conducted* (*tour in Europe*), illust. 7s. 6d.

——— *Rudder Grangers Abroad*, 2s. 6d.

——— *Schooner Merry Chanter*, 2s. 6d. and 1s.

——— *Squirrel Inn*, illust. 6s.

——— *Story of Viteau*, 5s., 3s.6d.

——— *Three Burglars*, 2s. & 1s.

——— See also Low's Standard Novels.

STODDARD, W. O., *Beyond the Rockies*, 7s. 6d.

STOKER, BRAM, *Under the Sunset*, Christmas Stories, 6s.

——— *Snake's Pass*, 3s. 6d.

STORER, F. H., *Agriculture and Chemistry*, 2 vols., 25s.

Stories from Scribner, illust., 6 vols., transparent wrapper. 1s. 6d. each; cloth, top gilt, 2s. each.
1. Of New York.   4. Of the Sea.
2. Of the Railway. 5. Of the Army.
3. Of the South.   6. Of Italy.

Story of My Two Wives, 3s. 6d.

STOWE, MRS., *Flowers and Fruit from Her Writings*, 3s. 6d.

——— *Life . . . her own Words . . . Letters, &c.*, 15s.

——— *Life*, for boys and girls, by S. A. Tooley, 5s., 2s. 6d. and 2s.

——— *Little Foxes*, cheap edit. 1s.; also 4s. 6d.

——— *Minister's Wooing*, 2s.

——— *Pearl of Orr's Island*, 3s. 6d. and 1s.

——— *Uncle Tom's Cabin*, with 126 new illust. 2 vols. 16s.

——— See also Low's Standard Novels and Low's Standard Series.

STRACHAN, J., *New Guinea*, *Explorations*, 12s.

STRANAHAN, *French Painting*, 21s.

STRICKLAND, F., *Engadine*, new edit. 5s.
STRONGE, S. E., & EAGAR, *English Grammar*, 3s.
STUART, E. A. See Preachers.
—— Esmé, *Claudex's Island*, 6s.
STUTFIELD, *El Maghreb*, 8s. 6d.
SUMNER, C., *Memoir*, vols. iii., iv., 36s.
Sylvanus Redivivus, 10s. 6d.; new ed., 3s. 6d.
SYNGE, G. M., *Ride through Wonderland*, 3s. 6d.
SZCZEPANSKI, *Technical Literature*, a directory, 2s.
TAINE, H. A., *Origines*, I. Ancient Regime and French Revolution, 3 vols., 16s. ea.; Modern, I. and II., 16s. ea.
TAUNTON, *Celebrated Racehorses*, 126s.
—— *Equine Celebrities*, 25s.
TAYLER, J., *Beyond the Bustle*, 6s.
TAYLOR, Hannis, *English Constitution*, 18s.
—— Mrs. Bayard, *Letters to a Young Housekeeper*, 5s.
—— R. L., *Analysis Tables*, 1s.
—— *Chemistry*, n. ed., 2s.
—— *Students' Chemistry*, 5s.
—— and S. PARRISH, *Chemical Problems, with Solutions*, 2s. 6d.
Techno-Chemical Receipt Book, by Brannt and Wahl, 10s. 6d.
THANET, *Stories of a Western Town (United States)*, 6s.
THAUSING, *Malt & Beer*, 45s.
THEAKSTON, *British Angling Flies*, illust., 5s.
Thomas à Kempis Birthday Book, 3s. 6d.
—— *Daily Text-Book*, 2s. 6d.
THOMAS, Bertha, *House on the Scar, Tale of South Devon*, 6s.

THOMSON, Joseph. See Low's Stan. Lib. and Low's Stan. Novs.
—— W., *Algebra*, 5s.; without Answers, 4s. 6d.; Key, 1s. 6d.
THORNDYKE, Sherman's, *Letters*, 16s.
THORNTON, W. Pugin, *Heads, and what they tell us*, 1s.
THOREAU, H. D., *Life*, 2s. 6d.
THORODSEN, J P., *Lad and Lass*, 6s.
TILESTON, Mary W., *Daily Strength*, 5s. and 3s. 6l.
TINTORETTO. See Gr. Art.
TITIAN. See Great Artists.
TODD, Alphaeus, *Parliamentary Government in England*, 2 vols., 15s.
—— Eyre, *Anns of Argyle*, 6s.
—— M. L., *Total Eclipses*, 3s. 6d.
TOLSTOI, A. K., *The Terrible Czar, a Romance of the time of Ivan the Terrible*, new ed. 2s. 6d.
TOMPKINS, *Through David's Realm*, illust. by author, 5s.
TOURGEE. See Low's Standard Novels.
TRACY, A., *Rambles Through Japan without a Guide*, 6s.
TRAILL. See Prime Ministers.
—— Mrs. C. P., *Pearls and Pebbles*, 8s. 6d.
TURNER, J. M. W. See Gr. Artists.
Twentieth Century Practice of Medicine, 20 vols., 420s.
TYACKE, Mrs., *How I shot my Bears*, illust., 7s. 6d.
TYTLER, Sarah. See Low's Standard Novels.
UPTON, H., *Dairy Farming*, 2s.
Valley Council, by P. Clarke, 6s.
VANDYCK and HALS. See Great Artists.

In all Departments of Literature. 29

VAN DYKE, J. C., *Art for Art's Sake*, 7s. 6d.
VANE, DENZIL, *Lynn's Court Mystery*, 1s.
—— See also Low's St. Nov.
Vane, Young Sir Harry, 18s.
VAN HARE, *Showman's Life, Fifty Years*, new ed., 2s. 6d.
VELAZQUEZ. See Gr. Artists.
—— and MURILLO, by C. B. Curtis, with etchings, 31s. 6d.
VERNE, J., *Works by.* See page 31.
Vernet and Delaroche. See Great Artists.
VERSCHUUR, G., *At the Antipodes*, 7s. 6d.
VINCENT, DR. C., *Chant-book Companion*, 2s. and 4s.
—— MRS. HOWARD, *40,000 Miles over Land and Water*, 2 vols. 21s.; also 3s. 6d.
—— *Newfoundland to Cochin China*, new ed. 3s. 6d.
—— *China to Peru*, 7s. 6d.
WAGNER. See Gr. Musicians.
WAHNSCHAFFE, *Scientific Examination of Soil*, by Brannt, 8s. 6d.
WAKEFIELD, BISHOP OF. See Preachers.
WALFORD, MRS. L. B. See Low's Standard Novels.
WALL, *Tombs of the Kings of England*, 21s.
WALLACE, L., *Ben Hur*, 2s.
—— PROFESSOR, *Australia*, 21s.
WALLACK, L., *Memoirs*, 7s. 6d.
WALLER, *Silver Sockets*, 6s.
WALTON, Iz., *Angler*, Lea and Dove edit. by R. B. Marston, with photos., 210s. and 105s.
—— T. H., *Coal-mining*, 25s.
WARBURTON, COL., *Racehorse, How to Buy, &c.*, 6s.
WARDROP, OL., *Kingdom of Georgia*, 14s.

WARNER, C. D. See Low's Stand. Novels and Low's Stand. Series.
WARREN, W. F., *Paradise Found*, illust. 12s. 6d.
WATKINSON. See Preachers.
WATSON, J., *Handbook for Farmers*, 4s. 6d.
—— J. B., *Swedish Revolution*, 12s.
WATTEAU. See Great Artists.
WEBER. See Great Musicians.
WELLINGTON. See Bayard Series.
—— *Rise of.* See Roberts.
WELLS, H. P., *Salmon Fisherman*, 6s.
—— *Fly-rods & Tackle*, 10s. 6d.
WENZEL, *Chemical Products of the German Empire*, 25s.
WESTGARTH, *Australasian Progress*, 12s.
WESTOBY, *Postage Stamps*, 5s.
WESTON, J., *Night in the Woods*, 3s. 6d.
Whincop's Pocket Chess Board, 5s.
WHITE, R. GRANT, *England Without and Within*, 10s. 6d.
—— *Every-day English*, 10s. 6d.
—— *Studies in Shakespeare*, 10s. 6d.
—— *Words and their Uses*, new edit. 5s.
—— W., *Our English Homer, Shakespeare and his Plays*, 6s.
WHITNEY, MRS. See Low's Standard Series.
WHITTIER, *St. Gregory's Guest*, 5s.
—— *Life, by Pickard*, 18s.
—— *Text and Verse for Every Day in the Year*, selections, 1s. 6d.
WILCOX, MARRION. See Low's Standard Novels.

WILKIE. See Great Artists.
WILLS, *Persia as it is,* 8s. 6d.
WILSON, *Health for the People* 7s. 6d.
—— Mrs. R., *Land of the Tui,* 7s. 6d.
—— H. W., *Ironclad Warfare.*
WINCHESTER, BISHOP OF. See Preachers of the Age.
WINDER, *Lost in Africa.* See Low's Standard Books.
WINGATE. See Ohrwalder.
WINSOR, J., *Columbus,* 21s.
—— *Cartier to Frontenac,* 15s.
—— *History of America,* 8 vols. per vol. 30s. and 63s.
—— *Mississippi Basin,* 21s.
With Havelock from Allahabad, 2s. 6d.
WITTHAUS, *Chemistry,* 16s.
WOLLASTON, A. N., *Anwar-i-Suhali,* 15s.
—— *English-Persian Dictionary,* 31s. 6d.
—— *Half Hours with Muhammad,* 3s. 6d.
WOLSELEY, LORD, *Decline and Fall of Napoleon,* 3s. 6d.
Woman's Mission, Congress Papers, edited by the Baroness Burdett-Coutts, 10s. 6d.

WOOD, ESTHER, *Dante Gabriel Rossetti and the Pre-Raphaelite Movement,* with illustrations from Rossetti's paintings, 12s. 6d.
—— SIR EVELYN, *Life,* by Williams, 14s.
Cavalry in the Waterloo Campaign, 3s. 6d.
WOOLSEY, *Communism and Socialism,* 7s. 6d.
—— *International Law,* 18s.
—— *Political Science,* 2 v. 30s.
WOOLSON, C. FENIMORE. See Low's Standard Novels.
WORDSWORTH. See Choice.
Wreck of the "Grosvenor." See Low's Standard Novels.
WRIGHT, H., *Friendship of God,* 6s.
—— T., *Town of Cowper,* 3s. 6d.
WRIGLEY, *Algiers Illustrated,* 100 views in photogravure, 45s.
Written to Order, 6s.
YEATS, S. LEVETT, *Honour of Savelli,* 6s.
YORKE DAVIES, DR., *Health and Condition,* 2s. 6d.
Ziemssen's Medicine, £18 18s.
YOUNGHUSBAND, CAPT. G. J., *On Short Leave to Japan,* 6s.

.*.* Messrs. SAMPSON LOW, MARSTON & CO., Ltd., are the publishers of a number of works in the Eastern Languages —Hindustani, Bengali, Sanscrit, Persian, Arabic, &c.—which were formerly issued by Messrs. W. H. ALLEN & Co., Ltd.

Many of these books are used as Text-books in the Examinations for the Indian Civil Service and the Indian Staff Corps, also as Class-books in Colleges and Schools in India.

Complete Catalogue of Works in the Oriental Languages forwarded on application.

London: SAMPSON LOW, MARSTON & COMPANY, LTD., St. Dunstan's House, Fetter Lane, Fleet Street, E.C.

BOOKS BY JULES VERNE.

WORKS.	LARGE CROWN 8vo. Containing 350 to 600 pp. and from 50 to 100 full-page illustrations.		Containing the whole of the text with some illustrations.	
	Handsome cloth binding, gilt edges.	Plainer binding, plain edges.	Cloth binding, gilt edges, smaller type.	Limp cloth.
	s. d.	s. d.	s. d.	s. d.
20,000 Leagues under the Sea. Parts I. and II.	10 6	5 0	3 6	2 0
Hector Servadac	10 6	5 0	3 6	2 0
The Fur Country	10 6	5 0	3 6	2 0
The Earth to the Moon and a Trip round it	10 6	5 0	2 vols., 2s. ea.	2 vols., 1s. ea.
Michael Strogoff	10 6	5 0	3 6	2 0
Dick Sands, the Boy Captain	10 6	5 0	3 6	2 0
Five Weeks in a Balloon	7 6	2 6	2 0	1 0
Adventures of Three Englishmen and Three Russians	7 6	3 6	2 0	1 0
Round the World in Eighty Days	7 6	3 6	2 0	1 0
A Floating City	7 6	3 6	2 0	1 0
The Blockade Runners		& 2 6	2 0	1 0
Dr. Ox's Experiment	—	—	2 0	1 0
A Winter amid the Ice	—	—	2 0	1 0
Survivors of the "Chancellor"	7 6	3 6	3 6	2 0
Martin Paz			2 0	1 0
The Mysterious Island, 3 vols.:—	22 6	10 6	6 0	3 0
I. Dropped from the Clouds	7 6	3 6	2 0	1 0
II. Abandoned	7 6	3 6	2 0	1 0
III. Secret of the Island	7 6	3 6	2 0	1 0
The Child of the Cavern	7 6	3 6	2 0	1 0
The Begum's Fortune	7 6	3 6	2 0	1 0
The Tribulations of a Chinaman	7 6	3 6	2 0	1 0
The Steam House, 2 vols.:—				
I. Demon of Cawnpore	7 6	3 6	2 0	1 0
II. Tigers and Traitors	7 6	3 6	2 0	1 0
The Giant Raft, 2 vols.:—				
I. 800 Leagues on the Amazon	7 6	3 6	2 0	1 0
II. The Cryptogram	7 6	3 6	2 0	1 0
The Green Ray	5 0	3 6	2 0	1 0
Godfrey Morgan	7 6	3 6	2 0	1 0
Kéraban the Inflexible:—				
I. Captain of the "Guidara"	7 6	3 6	2 0	1 0
II. Scarpante the Spy	7 6	3 6	2 0	1 0
The Archipelago on Fire	7 6	3 6	2 0	1 0
The Vanished Diamond	7 6	3 6	2 0	1 0
Mathias Sandorf	10 6	5 0	3 6	2 vols 1 0 each
Lottery Ticket	7 6	3 6	2 0	1 0
The Clipper of the Clouds	7 6	3 6	2 0	1 0
North against South	7 6	3 6	—	2 vols 1 0 each
Adrift in the Pacific	6 0	2 6		
The Flight to France	7 6	3 6	2 0	1 0
The Purchase of the North Pole	6 0	2 6		
A Family without a Name	6 0	2 6		
César Cascabel	6 0	2 6		

Mistress Branican; Castle of the Carpathians; Foundling Mick; Captain Antifer; Screw Island (*in the press*), 6s. only.

*** Special issue in eight cases of five books each, in a box, 4s. per box.
CELEBRATED TRAVELS AND TRAVELLERS. 3 vols. 8vo, 600 pp., 100 full-page illustrations, 7s. 6d., gilt edges, 9s. each:—(1) THE EXPLORATION OF THE WORLD. (2) THE GREAT NAVIGATORS OF THE EIGHTEENTH CENTURY. (3) THE GREAT EXPLORERS OF THE NINETEENTH CENTURY.

SAMPSON LOW, MARSTON & CO.'S
PERIODICAL PUBLICATIONS.

THE NINETEENTH CENTURY.
A Monthly Review. Edited by JAMES KNOWLES. Price Half-a-Crown.

Amongst the Contributors the following representative names may be mentioned: The Right Hon. W. E. Gladstone, Mr. Ruskin, Mr. G. F. Watts, R.A., Earl Grey, the Earl of Derby, Lord Acton, Mr. Herbert Spencer, Mr. Frederick Harrison, Mr. Algernon C. Swinburne, Mr. Leslie Stephen, Sir Theodore Martin, Sir Edward Hamley, Professor Goldwin Smith, and Professor Max Müller.

SCRIBNER'S MAGAZINE.
A Superb Illustrated Monthly. Price One Shilling.

Containing Contributions from the pens of many well-known Authors, among whom may be mentioned, George Meredith, Thomas Hardy, J. M. Barrie, Sir Walter Besant, Bret Harte, Henry James, Thomas Bailey Aldrich, Sir Edwin Arnold, Andrew Lang, Sarah Orme Jewett, H. M. Stanley, R. H. Stoddard, Frank R. Stockton, &c.

THE PUBLISHERS' CIRCULAR
and Booksellers' Record of British and Foreign Literature. Weekly. Every Saturday. Price Three-Halfpence. Subscription: Inland, Twelve Months (post free), 8s. 6d.; Countries in the Postal Union, 11s.

THE FISHING GAZETTE.
A Journal for Anglers. Edited by R. B. MARSTON, Hon. Treas. of the Fly Fishers' Club. Published Weekly, price 2d. Subscription, 10s. 6d. per annum.

The *Gazette* contains every week Twenty folio pages of Original Articles on Angling of every kind. The paper has recently been much enlarged and improved.

"An excellent paper."—*The World.*

ON WATCH!
A High-Class Monthly Journal of Naval News and Literature. Price 1d.

OUR CELEBRITIES.
Photographs of Celebrities by Walery, accompanied with biographical letterpress. 2s. 6d. per number

LONDON: SAMPSON LOW, MARSTON & COMPANY, LIMITED,
ST. DUNSTAN'S HOUSE, FETTER LANE, FLEET STREET, E.C.

www.ingramcontent.com/pod-product-compliance
Lightning Source LLC
Chambersburg PA
CBHW022041230426
43672CB00008B/1035